D0081679

Philosophy and Its Place in Our Culture

CURRENT TOPICS OF CONTEMPORARY THOUGHT

A series devoted to the publication of original and thought-evoking works on general topics of vital interest to philosophy, science and the humanities.

Edited by **Rubin Gotesky** and **Ervin Laszlo**

Philosophy and Its Place in Our Culture

J. O. WISDOM

University Professor of Philosophy and Social Science,
York University, Toronto.

GORDON AND BREACH SCIENCE PUBLISHERS

New York   London   Paris

B
53
.W57

Preface

THESE ARE days when relevance is called in question. To question the relevance of philosophy is not, however, simply a matter of discontent, rebellion, utility, or whatever. It is a significant and interesting question in its own right. What is the relevance of philosophy to knowledge in general? What is its relevance to human beings as individuals? What is its relevance to society (if any)?

The culmination of this book in Part IV concerns the place of philosophy in the life of the individual and the peculiar and usually unsuspected influence it has upon society.

Such an enterprise can be undertaken only if we dissect out various modes of philosophy, for we must know which mode(s) we are dealing with in connection with persons and society. This is carried out in Part I. I have been rash enough or brash enough to think I have at last solved the problem of what philosophy is about (which is one of the problems that has been constantly with me for forty years). By distinguishing seven modes in a new way—without regard to whether I regard any as outmoded—I believe I have explained why philosophers of various modes, or three or four at any rate, cannot have an intelligible philosophical conversation with one another, and why some scientists brush philosophy aside as useless and stupid while others look to it for scientific salvation.

Doing this seems to me partly a moral obligation for a teacher: a teacher has a right to his own philosophy, has a right to peddle it to the exclusion of other philosophies, has a right to hold that other modes are ridiculous; he has no right to withhold the information that other modes exist, that other thinkers have held them, and he has a duty to be able and willing to state what these other modes are about, to try to do so fairly from their own point of view.

Distinguishing the modes had for me, however, another goal: it enabled me to answer the question—so I thought—what philosophy is about. And, indeed, so far as it goes I think I have more or less done this (making allowance for deficiencies, oversights, etc.). But I discovered that there may always be yet another mode that has not been thought

v

of. In fact, over and above the seven modes of Part 1, there is an eighth mode, which I have kept back to the end of the book; not because it has never existed in the past, but because it was never explicit. These eight are all I know. One could catalogue them differently, lump some together or subdivide some according to the requirements of the matter in hand (and the family resemblance of some of them leads me to think there are only five that are deeply different). But by the discovery of new modes I do not mean mere elaboration of these, but something as different from all these as some of them are from one another. I cannot help wondering if there will be some vastly new modes during the next 500 years.

The outcome of Part I is that there are two modes, utterly different from one another, that will bear on Part IV.

Part II is concerned with evaluation of the heritage of philosophy. First results may appear negative—"proving" that philosophical propositions can be neither proved nor disproved, neither the "metaphysical" modes of the past nor the anti-metaphysical or positivistic modes of the twentieth century.

Despite grave and even gross defects, I think there is value (truth being questionable) in all these modes; I have tried to state the modes and also to evaluate them, but attempted to keep the evaluations separate. I have also tried to separate out the "living issues" to see what from the past is vital even now (though this is relative to one speck of time only).

Chastened in our expectations from philosophy, we proceed in Part III to its roots both in the unconscious of individual philosophers and in the climate of outlook of society. From previous investigations it transpires that philosophy in some modes is much bewitched and even largely created by unresolved, unconscious personal problems. But it transpires also that in a given intellectual epoch, a philosophical mode springs from a standard root which is apparently characteristic of the period. I have unearthed a societal factor characterizing philosophers, which is of some peculiarity, and have decided to call it the Hippolytus Complex—meaning that there is a communication barrier between man and man due to failure of the process of identification that normally unites men.

The question of what light these psychological and societal investigations throw on philosophy is carefully examined; for clearly they provide no disproof, but nearly as clearly they undermine, and it is a matter of some delicacy to square these results.

In Part IV, a modest role is alloted to one classical mode which may be described as a priori natural science: instead of focussing this on matters that are sometimes answered by natural science, let us try it, so long as we have nothing better, on the large societal problems—unlike

the ancients, however, recognizing its fallibility. But the main mode
utilized concerns "way of life" (existentialism).

Now as a mode, this concerns the individual. But it springs, in part,
from a societal root, the downfall or at least twilight of Western man's
Weltanschauung and the search for a new, interpersonal, one. This
eighth mode, philosophy as a Weltanschauung, differs from the earlier
modes in being a presupposition of them; for this reason, though more
for societal reasons, it has largely passed unnoticed. I have suggested
there is much to be gained by making Weltanschauungen explicit, and
by making an explicit examination of them, notably towards understanding basic societal problems, both theoretical and practical. I have
attempted to delineate three Weltanschauungen which have been and
are dominating Western societies, with a view to bringing to light what
basically underlies our states of unrest, what the most forward-looking
of Western man are groping for, what the more nostalgic repine; but
also to indicate that this conflict of outlook holds, moreover, between one
part of an individual person and another part of himself.

Though he has asked it, never before has man asked on such a scale,
"What path shall I pursue?" To this question, philosophy as a way of
life, philosophy as a Weltanschauung, and even philosophy as cosmological ontology of old tradition, provide the means, not of getting firm
answers, but of enquiry. A specific value-structure is outlined as a possible new Weltanschauung.

NOTE

For convenience of printing, acknowledgements appear at the end on page 263.

As regards the convention of printing foreign words in italics, I decided quite deliberately to treat them as naturalised and put them in roman type. Thus italics are kept for emphasis alone. I also thought of dropping the capital from German nouns, but printing was too far advanced to make the change in this book.

Contents

PART III

What Are Philosophers' Goals?

PART IV

Philosophy as a Social and Personal Weltanschauung

Part 1

MODES OF PHILOSOPHY

On Mapping the Ground in Philosophy

THE twentieth century has boasted many philosophers who believed there are no living issues in philosophy. They spread the gospel widely, enthusiastically, and even aggressively. Although they earned their livelihood under this banner, they were, almost to a man, as sincere (though a subtle qualification might be appropriate) as any of their great philosophical forefathers. There were the so-called logical positivists who reigned from about 1920 to 1940, and they were succeeded after World War II by a new dynasty, or a new house belonging to the same dynasty, which upheld the tradition that there were no living issues in philosophy.

The logico-positivist dynasty was of great importance. Although I hold that every one of its major contentions was false, it introduced a regimen of hygiene into philosophy that was badly needed, though it should not be forgotten in these hypochondriacal days that excessive hygiene is tiresome, psychologically damaging, and physiologically dangerous. Perhaps the dynasty in some measure got the right answer by the wrong means. For though there are, I think, some living issues from our philosophical heritage, perhaps there are only a few.

I am interested in finding out what the living issues in philosophy are, and to see them in a perspective.

By living issue I mean an issue for which strong reasons can be found for regarding it as a problem, not just that it is currently discussed.

I am also interested in the queer question of what philosophy is. Because, after studying it, teaching it, and researching in it for the greater part of my life, I found I still did not know. No clear and generally acceptable answer to this exists.

I am also interested in the question of what philosophers are trying to do by means of philosophy.

The first essential seems to me, therefore, to put various kinds of philosophical enterprises on the table and sort them out.

Moreover I think this should be done for all students. Philosophy is conceived parochially on an international scale. It is a subject that means different things in different continents, in different countries within one

1

continent, in different universities within one country, in departments within one university, in different teachers within one department—in different parts of the mind, perhaps, within one philosopher. (I do not write merely of the differences between political philosophy, ethics, logic, aesthetics, and so on, but of the differences of interpretation found in the "central" area of the subject, metaphysics and epistemology.) The differences are so great that philosophers of different genre cannot communicate at all. Not so elsewhere, despite specialization. A quantum physicist may get out of touch with the detailed development of low temperature physics but he knows what it is about and can follow it reasonably well if he takes the trouble. In philosophy, not only is there no communication—there is even a widespread obliviousness to the existence of a barrier and of some sort of philosophy on the other side of the barrier. Philosophy at a college is taught as the college sees it. I do not object to a college developing a "school" pressing its own point of view. I think only that this should not be done as if the view-point were the only one in existence. It is right to argue for a view-point and to reject other view-points which have come from philosophers of stature. But the various view-points should be put on the table first.[1]

There are, for me, significant additional reasons for doing this.

Since not only philosophers do not know what philosophy is (though in an esoteric sense), and since the same is true of scientists and others (in a less esoteric sense), and since I happen to attribute great importance to communication between philosophers and thinkers in other disciplines (because of possible gains for *both*), I have sympathy with the scientist (say) who either cannot make head or tail of philosophy or thinks of it as waffle or bunkum. A lot of it is, I think, waffle or bunkum—what can you expect, at least at first sight, of a subject with no criteria for telling when you may be right or wrong, that is to say, of a subject with no standards? But something could be done for colleagues to sort out the different—virtually unrelated—modes of activity that all come within or near the central area of what is called philosophy. One may gain a different perspective thus, granting the validity of some mode in which one will have no interest, or select some mode for further use.

The seven modes, which I shall now describe and characterize, are not philosophical schools, points of view, or positions (or theories). They are ways in which philosophy has been carried out (of course they presuppose goals and points of view), and which will be laid out in the first instance mainly without value judgment.[2] They are for the most part abstractions, in that a philosophical discussion will usually contain a blend of two or more of them. But this is not necessarily so; they are separable. Even if they were not, that would not detract from the value of isolating them.

The order of presenting them is of little significance. The first one is selected partly because it is unusually easy to explain, but mainly because it provides a way of differentiating several others.

FOOTNOTES

[1] I like to tell my students that for every philosophical statement I make or subscribe to, I can name a highly distinguished, intelligent, and competent philosopher within a few hours' distance who would think it false and perhaps even stupid.

[2] Value-comments will indeed not be wholly excluded from exposition, but they will be explicit and not covert. General assessment will be postponed.

CHAPTER I

Mode (1): Philosophy Looks at Scientific Reasoning (Metascience)

IF WE do not know what philosophy is about, we do know what a great many other studies are about. Let us scrutinise these and note a certain contrast.

Take mathematicians for instance. They know very well what mathematics is about. Other people think they do too (though this is somewhat questionable). It is concerned at least with deduction and proof. If you take physicists, they know very well what physics is about, and I think other people, outside physics, really do know what physics is about. It concerns the motion of matter. Again, biologists know what biologists do, what biology is about, and I think other people also know what it is about. It is concerned with living processes. Historians know what history is about and I think other people know, more or less, though a doubt enters here, what history is about. The strange thing is, all these people—that is to say the vast majority of those who teach in a university—know what they are doing and other people know fairly well what they are doing. And yet, when you come to philosophy, people do not know what philosophers are doing and—may one dare to admit it—philosophers themselves sometimes are at sixes and sevens about knowing what they themselves are supposed to be doing.

Let us take a cue from a saying of William of Stratford: "All the world's a stage," quoth he, to which one may add, "and most professors merely lookers on." Thus if the world of reality is a stage, then the professors of physics, the professors of history, the professor of biology, and so on, all the people with definite jobs are sitting in the front row of the theatre looking on at what is happening in the real world, studying it, understanding it, explaining it, raising questions about it, and so on. Now where does the professor of philosophy fit in? When they are looking at science, its procedures and especially its type of inference, philosophers, I suggest, are sitting in the second row.

Then the question arises, what are they doing there? They are studying the capers of the people in the first row.

Some of them myopically only see what is going on in the front row, the row in front of them—they only discuss the remarks and activities of the physicists, chemists, biologists, and historians in front of them— and never see what is happening on the stage. This, I might add, is what takes place in a number of diverse places in England and America. There are other philosophers or metascientists who watch the capers of those in the front row just the same as the first lot, but they also take into account what is happening on the stage. This helps maintain a sense of realism. It, too, is widely represented throughout the world. The importance of metascience is that it can throw some light on the workings of science. It raises the question of what scientific explanation really consists of, how testing in science is carried out, what is the role of experimentation at all (which is not so obvious as we sometimes think); even such questions as, "what is the part mathematics plays in doing science?" This may be a modest role, but it is a role. And it isolates a subdiscipline within the field of philosophy of science and perhaps even of philosophy.

We have, then, that physicists, historians, etc. are in a sense operators : they know what they are doing; they know what their subject is about and they do it. By contrast, philosophers who are metascientists are eavesdroppers, sitting behind the others in the second row.

The point behind this metaphor is widely recognised; for philosophy is often referred to as a "second-order" subject, meaning that the subject-matter it deals with comes not from the world but from ideas or statements about the world.

The word "metascience" I coined from an obvious source. Hilbert, in the twenties, had drawn a fundamental distinction, now a standard one for all logicians, between an object-language and a metalanguage. In the object-language you can refer to anything under the sun—fact, existent, situation, state of affairs—with one and only one exception : you do not refer to your language (sentence, statement, word, phrase, or any part of it). To refer to your language (or some component of it) you use a metalanguage. And this is lopsided, for you are not precluded from referring also to the things the object-language refers to. Similarly, metascience, conducted in the second row, though focussed on the first row, is not precluded from studying the stage as well.

This distinction reflects something in rerum natura. Consider a set of tools. They are used on objects in the world : a saw cuts down a tree, a wheel enables something to be moved. New tools are made in factory. In order to make them, the factory has to have certain tools—tools to make tools. Tools that make tools, or in a general way operate on tools, are metatools. Thus a screw is (usually) a tool, and a screwdriver is (usually) a metatool. A metatool is not precluded from operating on things in the world as well as on tools. Thus a screwdriver, which is a metatool to a screw-tool, may be used as a tool to open a box.

Metatools also have to be made. And they are made by means of meta-metatools. When I referred to the word "metascience" I did so in a meta-metalanguage.

This chapter, examining philosophy carried out in the second row, is metascience, is a meta-meta-investigation. Accordingly it is an activity belonging to the third row.

We now know where metascience is in the hierarchy of knowledge. (We can likewise have metamathematics, metabiology, etc,; "metaphysics" in the classical sense will be discussed in Mode (5).) This does not, however, tell us anything about its content. An elaboration of the details can be found in works in metascience,[1] and only a few cursory remarks will be made here by way of illustration.

You may wonder whether the causal relation consists of some nexus or tie in the nature of things, connecting cause and effect; you may consider how the accumulation of evidence strengthens a piece of knowledge and whether it is possible to attain certainty; you may compare the inductive method of building up a structure of knowledge upon foundation stones consisting of sensory observations with the method of hypothesis and conjecture surviving refutation.

But my aim is not to map the highways and byways but rather to produce a relief map—to carry out a sorting operation; so that if you meet some question in philosophy, you will know where to put it—not to zipcode it to a place but to know what sort of creature, fish, fowl, reptile, animal, or man, it may be.

Further, although we have found an answer in distinguishing metascience as a second-row study, we have by no means obtained the final boundary for the subject. A metabiologist and a metahistorian will of course also occupy the second row, as particular kinds of metascientist. But a grammarian, for instance, might also eavesdrop on the front row (picking up such scraps as that mathematicians always say "mathematics is . . ." whereas others say "mathematics are . . ."). The question arises whether he is a metascientist in the same sense. So, if there are other second-row colleagues of the metascientist, there is the problem of distinguishing metascience from other second-row subjects; but it is not my aim to go into this.

Some progress will have been made if we know how to ticket metascience: that is, if we know how to distinguish if from physics, history, biology, and so on; but we shall not understand it satisfactorily until we can also see its relations to other modes of philosophy.

REFERENCES

[1]Popper, K. R. (1959), *The Logic of Scientific Discovery*, London; Wisdom, J. O, (1952), *Foundations of Inference in Natural Science*, London; Woodger, J. H. (1952). *Biology and Language*, Cambridge.

CHAPTER II

Mode (2): The Nature of Human Knowledge (Epistemology)

PREVIOUSLY I tried to explain one of the activities that goes on under the name of philosophy, namely that branch of the philosophy of science called methodology or metascience; it is an activity that can be understood fairly easily compared with other sorts of philosophizing. I spent some time explaining this in terms of the following model. Namely, if you regard the world of reality as the stage and if professors of the learned subjects in the university occupy the front row, with the professor of physics watching the motion of bodies on the stage, not necessarily human bodies but billiard balls in motion, and if the professor of history is studying the history of the beings on the stage, and the professor of biology is studying living things on the stage, the question arises where to seat the professor of philosophy. The brief answer that I gave was that he would not be sitting in the front row at all with his colleagues, studying what is going on on the stage, but he would be sitting in the second row watching the capers of his colleagues in the front row. His primary interest would be the things that he eavesdropped upon coming from the people in the front row: he would be discussing their theories, their observations, and so on, e.g. the relation of evidence to a theory, what constitutes evidence, and how to recognize science for what it is. From time to time he would perhaps cast his eye a little distantly at the stage as well, but that would not be the primary objective. This will give a rough picture of that branch of philosophy which is methodology or metascience; and it is readily understandable.

Here we come to another mode of philosophy: "epistemology" or "theory of knowledge", which is concerned with the nature of knowledge in general; for this mode is largely analogous to metascience.

An epistemologist also sits in the second row, and like the metascientist he is not much concerned with what happens on the stage; but unlike the metascientist it is not in the main scientists he overhears, at least not their more abstract remarks. What kind of conception does he study and who provides it?

Some sorts of examples are easily come by. People are heard remarking on the paradoxical fact that a straight stick partly immersed in water looks bent or that a star one looks at may have ceased to exist by the time the light from it by which we see it has arrived. These strange phenomena may be remarked upon by anyone, though they stem from elementary science. What they arouse in the second-row epistemologist is a question whether there may not be some equally insidious interference at work disturbing *all* our perceptions and rendering them *all* unreliable. The stick looks bent, which is false, we see a star, but there may be nothing there to see; perhaps *all* perception is untrustworthy, or, as it was traditionally put, our senses deceive.

Other sorts of questions arise not directly in this way but generated out of such questions as a further development. Thus the epistemologist may raise a further question arising out of the foregoing sort: if our perceptions are inherently untrustworthy, while seeming true, what is the mark of *truth*? If what is seemingly true does not accord with reality, is there any other way than by deceptive appearance by which truth can be judged? Could it be that a number of appearances, no one of which is reliable, may fit together into a coherent whole and may therefore be true?

Or again, since the doubt affecting the trustworthiness of the senses implies that *knowledge* cannot be reliably built upon what our sensory channels of information tell us, what is the basis of knowledge? If it has no reliable source in experience, does knowledge come from our reason?

And, in view of these problems, if satisfactory answers are difficult to achieve, might it be that knowledge is subject to limitation, i.e. that we can obtain reliable knowledge in some areas, such as mathematics, and not in others, such as about life beyond the grave?

Many philosophers in this century have questioned the validity of these very questions—that when examined the questions disintegrate and turn out not to be questions at all. However this may be, it is in some such way as that described that the questions, legitimate or not, have arisen. Let us look at their differences a little more closely.

Traditionally, epistemology, as its stock and trade, is concerned with the *kinds* of knowledge, the *limits* of human knowledge, the *origin* of human knowledge, and the *certainty* of human knowledge. Some of these overlap and some of them are less interesting than others. A little more is now needed about what they mean. The idea of kinds of knowledge is a very old one which occurs in Plato. He held that there is a difference between one kind of knowledge, which is genuine knowledge, and another kind of thing which he rather looked down upon as mere opinion. Nowadays few would make such a sharp distinction between them as Plato did; and it would seem rightly, for both kinds are genuine, and a new line of demarcation would be drawn, to discriminate kinds of knowledge, not by their value, but by the characteristics of the ways of assessing them; so this is hardly a living issue. The question of the limits of human knowledge is something that has exercised mankind for thousands of years, and still does. For instance, one of the earlier papers that I listened to when I was a young man was a paper by Bertrand Russell (1936) entitled "The Limits of Empiricism", and he has been very much concerned in some of his books with the limits of human knowledge. What this means is whether we could only have knowledge of the things around us or whether we could have knowledge of things beyond the reach of the senses (whether the world of matter or an after life and things of this sort). Now the question of the origin of human knowledge concerns what knowledge is built upon or how it is constructed. At one time the question would have been answered by saying that knowledge was built upon authority, say the authority of sacred tablets. From the time of Locke, however, and even earlier, the origin of knowledge became a different kind of question altogether. It concerned whether knowledge was rooted in common experience or in rational thought. Now in our time, in the last ten years, a different kind of answer has been given altogether, namely that knowledge has no origin at all (Popper 1962).

Not all of these are living issues. I would say the question of the kinds of knowledge has changed its form. The traditional form is no longer anything like so interesting as it used to be, because, for most philosophers now, apparently with reason, most knowledge is fairly uncertain. Nonetheless it has been replaced by a new form, namely the difference in kind between scientific and philosophical knowledge. As regards the limits of human knowledge, most philosophers would suppose that in principle there are no limits to our knowledge of the world, but they might be modest enough to think that they might never be lucky enough to get it all. In fact, some would hold that we certainly never shall gain it all, but you could never tell what part we would never know about. So that question has lost a good deal of its interest. But in a new form it has revived: namely whether there are questions that are unanswerable in principle. The question of the origin of knowledge, whether knowledge is built up on experience or can be gained in some other way, is still a living issue. The question of certainty has, however, been replaced by the question of how knowledge is possible where there is total uncertainty. So, the issues that are living, I would say, concern the question of whether knowledge has an origin at all or not, and whether there are certain forms of unanswerable questions.

Now coming back to the metaphor I drew before, we can see that epistemology is a study that is conducted by somebody sitting in the second row. He is concerned with the knowledge that those sitting in the front row express. The reason for this is that what is being discussed is not the world itself, but claims or statements made about the world, claims to do with our knowledge of the world, different kinds of knowledge, its limits, origin, and certainty.

Who is it that is sitting in the first row and what kind of activities are going on there? Evidently, one thing that is going on is that the people sitting there are making perceptual statements about the world, and remarking, for instance, that square towers in the distance look round and that straight sticks look bent in the water, and that these strange things make them doubt the evidence of their senses. And they start asking whether they can ever rely on the evidence of their senses. Now there can be other kinds of questions asked too. Maybe remarks asked about the peculiarity of certain sorts of numbers, or questions about scientific concepts, may be raised, or even questions about metaphysical entities. But typically they are questions that have to do with matters of commonsense or unarticulated assumptions of common life as exemplified by perceptual statements. Hence we get in the second row epistemological discussions which constitute a philosophy of perception, and this is the second row discussion of the comments overheard coming from the front row.

Since an epistemologist is sitting in the second row, it may look as though he is exactly like a metascientist discussing the remarks he overhears coming from scientists. But this is not exactly the case, although there is some truth in it. For the metascientist treats only of statements that come from the sciences, whereas the epistemologist in general is treating of something wider than this. He is taking statements made by the ordinary man or by somebody given to intellectual reflection.

In the second place the ideas that the epistemologist comes up with are rather different from those of a metascientist. He does not deal with theories and their testing, for example; he deals with perceptual statements about perceptual structures which are not testable in the way scientific theories are. So there is some difference of content in the subject matter that the epistemologist treats of.

In the third place, his method of doing this is unlike the metascientist, for the metascientist is constantly appealing to scientific practice to use as a standard against which to measure his metascientific view, whereas the epistemologist does nothing analogous to this; he uses purely logical means for arriving at his results.

In the fourth place, the two types of philosophers tackle different types of questions. The metascientist is concerned very centrally with problems such as that of testability of a theory about the way things happen, whereas the epistemologist is concerned typically with structure, or the way things are related, as for instance in the structural content of a perceptual situation, involving the relation between an object and the ways it appears to us.

Here it is worth adding parenthetically that classically or traditionally metascience was largely equated with induction, and was therefore very similar to epistemology and used to be virtually assimilated to it. Now, however, there is a reverse tendency to try to interpret epistemology as a not very refined form of metascience. On this one may comment that, while there is a certain justification in reversing the process insofar as certain epistemological questions can best be treated in a metascientific way, this tendency might well go too far, because epistemology does, in fact, treat questions that are wider or different in content from those that are covered by metascience.

To sum up so far, we might say that epistemology is the metascience of non-scientific knowledge or if you like it is metacommonsense. Further it is concerned with different questions, uses a somewhat different method, and tends to be more interested in questions of structure than of function.

On the other hand, there is a certain overlap. Thus both metascience and epistemology are concerned with the kinds of knowledge, the limits of knowledge, the origin of knowledge, and the certainty of knowledge. Further, questions of truth and rationality can occur in both domains, but are peripheral in metascience.

It would seem that from one point of view the difference between the two areas is not very great, they belong to a somewhat similar family, but they are more like cousins than brothers. There is a difference of spirit informing the two approaches. Although they are both in part second row activities, epistemology is concerned with some similar questions, but largely with different sorts of questions.

However there is a greater generality about epistemology: truth and rationality are not part of metascience but an epistemological crown to it. Now questions of truth and rationality can arise out of metascience as well as metacommonsense, though this has been less in evidence in traditional writing. So we could say we have metascience and metacommonsense studied in the second row, and epistemological questions arising out of them dealt with in the third row.

BIBLIOGRAPHY

Popper, K. R. (1962), "On the Sources of Knowledge and of Ignorance", *Conjectures and Refutations*, London and New York, 3–30.
Russell, Bertrand (1936), "The Limits of Empiricism", *Proc. Arist. Soc.*, **36**.

CHAPTER III

Mode (3): The Scientific Structure of the World (Embedded Ontology)

BY LONG tradition science is rooted in observation, or at least cannot go against observation, and owes whatever truth it possesses to observation. Thus on the Bacon-Mill inductive tradition, scientific laws are precipitates of observations; on the logical positivist approach of the second quarter of this century, truth and falsity of laws hinged on the possibility of being verified by observation; on Popper's more recent criterion of demarcation of what constitutes science, it consists of what is open to falsification by observation. For all these approaches, the empirical content of science relates at least to the possibility of observation whatever else it might also have to satisfy. Such content is always confirmable by observation, and usually refutable (always on Popper's view).

Now it transpires that there are components of science that do not relate to observation: even indirectly some can be neither confirmed nor refuted thus, though there are some that are half-way between (Watkins, 1958), which can be confirmed but not refuted.

Thus there are parts of science that are refutable and parts that are irrefutable.

EMPIRICAL CONTENT

In this connection Popper (1959) has provided a demarcation criterion to decide whether a general theory (understood in the broad sense of a theoretical system) belongs to science or not. It depends upon whether the theory is falsifiable or not. That is to say, a theory is scientific if it is possible to specify what observation[1] would refute the theory should it happen to be false. Although I hold that Popper has thus provided a superb criterion for empirical content,[2] this does not have to be assumed in what follows. My thesis requires, not that falsifiability is a *criterion* for empirical content (though I happen to think it is), but only that there exists a part of science of which falsifiability is a *property*.

What requires to be brought out first is that, as well as empirical content, science contains other components, which I hope to specify, but which his criterion was not designed for, and which are *not* falsifiable like empirical content. Otherwise put, we are concerned first with those parts of science that are falsifiable and those that are not, to lead up to the discrimination that which is irrefutable is *ontological* in character.

To approach this, consider an example of empirical content, say the Newtonian law of gravitation, $F = M_1 M_2 / r^2$. From this (together with other appropriate laws and especially initial conditions) observational consequences, such as the motion of the tides, can be deduced.[3] If actual observations conflict with such consequences, the theory is refuted. And the motion of the planet Mercury does refute Newton's law. Other examples of content of laws would be Galileo's law for the height of the falling bodies, $s = \frac{1}{2} g t^2$; or Kepler's law that the planets go around the sun in ellipses; which can be applied to the real world and could be refuted by observational means.

I would sum up this property, due to Popper, as refutability by means of observation.[4] In other words, *the empirical content of a scientific theory is observation-refutable*.[5] This way of putting it will lead up to the next component of scientific theory.

EMBEDDED ONTOLOGY

Hard-headed scientists may think of science as consisting solely of its empirical content—all else being a blemish to be liquidated. My task is now to show that scientific theories have ontologies associated with them, in fact actually shot through them. The first step is this. These ontologies are not refutable by observation : thus they carry the awful overtones of old-fashioned metaphysics about them. So it is at least important to examine scientific theories to see whether this is so or not, whether or not they do carry an "embedded ontology".

I shall now consider a number of examples (see Wisdom, 1963). Take the general law of conservation. If you say the sum of kinetic and potential energy is constant, that is refutable in Popper's sense. And it has in fact been refuted. You then make a new conservation law involving heat energy. This again is falsifiable—and has in fact been falsified. You continue to make new conservation laws with a new form of energy added to the old ones to preserve the constancy. That is quite in order; it is scientific. When a *specific* conservation law is found to be false, it is replaced by another *specific* one. But the *general* conservation law is in a different position. It is very hard to do without postulating that there is always energy in some form to make the total energy constant. But this is untestable; there is no observation, as was pointed out by Poincaré (1952), that could refute it in its most general form. For, if you find that there is evidence against a specific conservation law, yet you cannot find a new form of energy to add to preserve the constancy, the general law means that if we are lucky tomorrow we shall find some new form of energy that will do this; and you can never know that this will not happen. In other words, the general law is not observation-refutable.

Again a principle that has animated physiology (and rightly so) is that all bodily changes are due to physical causes. You will not find this down in textbooks, but you can suppose that it is written in invisible letters over all physiological laboratories. If a physiologist did not subscribe to it he would be out of his job or he would not be given a grant for his research. This principle may sound awfully thin and uninteresting, but if you think back a few hundred years to what it replaced, you will see that at one time it was of great significance. If you had warts, for example, you asked "Who done it?", for you suspected an unfriendly witch; nowadays, you ask "What done it?", for you suspect a virus. This was an important change in the history of thought. But what I want to point out even about the new principle is that it is not refutable by observation. If you find some bodily change for which you cannot track down a physical cause, you may take the line that a physical cause will turn up sometime, if not in the next 10 or 20 years then in the next 100 years, and if not in 100 years then later. Thus there is no way of specifying what would be allowed as refutation. So this principle is not observation-refutable. Perhaps a more interesting example would be that energy-values occur in all degrees. Again, this is not written down in any book on physics, but it certainly is presupposed by all classical physics, Newtonian and the various kinds of physics concerned with kinetics that preceded. No one would ever have thought of writing it down as a part of physics, for it is only with the advent of quantum physics that it becomes interesting; but it is a presupposition of classical physics nevertheless. Now if a certain energy-level *is not* to be found, there is no way of showing that it *could not* be found—it may turn up tomorrow. Hence this part of classical mechanics is not refutable by observation.

I would call this an example of a continuity-principle.

Another instance of the continuity-principle is that matter is infinitely divisible—again not observation-refutable.

Another example is that space is infinite. There is no way of refuting this by observation. Yet it is a presupposition of Newtonian mechanics.

A highly interesting example is that space is absolute—again not observation-refutable. The cash-value of Newtonian mechanics for hard-headed scientists is the empirical content (of) $F = M_1M_2/r^2$. But Newtonian theory essentially involves both empirical content and the absoluteness of space. That space is absolute is not written down in the deductions, but it permeates them. For you cannot carry out any of the work of Newtonian mechanics without supposing bodies that are absolutely rigid; as you move a measuring rod from here to there it stays rigid; i.e. stays the same length in a classical sense. This may be taken to be one form of the absoluteness of space. Another interpretation would be that velocities are compounded according to the ordinary algebra of vector addition. So the introduction of the irrefutable idea of the absoluteness of space is not just an aberration of Newton's but a presupposition that is actually, even though covertly, used in Newtonian mechanics.

Some of these examples are confirmable but not refutable; others neither.

Thus empirical content is not pure: it contains what may be called an *embedded ontology*.

PREMISSES, INFERENCES, AND REFUTATION

The situation thus involves a premiss about empirical content plus another premiss which perhaps is better not stated as a separate premiss, because usually you think of premisses as independent of one another. However, the one about absolute space is impregnated in the one about content. And this fact has a logical implication of significance.

Suppose now you get an observation-refutation of, say, Newtonian mechanics, and let us agree that the premisses consist of the empirical content of $F = M_1M_2/r^2$ and the absoluteness of space. An observation-refutation means that some conclusion is false, and therefore in a valid inference that one of the premisses is false (possibly both but certainly one). But you do not know *which* premiss is refuted. Could we get a refutation of the content, with the premiss about absolute space left untouched? This would seem to be possible. Clearly if the premisses are independent of one another and a false conclusion is obtained (the inference being valid), any one of the premisses may in general be false, and there may sometimes be a reason for judging one of them to be false rather than another. Why not here? Given that the ontological premiss pervades the content, it is possible for the content to be false and the ontology true. When Newton's theory was refuted by the observation of Mercury, it would have been possible to replace it with a theory having a different content yet retain the ontology of absolute space. But the converse is not possible : you cannot give up that ontology without altering the content and therefore giving it up too; i.e. you cannot give up the ontology and retain the content. That is to say, the ontological premiss cannot be false and the content true. Hence an observation-refutation of Newtonian mechanics can only refute the content but not the ontology. This result is not, of course, news : metaphysicians have held for centuries that ontology is not refutable by observation. My aim has been to show that ontology is part of empirical science although not refutable in Popper's sense. (We are therefore faced with a highly interesting problem : how is the validity of the embedded ontology of science, which is not testable by observation, to be decided? But this is not the issue here.)

CONCLUSION

In scientific theories the ontology is not testable by observation. But it is not expendible—it is an integral part of a scientific theory. In fact the ontology is *embedded* in the theory, in the following sense. If you alter the content by means of some adjustment, you can do so without altering the ontology; refutation of the theory by observation refutes only the empirical content, not the ontology; but if you alter the ontology you ipso facto alter the empirical content. Hence the empirical content *presupposes* the ontology—or the ontology is embedded in the content.

Such ontology is a form of metaphysics that concerns scientists. They discuss it, sometimes as a matter of course, sometimes without realising they have entered upon philosophy; the exegesis of a theory is incomplete without it. Sometimes it has a technical flavor, and may even be relegated to an esoteric corner of philosophy of science, hardly considered by middle-of-the-road philosophers of science who are not interested in the details of science.

In the present context, its significance is mainly that such an ontology forms a touchstone by which we can understand various other forms of ontology that are either near to or in the centre of philosophical interests. Also we have found a method for assessing embedded ontology which may turn out to be applicable to the most full-blooded kind of metaphysics.

APPENDIX

There are other trends also in the philosophy of science. The present breakdown into seven modes is not, however, intended to exhaust all subdivisions; and, since this is not a work in philosophy—it is rather a work in metaphilosophy—it would be irrelevant to pursue them. Nonetheless, I would make a brief mention of a form of ontology to be found in science, which is not embedded in it in the sense of being created along with the content and being inseparably linked with that content, but which is *prescribed* in some way. Thus, the outlook according to which action at a distance was impossible proscribed theories from counting as science if they violated this principle and thus prescribed e.g. an ontology that a force and its point of application are ontologically filled with emanations of the force, or an ontology that all physical change must be explained on mechanical lines, i.e. that nature is essentially linked by mechanical means. Such ontologies do not spring from the content of a scientific theory but are imposed upon it. Attention is drawn to this feature of scientific investigation, because it reveals a more arbitrary aspect of science than is commonly recognized, and because it has much in common with non-scientific metaphysics.

Such ontologies, prescribed or proscribed, arise from what I have called the Weltanschauung of science (Wisdom, 1968, 1972)[8]. It has affinities with both modes (4) and (5).

FOOTNOTES

[1]Strictly, Popper formulates in terms not of observation but of an intermediary, which is itself falsifiable by observation (this also can be more strictly presented), so that by transitivity it comes to the brief version given above; the stricter amplifications are not relevant in the present context.

[2]Popper identifies "empirical" with "falsifiable" (Popper, 1959).

[3]This is not a rigorous formulation; but it suffices to bring out the most central part of his criterion, though so far as the present thesis is concerned, it leaves a trivial hole unplugged.

[4]Agassi (1964), also has pointed out that science contains more than empirical content, and that it is the empirical character of science to which Popper's criterion applies. (He attributes this to Popper in unpublished lecture courses.)

REFERENCES

Agassi, Joseph (1964), "The Nature of Scientific Problems and their Roots in Metaphysics", *The Critical Approach to Science and Philosophy*, ed. Bunge, Glencoe, 198, 200.

Poincaré, Henri (1952), *Science and Hypothesis*, New York, Ch. 8.

Popper, K. R. (1959), *The Logic of Scientific Discovery*, London, sec. 21, 86.

Watkins, J. W. N. (1957), "Between Analytic and Empirical", *Philosophy*, **32**.

Wisdom, J. O. (1963), "The Refutability of 'Irrefutable' Laws", *British Journal for the Philosophy of Science*, **13**, 303–06.

———————— (1968), "Scientific Theory: Empirical Content, Ontology, and Weltanschauung", *Proc. Inter. Congr. Philosophy*, Vienna, 1969.

———————— (1972), "Scientific Theory: Empirical Content, Embedded Ontology, and Weltanschauung", *Philosophy and Phenomenological Research*, **33**.

CHAPTER IV

Mode (4): Armchair Science (Parascientific Ontology)

A CONTRAST should be made between two kinds of philosophers of science. There are metascientists, sitting in the second row, who discuss such questions as the nature of the theories produced by scientists, the nature of evidence, and what constitutes testing. And there is another kind of philosopher who deals almost altogether with the nature of the universe itself. So he sits in the front row, and may seem to be like a scientist, yet he is evidently not one. The metascientist is only very secondarily concerned with nature. He is primarily concerned with the ideas and theories of his colleagues. Now the kind of philosopher just about to be considered is wholly different in this respect. He may utilize the theories of his colleagues, but not discuss them; if he concerns himself with them at all, it is solely for their implications about nature itself. We have seen one form of this in embedded ontology. Here we shall examine something that is superficially similar but actually very different. The best way to bring out this is by means of examples.

For a very long time, not just centuries but millennia, philosophers have been interested in certain very general questions about the universe. One would be the question *whether space is infinite or finite*. Another would be *whether the universe had a beginning in time or has always existed* (and of course similarly whether the universe will have an ending in time or will always exist). Another such question which has exercised philosophers from very early on is *whether matter is infinitely divisible*. Yet another, though of a rather different kind, would be *whether nature is subject to the unbroken rein of deterministic law*. These examples are enough to give at the moment, though more may be added later. It will be useful to say a little about each in turn, not with the aim of discussing the problems but to show what kind of problem was involved, and how philosophers have viewed them.

Some philosophers have held that space was infinite and others have held that space was finite. However such a matter is to be settled, a question of this kind looks like a question in physics. Physics, it is true, is for the most part concerned with explaining or investigating motion, but it can also be concerned with the nature of space. So one might very well think that the question of the finitude or otherwise of space was a question in physics. And yet physicists have not really raised this question overtly; or rather they discuss it only as a by-product of other questions.

Such questions have been discussed by philosophers, and a very notable example of such a discussion is that given by Kant. Kant in this regard was a forerunner of the twentieth century logical positivists. For he held that the question whether space is infinite or finite could not be answered in principle. What he tried to show was that, if one starts with the supposition that space is finite, one is led to a contradiction. This might, of course, be only an indirect method of proving that space is infinite, but in fact he goes on to try to show that, if space is supposed to be infinite, this also involves a contradiction.[1]

Hence, so far as Kant's argument goes, we are in the position that space can be neither infinite nor finite; which amounts to saying that no statement can be made about the finitude or infinitude of space. However, our concern here is not with Kant's conclusion but about his problem and about his method of handling it.

We may notice two features that are involved here. One is that Kant is speaking about some whole; he is, however, speaking not about something in the universe, but he is speaking about *space as a whole* and not just parts of space. *Further, the method he is using consists of what is in some broad sense logic or considerations of pure reason alone.* He is not making use of any conclusions arrived at from science, nor is he relying upon common knowledge; in particular, he is not making use of any empirical observation. In this respect his procedure is obviously completely different from what would be adopted by a physicist. Moreover, physicists do not normally discuss space as a whole.

Although the problem may appear to be somewhat similar, it is worth devoting some consideration to the problem of time. Kant also gave his attention to this problem, and in a somewhat similar way it transpired that the universe could neither have a beginning in time nor could it have always existed.[1] Now in this case the philosophical enquiry about the origin of the universe looks very like a question in physics or cosmology, or perhaps more like a question in history. It was not, of course, like an ordinary question in history because no documents are involved, nor can it be settled by a different kind of historical method such as might be used in geology, i.e. no method of carbon-dating, for example is relevant. So the method of enquiry is altogether different from those employed in history, either human history or the history of the universe scientifically conceived. The philosophical enquiry is conducted by consideration of logic or reason as in the case of space.

It is now appropriate to draw attention to such answers to these questions as may be obtained from some of the sciences. Classical mechanics is compatible with the idea that space is infinite, at least potentially, but interestingly enough a very different answer comes out of the general theory of relativity. According to this theory the universe is finite but unbounded. This very sophisticated notion can be explained by a model. It means that the universe is finite, but that, although finite, no matter how far you go in any direction, you will never meet a boundary. The model commonly used to explain the relativity idea is that of a two-dimensional being living on the surface of a sphere, a being who can look neither up nor down, but only horizontally over the surface of the sphere. Now the sphere on which such a being lives is certainly finite, but however far this being wanders in any direction it never meets with a boundary—hence the expression, "finite but unbounded". *And this conclusion from the general theory of relativity has to be accepted so long as we accept the theory as having been tested and corroborated by observation.* It will be observed that this is at variance with Kant's very natural assumption that if space is finite there must be a boundary to it.

The conclusion drawn from relativity might seem to be about the nature of space; and if this were strictly the case one would have to go on to the question of time to which there is no corresponding answer. But strictly speaking the answer that comes from relativity does not concern space alone, but concerns space in close conjunction with time—what is commonly known as space-time.

The concepts of space-time and matter go closely together. Dwell for a little while on the notion of matter. Philosophers for millenia have been raising the question whether matter was infinitely divisible. That is to say, they wondered whether you could carve it up into smaller and smaller pieces without end. Now this idea has given many philosophers considerable difficulty. It has seemed to many that if you could go on dividing matter indefinitely, this would presuppose that matter must exist in the form of an actual infinity of tiny little pieces. Now this would be a contradiction in the same way as an actual infinity of numbers. So, on the whole, philosophers have opted for the idea that matter was not infinitely divisible, and they have therefore tended to hold that there is a smallest piece of matter beyond which you could get nothing smaller. Such a piece of matter has traditionally been known as the atom. And from classical times up to the beginning of this century it has been held that an atom could not be divided into parts. On the other hand this notion has seemed to be contradictory because no matter how small an atom might be, so long as it has some size, that size could be divided up, just as a number, however small, can be divided by two.

This age-old problem has likewise been given an interesting answer by modern physics. Since quantum mechanics arose there has been a new conception of matter. The foundation stone of the earliest quantum theory consisted of the fact that a certain sort of entity existed only in amounts with a fixed minimal size. And this had as repercussions that there would be a smallest piece of space, a smallest duration of time, and also a smallest piece of matter beyond which there would be nothing smaller. Now when the study of the atom progressed, it was found that an atom could be divided, contrary to what had already been supposed. Nonetheless, on continuing the process of dividing up an atom it became clear that what happened was not the occurrence of two half atoms but a change from material atoms to something quite different. In other words we ceased to have matter. Thus, matter existed down to molecules and even further down as far as atoms, but on further breaking up it ceased to be matter and became electric particles or energy or something of that sort. So the answer to the old question about the infinite divisibility of matter that has come from modern physics is that matter is indeed capable of being divided only to a limited extent. In other words it is not infinitely divisible. (However, it does not follow that there is nothing that cannot be further subdivided.) It may very well be that the subatomic particles may be capable of being subdivided over and over again. This is a matter for which current physics has as yet provided no answer.

These three questions have a family resemblance and we can see that they are all about something general. The last question concerns *matter as a whole*. It is not concerned with the subdivisibility of a piece of wood, but of matter. *Moreover, the enquiry was traditionally carried by means of reasoning, without appeal to scientific results or to observation.*

Let us turn now from these three closely connected questions to one that is rather different, namely that of determinism. Philosophers have long wondered whether the universe was deterministic or not, and on the whole they have favoured the deterministic answer. What this means, put very broadly, is that everything that happens is due to a cause which inevitably had that thing as its effect. Determinism is the unbroken rein of cause and effect. Its nature comes out very sharply in the saying of Laplace, who expressed the matter brilliantly if omnipotently when he said in effect

"Give me the laws of physics and the conditions now prevailing and I can predict the entire future of the universe to the end of time."

Modern physics again gives a totally different answer, for, as is well known, quantum mechanics implies that there is an intrinsic uncertainty about the motion of particles. It should be noted, moreover, that, from the point of view of quantum mechanics, the uncertainty is due not to the imperfection of scientific work or the limitations of instruments, but is inherent in the nature of the universe itself, for it is inherent in the structure of quantum theory.

Once again, this is not a question that physicists themselves ask, at least while they are doing physics, but it looks like a question that a physicist might ask. What, then, is the difference? Again I think we may find the difference in the fact that *determinism is a principle attributed to the entire universe.* The philosopher who raises the question is not simply asking whether an explosion, for example, has a certain cause, which is something a physicist might ask. He is asking, rather, whether *everything* that has come to be has been caused. *He is therefore dealing with causation as a whole.* And further there is no appeal either to scientific results or to observation as ways of settling the question. *The philosopher is thus attempting to deal with it by means of logic or reason alone.*

Having considered certain questions, some rather like one another and another rather different, it may now be appropriate to consider a few more. A further example of a very general problem about nature is *whether or not there exists physical necessity.* This may seem to be the same problem as that of determinism all over again, but it is somewhat different. Determinism is concerned with whether or not all phenomena have causes. Physical necessity on the other hand, concerns the *nature* of the casual relation. In other words determinism is concerned with how widespread the causation is, physical necessity is concerned with its *nature.*

Put still more specifically, given that two events are connected by the causal relation, that is that one event is the cause of the other, different theories may be given about the nature of this causal relation; in fact, theories may be grouped into two classes. There are those who hold that there is a necessary relation between them and there are those who hold that there is not. Those who hold that there is no necessary connection between events would mean by causation simply that cause and effect constantly accompany one another, and they would imply that there is no particular reason why they should. On the other hand those who hold that there exists necessity of a physical kind imply that there is some sort of tie or *nexus* connecting a cause with its effect such that there is some inherent basis for concluding that the effect will occur given that the cause occurs.

It is very difficult to formulate just what is meant by physical necessity. One may lead up to this by using the model of logical necessity. As is well known the various terms of an analytic proposition are connected by a necessary relation. Nonetheless, the conclusion is not physical necessity is exactly like this; but there are some who have maintained that it is something like it, that is to say that there is a family resemblance between logical necessity and physical necessity. The main reason for this is that no one has been able to think of any other way of describing physical necessity. (It may be, of course, that the idea of physical necessity carries overtones of mythology—the necessity being characterized, for example, by the way in which Oedipus met his fate, the dread necessity of which the classic speak. Naturally few philosophers would admit that this is what is meant. But it could be that some such idea has contributed to the concept.) Otherwise expressed, we can say with assurance that if there is physical necessity then given an event potentially causal, an effect must occur and its absence is impossible; hence there is at least this resemblance to the relation of logical necessity in which given a premiss the conclusion must follow.

About this subject, we are less well off than in the case of the others already described, partly because it would seem that the notion of physical necessity is not in fact used even ostensibly by any science. It may appear on occasion to be presupposed by the use of causal explanation, but it could be done without. A mere regularity, events just happening together, mere concomitants, would do just as well so far as science is concerned. So on this question apparently, no contribution can be derived from any scientific theory ancient or modern.

If we care to ask why the question has some life in it, the answer is that, if there is a merely accidental concomitant relation between a cause and its effect, it would seem fantastic that there should be any such thing as uniformity in nature at all. Thus to say, even if the uniformity does not prevail through the entire extent of nature, but is only fairly widespread, it would be very hard to understand how this was so. It would appear to be merely a matter of chance. This would seem to be the main reason why philosophers have held that there exists something like physical necessity, though there may, of course, be other reasons as well. On the other hand, philosophers have been defeated by the task of trying to give any understandable account of what physical necessity may consist of, and here there is an *impasse*. However, the question would seem to be a genuine one, even if no progress has been made about it.

It is now appropriate to mention a problem of a very different kind, mainly that of *teleology*. This means, that, *events are determined by some goal towards which they are drawn in the future.* This is a very old conception. The idea of teleology in the physical inanimate world has long been given up by physicists, chemists, and natural scientists generally, for hundreds of years. But in the realm of living things, biology works in practice by treating living bodies *as though* they are teleological. Nonetheless modern scientists do not use a teleological principle in their work; they think not of a teleological pull from the future but of a mechanical push from the past. To this it is worth adding that the modern development of cybernetics has added a nail in the coffin of teleology so far as biology is concerned, because at last there is a theory explaining how the apparent purposiveness of organisms can be brought about by purely mechanical means (Wisdom, 1951).

The question of whether or not nature is teleological is a question about the real world. Nonetheless, it is a question that is very easily converted from being about the real world into one of metascience. That is to say, the discussion would be not one about the real world but one about the nature of biological theories. In short, the question is whether the concept of teleology is needed by biological theory. This brings out a point of some importance: i.e. that there is a close relation between metascientific questions and questions such as those that are being discussed here. It is very hard to discuss an ontological question for long without discussing the questions about knowledge, and it is very hard to discuss questions of knowledge for long without discussing questions of an ontological kind. In practice the two often shade into one another, but this does not mean that they are not conceptually distinct. Though the metascientific question is concerned with the workings of science and therefore with the nature of scientific knowledge, the questions exemplified here concern nature in itself. *Such questions are thus ontological in character.*

From teleology it is a short step to an interesting question, now somewhat out of fashion, concerning what it is that animates organisms. This is the problem of vitalism. *Vitalists have maintained that all biological organisms are driven by some vital force or élan vital,* whereas their opponents deny this and hold that non-vital, that is mechanical, forces suffice to account for all biological change.

The vitalists have come under severe attack historically and have been very easy targets. Nonetheless, the mechanists, though they have had an easy time in conducting their attacks, have not been able so far to give a complete answer to the explanation of life, although the advent of cybernetics has made their task somewhat easier. Of recent years only very few have sought to defend vitalism; nonetheless it may be doubted whether the criticisms of it are yet decisive.

Here again philosophers are discussing a question about the real world, namely whether in fact the forces of nature contain a vital force over and above physical and chemical ones that make living matter living.

Let us now briefly reflect upon the last two examples. Teleology concerns a very general question about nature: not indeed nature itself as a whole, but the question *whether all organisms are subject to teleological explanation.* In this respect something as a whole is being considered, namely the nature of biological causation. Again with regard to vitalism, the problem is about all organisms: i.e. whether their activity is due to a motive force other than physical or chemical; *the problem of vitalism is dealing with motive force as a whole.* Now it does so happen that in the latter case biologists themselves have become involved in these controversies as well as philosophers; nonetheless *the issue is not one that biologists consider capable of being settled by biological theory or by biological observation. The argument,* as always, *centres on questions of logic or reason;* so here again we have the same two characteristics turning up as with the other examples.

The conclusion at this stage would be that the present area of philosophical problems may be considered delimited by two characteristics. One concerns the subject of enquiry: *is it holistic in character.* The other concerns the method of enquiry: *it is one of logic, in some broad sense, or reason.* But the method makes use neither of empirical theory nor of observation.

A question that arises here is what name should be given to questions of this sort, and it seems natural to call them ontological. They are concerned with the nature of some general feature of the universe. They are concerned with a very general enquiry about whether something is or is not so about the universe, whether about space or about matter or something else. On the other hand enquiries in physics do not normally take this form. They are concerned with enquiring into the operations of nature. Typically physics is concerned with the *explanation of motion.* Hence, there does seem to arise a distinction between structural and functional aspects of the entities in question. *The philosophical, that is the ontological, enquiry may be said to be concerned with something structural about the universe whereas physics is usually concerned with something functional.*

These questions seem to bear a first cousinship relationship with scientific enquiries, whereas in philosophy there are other kinds of ontological enquiries that differ very markedly from these, and have no such relationship. The nature of these other enquiries will be relevant on another occasion. Here it will suffice to illustrate by means of one example. It would be an ontological contention of this further sort to claim that the universe of matter was constituted by mental ingredients. For the latter kind of question, which looks as if it belonged to physics but handled by pure reason, it will be appropriate to introduce a new name : we may conveniently speak of ontological structure or, because of its breadth, we may speak of *cosmological ontology*. Because of the scientific overtones of the examples given in this chapter, I shall describe them as *parascientific ontology*.

Thus I have offered a broad conclusion about the subject of the enquiry, the method of conducting it, and (having characterized it roughly) given it a name. We must now consider whether the characterization is sufficiently accurate. The claim was made that the enquiry is holistic in character in concerning some feature of the universe as a whole, e.g. the character of space as such, or whether matter as such is infinitely divisible, and so on. Now it might be questioned whether this is not also sometimes so with questions of physics. Physics for example is concerned with the explanation of all motion without exception. Is it not therefore concerned with some feature of the universe as a whole? The parallel does not, however, really hold. It is true that physics is concerned with motion as a whole. But physics is not precluded from dissecting this into bits and considering the motion of parts of different kinds. So a problem in physics that is concerned with the whole is also applicable to different kinds of parts of the whole. On the other hand, in the present enquiry, the questions raised concern features of the universe as a whole, of which the parts have no relevant difference from each other or from the whole.

A further qualification is that physics, although prominently concerned with function, does enquire into questions of structure (whether as an ultimate aim or merely to assist in answering questions about function); for it contains postulates such as that of electricity consisting of two fluids. And such postulates are ontological and concerned with some aspect of the world as a whole.

To summarize the characterization of the present area of philosophical problems : the enquiries are concerned with some aspect of the universe as a whole, such that neither the questions nor possible answers to it are independent of all differences between parts of that whole. Secondly, the enquiry is restricted to the structure of the whole in question and has nothing to do with its function. Finally, as regards method, it would seem that science is concerned largely with the functioning of the universe, which can be appropriately investigated by means of empirical methods, but the reason why these other ontological enquiries are conducted by means of logic or reason alone is that structural questions, when isolated from functional questions, cannot be pursued by the empirical methods appropriate to questions of function.

Thus the parascientific ontologist, sitting in the front row, may seem to be like a physicist. His answers may indeed use physics at times, but for the most part they come from himself and appear to be, as it were, an *a priori* physics.

FOOTNOTES

[1]The reason why space cannot be finite is this. If space is finite it must end at a boundary, but if there is a boundary there must at least be the other side of the boundary and there would have to be not just the other side of the boundary but empty space beyond the boundary. Hence, the supposition that space is finite contradicts itself because the notion leads inevitably to the idea that space is extended beyond the limits allowed to it. Again, if space is supposed to be infinite, this is inconceivable, according to Kant. And the way of explaining this would be as follows. Let us take the model of the series of ordinary numbers. They are infinite in extent because we never reach an end no matter how far we count. On the other hand no actual infinity of numbers can be set down in front of us because however long we may be able to go on counting we can never reach the end, and therefore an actual infinity of numbers cannot be actually present to us. A way of expressing this is to say that the quantity of numbers is a potential infinity but not an actual infinity. Likewise, if we apply this model to space, we conclude that space may be potentially infinite but cannot be actually infinite, that is to say, an infinite space cannot exist laid out in front of us.

[2]If the universe is supposed to have had a beginning in time then the question arises, "what was happening one second or ten seconds before the beginning of time". Of course the answer is that nothing was happening. Nonetheless, the idea of the beginning of time presupposes a time before the beginning of time and this presupposes a universe even though an empty one. Hence, the idea of a beginning in time for the universe is self-contradictory. However, just as in the case of space, an infinity of time, stretching backwards without end, is equally a self-contradiction.

REFERENCES

Wisdom, J. O. (1951), "The Hypothesis of Cybernetics", *Brit. J. Philos. Sc.*, **2**, 1–24

CHAPTER V

Mode (5): The Nature of All Things (Cosmological Ontology)

I HAVE described the activity of metascientists who are primarily concerned with discussing the ideas, theories, concepts, evidence, and so on, of natural scientists who in their turn are viewing the world of reality. This led to the investigation of the ontology embedded in science. In contrast with that I have described another activity of philosophers of science who view the world of reality direct without considering the nature of the theories of their scientific colleagues. The latter who are directly concerned with the world might perhaps be called philosophers of nature or parascientific ontologists who are concerned with the world in the large.

Now along comes the purest form of metaphysics. Pure metaphysics resembles this kind of philosophy of nature, in that a metaphysician does view the world itself, apparently like a scientist, historian, biologist, geologist, sociologist; but although he does this his canvas is much wider than that of the parascientific ontologist. The parascientific ontologist does seem to be concerned with questions that have all the look of being scientific, even though they are not exactly the kind of questions a scientist raises. The pure metaphysician is concerned with still wider questions. The only way to bring this out at this point is by giving specific examples.

The parascientific ontologist may ask questions about the divisibility of matter, for example, or the finitude of space, or the origin of the universe in time. Now these are questions that would seem to be concerned with physics. The pure metaphysician (for the parascientific ontologist is also a metaphysician), on the other hand, is concerned not so much with the divisibility of matter but with the *nature* of matter, the *nature* of space, and the *nature* of time, and in general, with the nature of *being,* which a metaphysician would consider to be common to all of these and other entities. He is also very concerned with the origin of the universe as well as its goal or purpose. Now it may be a little unclear whether the pure metaphysician raises the question of the

30

origin of the universe in a different way from the parascientific ontologist. Possibly there is an overlap here. Further, the metaphysician is concerned with what may be called, following Berkeley, the furniture of the earth. He is concerned to know what are the fundamental constituents that make up the universe. This is connected with the question of the nature of *being,* although it is not exactly the same. The nature of being would be concerned with what constitutes being of any sort whatever. To study the nature of the furniture of the earth is to enquire what sort of thing is fundamentally the stuff of which the universe is made. Otherwise put, the question is, "What is the nature of reality?" And this, perhaps, had better be illustrated straightaway by examples. Some philosophers in early Greek days have thought that the element *water* was a constituent out of which everything was made. Others thought that it was fire. A present day scientist might say that it was hydrogen (which is not after all so very different an answer). Other philosophers of contemporary times have held that the world was constituted by sense-data or patches of colour. Others in between have held that material substance was the fundamental stuff out of which everything was made. In addition to all these things the metaphysician is concerned with the laws of operation or the ultimate principles that determine how being and its various forms shall manifest itself.

These would seem to me to be the basic considerations in metaphysics, but there are a number of others that arise, which are generally regarded as very fundamental, but which seem nonetheless to be subsidiary or to arise out of these earlier questions. For instance, if it is held that the fundamental nature of the universe is to consist of material substance the question will arise about the nature of substance itself, and then there will arise a question about the number of substances that there may be, and whether they are independent. Connected with this would be a question known as individuation, that is to say what makes one thing different from another thing, and then there is a side issue question of some fame whether there can be two things that are distinct but quite indistinguishable, a question known historically as the identity of indiscernables. Connected with all these questions is the problem of the categories, which is a relatively sophisticated way of expressing some of the other problems, or of approaching them, or of providing a theory about them. A further problem that arises concerns the nature of universals. This arises ostensibly because it is puzzling that one and the same entity should exist in many things: e.g. that equinity is to be found in all horses. It seems to me unlikely, however, that this sort of puzzlement would have arisen had it not been against a background of something deeper. The phenomenon I suspect was *change.* There is birth, growth, decay, and death. How can one explain change? For if a thing remains itself it cannot change, and change is impossible; and if a thing changes it cannot remain itself and self-identity is impossible. Somehow a thing has to be twofold: it must have a factor of permanence; and it must have a factor of changeability. The permanence underlying all change may be isolated as what is "universal"; and the problem would be how it could exist one and the same in a multiplicity of changing things.

This description of the proliferation of metaphysical questions omits three historically very significant and famous problems, namely God, freedom, and immortality, which Kant regarded as the central problems of metaphysics.

The first of these, God, arises in connection with the problem of the origin of the universe, and possibly also in connection with its purpose. So this problem is a particularization of one that has already been described. Freedom concerns freedom of the individual person's will, that is to say it concerns a question whether he can influence the processes of the universe or whether he is simply one part of the universe, that is, under the complete domination of the ultimate metaphysical principles. This question, which may appear to be somewhat more on the fringe, arises because human beings have felt themselves for millennia to be part of the world but also to be part of God. It is not clear to them, therefore, where they stand, and whether they are obedient to the principles of God and his universe, or whether they, participating in some way in, or having some spark of, the divine, can enter into the controlling area. Further, the question of immortality arises because unlike earthly things, the divine spark attributed to man leads him to suppose that he may have some part that survives his material death.

An esoteric addition should be made, however. It consists of the most ultimate question conceivable, so ultimate that no one discusses it because of being unable to say anything about it—it is mentioned only by teenagers beginning philosophy.

"Why does anything exist?"

Or, more colloquially but more forcefully, "Why is there Something and not Nothing?"

I do not think our professional lack of expertise in handling a question is a reason for disregarding it—or for hinting that it is naive and not worthy of professional attention. Adam had an answer. So did Hegel. But twentieth century homo philosophicus?

That completes my description of the questions with which metaphysics deals.

We turn next to the question of what remains of each of these questions, which of them is dead wood, and what are the living issues. Now the question of the origin of the universe is one that is living in that philosophers discuss it and so do scientists. The typical contemporary attitude among philosophers of logical positivist inheritance is that the question has no meaning. Other philosophers hold that no question can be ruled out quite so simply as this, especially as scientists have some very interesting and relevant things to say about this question, which appears to be highly meaningful in their discussions of it. So it would seem that a question of this sort may just be left to scientists. Turning to the specific question of the origin of the universe attributed to God's causal action: none of the historical arguments bearing on this or offering a proof are accepted by any school of philosophy, with possibly one exception. There is certainly no unanimity of acceptance or anything near it. This tends to undermine interest in the problems of immortality as well. The question of freedom is one that is a living issue because, quite apart from its historical origins, man has other reason to believe that he initiates action in the real world, as well as reason to think that he is the plaything of material and other forces around him. Consequently, there is a real problem. Turning to the nature of being, the furniture of the earth, matter, space, and time, answers could not be arrived at by philosophical means alone. Now this leaves one fundamental question untouched, namely, whether there is such a general entity as being which science does not touch, and with it, whether there is some fundamental stuff or substance; for, if so, then the issue of the other questions would still be alive. It is worth pointing out, however, that if the problem of *being* should turn out to be a dead issue, then its ultimate principles, the nature of universals, the nature of substance, the number of independent substances, the nature of individuation, and categories, all lose a great deal of their force. Though, even here, there can be other reasons why one or two of these can survive, but I would say that only two do survive in practice. One is a question about the nature of universals because there is a living issue connecting it with modern logic. There is a question whether logic requires universals or can work only with particulars, or on the other hand whether it can work entirely with universals. The other is the question whether logic specifies or prescribes that there is some ultimate piece of furniture of the earth. The question of categories arises similarly in connection with the furniture of the earth, i.e. whether there are different levels of being which cannot be reduced to one another, and this question could have a meaning and a treatment independently of whether the general question has anything living in it or not, i.e. the question of the nature of being.

Now on the question of the nature of being itself, it is a living issue in the sense that there is an influential school of philosophy that gives it great attention, namely the school of phenomenology and existentialism. It is closely connected with a fundamental theory called by Popper "essentialism" which has dominated philosophy from early Greek times, at least from the time of Plato, to the present day. The idea of an essence had disappeared out of physical science from the time of Galileo, but it still persists in the social sciences and in metaphysical thinking. Now the question whether there is such a thing as being could be interpreted specifically in terms of the question whether there are essences, and in fact, whether there might be only one essence. It is most difficult to illustrate and explain just what exactly this problem really is. This would have to be done before coming to a conclusion whether, in fact, there was a living issue in it, and to this I shall devote myself on a separate occasion.

In short, while some of these questions are on the borderline, perhaps the ones that are definitely most living have to do with freedom, universals, categories, and with the nature of being.

We turn next to ask more specifically how these questions differ from those of parascientific ontology. Having specified the questions, it is clear that denotatively they are very different. They bear no resemblance whatever to the question discussed by scientists, particularly physicists, except possibly the question of the origin of the universe, although, even here, it would seem that the question is asked in a different sense. How then are we to characterize the difference?

One of the main characterizations is that the questions in philosophy of nature are related to science, even if they are not questions that physicists would themselves be likely to ask. They are more closely related to questions in physics. Further, information from physics might be used in trying to establish a position or answer regarding them. In the present context metaphysics may fall back on information culled from the sciences, but also makes use, though somewhat scantily, of ordinary commonsense knowledge.

I do not think it would be possible to bring out the difference until we face these questions of the meaning of being or essence. When the parascientific ontologist asks about the nature of being he means something about the structure of matter as seen by commonsense. But it is not this conception that underlies the metaphysician's ideas. With that we will have to be content for the moment.

The parascientific ontologist and a metaphysician do, however, have something in common. Their method of approach seems to be the same.

They seem to be concerned with wholes and their method of reaching conclusions seems to be based on pure reason alone.

We are now in a position to approach some sort of conclusion or summary. It would seem that metaphysics, being concerned with being, may more specifically be called ontology and this in its broad sense is a *non-scientific cosmology,* to which we may add that there is some very slight overlap of the questions asked, but that the method is the same, namely *pure reasoning about wholes.*

This examination, together with the examination of parascientific ontology enables us to make a threefold distinction in metaphysics or to delineate three different sorts of metaphysics: (i) the embedded ontology of science; (ii) para-scientific ontology; and (iii) non-scientific ontology, which is what is provided by the pure metaphysics and which I have now been trying to describe; since it is totally unrestricted I am calling it cosmological ontology. To these must be added (iv) a different kind of metaphysics altogether which has appeared from time to time in the history of philosophy, consisting of what I would call vacuous postulates. I will now describe this very briefly. Most of the great systems of metaphysics have made some very large claim about the nature of the universe as a whole or some global component in it. There are, however, a few examples of metaphysics which have appeared to make a claim about the nature of the universe, but which when examined turn out to be asserting postulates that are vacuous or very nearly so. I will give two examples.

Berkeley gave the most ingenious detailed arguments of any philosopher of his time and used arguments that many would consider valid and uphold today. But his overall philosophy was something very different. He wished to explain the appearances of the world of nature around him. This he did by postulating the existence of an entity, namely God, which he could scarcely specify, though he mentioned one or two characteristics of a very general and vague sort. This postulate was supposed in his philosophy to explain the world of nature by an entirely unknown mechanism of causation. Again, the process was almost entirely unspecified. In short, the Berkeleian philosophy consisted of postulating an unspecified or almost unspecified entity answering Berkeley's problem by an unspecified or almost unspecified relation of causation. In other words, he was falling back on what has classically been called a deus ex machina. In short, he relied on an unspecified entity put to unspecified use or, if you prefer, a postulate making an unspecified claim.

A further example of this sort would be the philosophy of the occasionalists.

This is undoubtedly metaphysics, but is not like either scientific ontology or non-scientific ontology. The difference lies in the fact that there would seem to be content in the first two, while the third is vacuous. Nonetheless, metaphysics as a general term covers these four very different kinds of enquiries, and if we are to try to understand metaphysics to find out what are the living issues in it, to support it, or criticize it, we have to disentangle these four differences and treat them separately.

APPENDIX TO MODES [3], [4] AND [5]

Modes (4) and (5) are at times poles apart, at times scarcely distinguishable. It may be questioned whether, even in the extreme case, they are essentially different. Should they not rather be classified as two varieties of one mode?

To consider this, let us look at the ostensible differences.

Let us reflect on some of the examples, already noted, of parascientific ontology, such as the infinite divisibility of matter or the finitude of space. While these are ontological components of certain scientific theories, and therefore qualify for inclusion in the embedded ontology of science, they are also questions that might arouse, and almost certainly have done so, the interest of a philosopher who lacked knowledge and interest in science; hence for such a philosopher they would resemble cosmological ontology. They would, however, involve the concepts of science, which concepts in cosmological ontology typically do not. Thus the denotation is somewhat different. Parascientific ontology is a selection determined either by the scientific interest engaged or by the scientific type of concept involved.

In short, parascientific ontology is infused with a scientific interest or else involves ideas that usually are of special, though not exclusive, interest to scientists. Whereas cosmological ontology eschews the scientific route, and involves ideas that lie outside science and that scientists tend to shun.

If this were the sole difference, would it be justifiable to have classified Modes (4) and (5) separately? The difference of interest alone leads to a problem of communication. And this is sufficient justification; for I am trying to render "the" field of philosophy intelligible, and to this end it does not matter if only some of the divisions are more or less logical while some are practical.

A further comment on Modes (3), (4) and (5). Mode (4) may sometimes seem nearer to (5), but it may sometimes seem closer to (3). Perhaps this depends on the agent involved: if he is more rooted in philosophy his work will have a tinge of (5); if he is a scientist his work may easily be mistaken for (3). Moreover a question can move to and fro between (3) and (4).

But there would seem to be a more fundamental difference between Modes (4) and (5). The parascientific selection imposes a restriction which makes cosmological ontology look much wider, more abstract, more general. One reason would seem to be that relatively few of our ideas have, at this early stage in man's history, become articulated in scientific theories, so that cosmological ontology is perhaps in part the presupposition/consequences of our non-scientific notions. More significantly, however, it also manifests an attempt to probe more deeply than parascientific ontology.

The difference in generality or depth leads to a further consideration. If the embedded ontology of science and parascientific ontology both concern properties of wholes—the absoluteness of space, the infinite divisibility of matter, a vital force—it is entities and their properties they are concerned with. That is to say they are concerned with cosmological furniture and what it is like. But cosmological ontology asks a further question about the cosmological furniture, namely *what is its nature*? It asks about this nature, is it substance, is it mental, is it accessible to reason, is it Being, is it self-creating, is it outside time?

CHAPTER VI

Mode (6): Philosophy as Meaningless (Meta-ontological Negativism)

THE NEED was felt during the whole of the 20th century to oppose all metaphysical questions dealing with the fundamental structure of the universe, its nature, origin, and so forth. This is characteristic of the 20th century; a great part of the philosophizing has been done under the anti-metaphysical banner; and I think one might fairly describe the philosophizing that has gone on from around the turn of the century as debunking, trying to liquidate all the metaphysical ideas of the past. One might wonder whether this was a new movement, particularly characteristic of the 20th century, unlike anything that had ever taken place before; for it is, after all, a century of disillusionment. The answer to that is simply *no*. There have been from time to time very great sceptics down the centuries and even millennia who have done the same thing, but scepticism has probably never been quite so widespread or wholesale or given to such broadsides as in the present century. In Greek times Protagoras was renowned for having said that man is the measure of all things; there was much scepticism in the Renaissance; and there was the classic scepticism of Hume in the eighteenth century. Thus a tendency towards scepticism was shown very early in the history of thought, although the great bulk of philosophizing has been the other way, in favour of trying to find some positive edifice of human truth and human knowledge. To pass over the millennia, to Hume, the most famous sceptic of modern times: It is very well known that he argued that there was mathematical knowledge which told you nothing about the world; and there were matters of fact; and beyond these nothing. All else, he said, in one of the famous purple patches of philosophical literature, which came at the end of the *Enquiry*, was mere sophistry and illusion. The spirit of Hume has had a re-birth in the 20th century, and I suppose he is the spiritual ancestor of the great majority of philosophers of this century. In his day Hume received no support; philosophers were concerned to oppose him in the intervening centuries; and his comeback did not materialize till the second quarter of the present century. In Hume we have the phenomenon of opposition to every kind of metaphysical thinking. It is very clear, I think, that the tendency of the recent past was fundamentally anti-theological in its aims as it was with Hume. Hume was quite openly sceptical about all matters connected with miracles and religion. And the philosophers of the earlier part of this century were similarly concerned, for they were attacking theology and metaphysics.

(I cannot help wondering whether there is not something sociological about this mass movement of scepticism, hostility to the idea of a positive philosophical position, because the widespread nature of the tendency seems to spread beyond the frontiers of any one country, and this could mean some sort of change in the outlook of man. But of this more in Part III.)

A parallel movement began in England and Austria. Interestingly enough it had almost identical consequences and almost identical methods and procedures. The movement that began in England was initiated at Cambridge by Bertrand Russell and G. E. Moore, of whom Russell is the more famous internationally, though Moore is also very well known and in some areas perhaps more influential among philosophers. They were not sceptics these two. They were avowedly and nakedly out to puncture the rather vague and perhaps pretentious kind of philosophizing that had gone on in the previous century. Certainly that is so, but they did not start out with the idea that there was no philosophical truth, because they thought there was: they thought they would have to begin at the beginning and devise a more accurate and precise way of attaining it. In Austria it had a similar sort of origin with Mach in Vienna. There is a long history in both countries and a certain intertwining, because after a while there was mutual influence.

The philosophical position that emerged has gone through three phases. All of them have reached America and have conquered perhaps three quarters of the universities in America; they were well-nigh the universal philosophical outlook of Britain, Scandinavia, Poland and Australia. It is the most worldwide general view, though not the only one. A very different approach concerns philosophy as a way of life, the existentialist approach, which is characteristic of Europe, excluding Scandinavia, Poland, and Austria (quite a large exclusion, for these countries have been very active philosophically), especially in France and Germany, which are both existentialist and phenomenological. This is a different approach; and it is an approach which is unintelligible by and large to the kind of Anglo-American-Austrian way of thinking— and vice versa. It is a case of two types of philosophizing which are so different that philosophical conversation is, unfortunately, almost impossible between the protagonists of the two sides.

Here I want to depict the three phases mentioned.

The first quarter of a century was occupied by what can be described as *logical analysis* in England, and a corresponding activity in Vienna. Logical analysis was designed to clarify the meaning of statements and the cogency of arguments or inferences. The protagonists of this were Russell and Moore, as already mentioned, together with a slightly younger philosopher, Broad. They believed that, by clarifying straightforwardly the words and statements that philosophers use and expressing them sufficiently sharply and clearly, it would be somehow evident whether the claims philosophers made were true or false. Indeed for Moore, in effect, the problem of truth was the problem of clarity. They were not fundamentally opposed to the idea that philosophical truth might be discoverable if one was lucky; they were opposed only to the vague and perhaps pretentious way of carrying it on that had been characteristic in the previous century both in Germany and Britain.

The second phase I suppose set in when the Austrian movement became a bit more extreme than the English one (it was not British throughout; in fact, I should say not even English but more narrowly Cambridge, because no other university followed along this particular line; there was only an isolated adherent or two at Oxford, very different from now when some 40 or more out of 50 Oxford teachers of philosophy have been reputed to follow the grandchild of this particular line). The movement in Vienna became known as *logical positivism*. It was started by Moritz Schlick, and it became imported into Britain, and stimulated the more radical wing of the logical analysis that had been active there, partly because of Wittgenstein, who though an Austrian, worked at Cambridge, and partly because Ayer visited Vienna and returned with Carnap's ideas and programmes. Wittgenstein's work was in tendency the same as the logical positivism of Vienna, although he never overtly subscribed to the central thesis of the logical positivism of the Vienna Circle.

Thus there was an interpenetration of the two trends in England and Austria. They more or less went parallel, from say 1925 to 1940, and that was the period of logical positivism at its height.

The intellectual reasons for the transition were two. First, the method of logical analysis failed to produce results: clarification and analysis of ideal examples worked beautifully, but extrapolation to philosophical questions could not be carried out. Second, the idea of meaningless statements began to become prominent. This led directly to logical positivism.

The problem might be said to be the undecidability of metaphysics, since no way could be found to establish truth or falsity; and this led to a doubt whether it was understandable at all. Thus arose the problem of meaning.

Logical positivism in a nutshell was a doctrine of meaningfulness. That is to say, the meaning of a statement is given by whatever perception you would use in order to check up on the truth or the falsity of the statement. A statement was *verified*, as it was put. Thus, if you wonder whether the statement "there are mountains on the other side of the moon" has a meaning or not, you would find that it has a meaning because you know what it would be like to have perceptions of mountains on the other side of the moon if you could go there. Thus that sort of statement is meaningful. But if you proffer a statement about the origin of the universe, whether the universe had a first cause, this is the kind of thing the positivists would have said was meaningless, because you would not be able to specify what sort of observation or perception would enable you to detemine whether the statement was true or false. In developing this approach they utilized two sources of inspiration. One was science, which was unquestionably meaningful and vouched for by observation. The other was *Principia Mathematica,* for, among other things, Russell, delving into the foundations of mathematics, found that certain statements were structurally meaningless.

All I am trying to do is to convey the broad idea and the more or less merciless attack on the whole of metaphysical thinking, the outcome of which was that all metaphysical thinking was regarded as without meaning. This had very many eminent followers; but they had all given up these extreme positions at the latest by about 1945. I remember Hempel in the mid-30's reporting that it was customary in the Vienna Circle to interject "metaphysical" if any member lapsed into a meaningless statement, and that this happened so often it had to be shortened to "m". By 1945 this was a thing of the past.

In this context, I have been concerned primarily with logical positivism but have given some consideration to logical analysis, its predecessor, mainly to show what led up to logical positivism. It is, however, worthwhile to summarize the differences and parallels between them.

Logical analysis still retained a classical aim of finding philosophical truth (even if this was expected to be of a modest variety and not some great ultimate metaphysical truth). There was also the aim of pricking metaphysical bubbles, but not the wholesale liquidation of metaphysics. Further grounds of certitude were sought; these were located, rightly or wrongly, in logic and in sense-data. Its method was to find solutions by clarification. In the outcome, however, the procedure of clarification, which evolved into clarification of statements, led to consideration of statements that were meaningless. This did not at first seem to carry very significant overtones, but in fact it was this that effected the transition to logical positivism; for logical positivism, so to speak, inflated this aspect into the dominating feature of the entire philosophy.

By contrast logical positivism was at least ostensibly a method of ascertaining whether or not a given statement has a meaning, as this was determined by whether or not the statement has a verification. Now this involved that only what is suceptible of being verified by sense-experience has a meaning. The obverse of this is that terms denoting metaphysical entities that do not manifest themselves in sense-experience are meaningless. Thus the method has a far-reaching result, namely an *ontological negativism.*

One could express this by saying that logical positivism was fundamentally opposed to all ontology. For instance, it was avowedly opposed to metaphysics and theology. Strictly speaking, however, some ontology is left because sensory observations exist; they alone constitute the "ultimate furniture of the earth" and therefore they constitute an ontology. This exception is not so significant. When philosophers discuss the possibility of something ontological, they have in mind, not the appearance, but some supposed entity underlying the appearance.

Thus the outlook and tendency of logical positivism was totally different from that of logical analysis from which it sprang. No logical positivist believed in metaphysical truth, all age-old metaphysics was scrapped, and scrapped on the grounds of being meaningless—a fate that was worse than false.

What then was the fate of logical positivism? Why did it fade away somewhere around the time of World War II?

The answer is fairly simple; the thesis of ontological negativism centred on the principle of verifiability. In fact, although there were certain other features of the philosophy, the most important was this principle. Naturally, therefore, it was a major task for the logical positivists to formulate this principle, and, if possible, to specify in what way it might be established. Over these two questions difficulties arose.

Reminiscent of the principle of induction of old, it was impossible to prove the principle of verifiability by observation of matters of fact; nor could it be held to be a logical tautology to be established on logical grounds alone; and no other source of proof was open to the logical positivists, because any other way would have to fall back, for example, on the notion of the synthetic a priori, which would be ruled out by this very principle as meaningless. So it was realized by logical positivists that no proof was possible.

The situation was much more interesting over the matter of formulation. The early attempts to formulate the principle that were strong enough to exclude metaphysics did their work only by excluding too much, that is, by excluding some of the things that the logical positivists wished to retain, as for example, abstract scientific statements. Logical positivists were in a quandary, for they could not find a formulation that would exclude the metaphysical and theological kind of statements they wished to exclude on the grounds of being meaningless, while including statements that they regarded as being meaningful. Thus Popper (1962)[1] showed that metaphysical statements, e.g. "God exists", could be formulated in Carnap's language, which was specially devised to exclude these. A climax was reached when in the end Church provided a proof that one of the chief formulations, due to Ayer, necessarily failed to have those two functions. Logical positivism in its undiluted form faded away.

(In addition, an attempt was made to show by myself (1963)[2] that, independently of the problem of formulation, it was impossible in principle to devise a method that would do what was assigned to the principle of verifiability, on the grounds that a successful principle would be equivalent to a piece of a priori knowledge, that certain particulars did not exist in the universe, a claim that would be as sweeping on the negative side as any of the great metaphysical systems made on the positive side. This is elaborated in Part II, Chapter II.)

Although a total failure, as regards specific aims, it should be recognized that logical positivism constituted a worthy attempt to grapple seriously with the question of what could be known. It attempted to handle this in a rational manner. It attempted to get philosophy to have its feet upon the ground. It opposed the a priori omniscience of old-time philosophy (even though in a negative sense it tried to do exactly the same thing). It could be said to have attempted to provide a rational account of what may be believed.

We turn, then, to the next phase of the movement. Logical positivism was very much concerned with the handling and use of statements. It is not surprising, therefore, to find that the use of statements and words became the central feature of philosophizing in the next phase of the development. The main stimulus for this—there may have been other local stimuli at various places—came from Wittgenstein's notebooks which were widely circulated among a narrow circle. And, in fact, what ensued became centrally language analysis or linguistic philosophy.

In the philosophy of language, the main routine developed into processes of disentangling linguistic usage. There are enormous numbers of attempts to work it this way, but very few really fine specimens. Perhaps some of the most striking are Ryle's (1933) paper entitled "Systematically Misleading Expressions" and his book (Ryle, 1949), *The Concept of Mind* (which whether mistaken or not has a significant thesis and is ingenious).

Now it might be thought that this was logical analysis simply expressed in a more specifically linguistic form, but in fact a change had come upon the scene. Since it was not found possible to devise a principle that would drive a wedge between the meaningful and the meaningless, the overt aim of showing metaphysical statements to be meaningless was more or less dropped (though at times it seems to be covertly retained). The consequence of this was that in general any statement could be made, provided one took pains to make clear what it did and did not imply. In particular, the later work of Wittgenstein set the model for this. Not quite everything could be allowed to be said, but nearly everything could. Anything could be said for which the words have in ordinary language a use. The curious result of this was that many metaphysical expressions, including theological ones, which had been ruled out as meaningless by logical positivism, now returned to the fold because linguistic expressions referring to them very often could be found to have a use.

BIBLIOGRAPHY

Popper, K. R. (1962), *Conjectures and Refutations*, "The Demarcation between Science and Metaphysics", (1955), 274f.
Ryle, Gilbert (1933), "Systematically Misleading Expressions", *Proc. Arist. Soc.*, **33**.
——————(1949), *The Concept of Mind*, London.
Wisdom, J. O. (1963), "The Metamorphoses of the Verifiability Theory of Meaning", *Mind*, **72**.

CHAPTER VII

Mode (7): Philosophy as a Way of Life

PHILOSOPHY AS a way of life is often an unarticulated idea with which young students approach the subject. And it is widely looked upon as falling outside the proper business of philosophy. Nonetheless, several examples make it quite clear that philosophy as a way of life began two thousand years ago and that this tradition has continued, even if only in a minor way ever since. The Cynics and the Cyrenaics in Greek days and the Stoics and the Epicureans in Roman days were concerned quite explicitly and nakedly and unashamedly with the idea of a way of life; they were concerned with the business of how to cope with the frustrations and difficulties of living and dying. So much was this so that one of the ancient thinkers has left behind him a saying to the effect that "When Death is with us we are not, and when we are, Death is not". This means that he was trying to cope with the problem of death or dying, with the fear of death. But the curious thing about this is that he coped with it by means of something that is almost a joke or, perhaps better put, is just a bad joke. When Death is here we are not, so that when Death has actually arrived, personified, we have ceased to be, and so death is no problem; and when we are still alive Death has not arrived, so again there is no problem. Thus by a logical twist, the fear of death ceases to be a serious problem. The device is, of course, fantastic, for you cannot get over a real problem by a mere trick of logic. The interest of it, however, lies not in the solution but in the attempt. Here was a really fine thinker who was trying to cope with the problem of living, or rather of ceasing to live. He knew that one of the few things we can be certain about is that life does come to an end, and he felt compelled to cope with this. Further, even Aristotle, who went in for metaphysics as a general study of the universe, promulgated a doctrine of the mean, according to which the reasonable man would avoid extremes. In other words, avoiding excess was his guideline in conducting one's life.

If you come to modern days after the long period of the middle-ages, you find once again that philosophers for over two centuries were concerned with very abstract conceptions, which appear to have nothing to do with life. At length you reach Schopenhauer and Nietzsche, who were very much concerned with the problem of living. Schopenhauer was one of the world's greatest pessimists who has ever lived. He thought that all life was dreadful, and that even what seemed satisfying was only a snare and ended in distress. His recipe for living, and he had one, pervading his metaphysics and epistemology, was to cease to have any desires at all. Other philosophers have written in this vein down the ages, but Schopenhauer was the most extreme. He held that one should not try to satisfy private desire, and in particular, he held that one should avoid sexual desire and any kind of relations with other people but subjugate the will. There was one redeeming feature, strangely enough, in Schopenhauer's philosophy, namely he thought one might find some sort of salvation in art. There is a close connection between the ideas of Schopenhauer and some Indian philosophy, according to which the world is illusion: what you should aim at is the ultimate disintegration. This is very foreign to the western world, in which a philosophy of disintegration is not the sort of thing that would reflect the sentiments of a go-getter—quite the contrary. But the philosophy of the Far East displayed an overwhelming tendency to want to lose oneself in oblivion. If I say that is far from what the Anglo-American go-getter wants, it may not be so far removed after all, because there are plenty of Anglo-Americans who want to lose themselves in oblivion, though it is not in the oblivion of the religious of the Far East, so much as in the alcohol or drugs of the Near West.

Schopenhauer advocated oblivion. He quite explicitly was concerned with a way of life and how to cope with the appalling distress in human life. And there is no doubt that he found life appalling. Great numbers of people have found it that way both now and in the past, and I am concerned to bring out that philosophers, although it has not been much talked about, have reflected this point of view; I do not want to give an exaggerated picture, but merely to bring it out that a proportion of philosophers have put it this way.

Close on the heels of Schopenhauer came Nietzsche, who wrote very famous aphorisms and had the most penetrating insights. These, I would say, concerned two things—human nature on the one hand and philosophical theories on the other, very penetrating things to say, for example about the unconscious and the philosophy of Plato. One runs something like this—that when my memory says it was so and my pride says it was not, finally my memory yields. This may not appear very striking to us now, because it has been a commonplace since Freud that memory slips and oblivia have some such meaning: if something is disagreeable it is a familiar mental mechanism to get rid of it by amnesia. Thus Nietzsche was able to penetrate into something of human nature before Freud. His concern with the way of life was very different from Schopenhauer's. He considered that morals (i.e. in the broad sense, not just sexual morals) were a grave danger to life, they ought to be superseded; they were really lowbrow, undignified, and in effect grossly immoral. He, in fact, advocated a world view which transcended all ordinary morals, because he regarded ordinary moral codes as essentially narrow and restricting to anyone of imagination and enterprise. One of his books is entitled *Beyond Good and Evil*, by which he meant beyond the ordinary mundane parochial sense of good and evil and beyond the supposedly exalted senses of religion or philosophy, and he invented his conception of a superman who would be beyond these. So here you can see that Nietzsche was creating a philosophy of life.

In the recent past and in the present there has been a resurgence of the same sort of ideas which may seem to have had their inspiration in Kierkegaard (a famous Danish theologian in the last century) but in my view he has been found to be a kind of father in retrospect. He might not have become so famous if it had not been for contemporary thought; and when philosophers get going they like to find ancestors just as people do who make their fortune and like to build up a family tree in retrospect. Philosophers are not immune to this human frailty also. The contemporaries are those known to the world at large as existentialists. Now we are getting to what is more familiar. Some of the best known are the French ones, though there are also German ones. This philosophy has some following in perhaps a tenth of the academic philosophers of America. It has practically no hold in Britain, but an enormous hold in Europe. The main work has come from Jean-paul Sartre and various others in France, and Heidegger and Jaspers in Germany. There are nuances in the ways they all put the matter, but in the large they are concerned with the problem of how they shall live.

In developing their point of view a number of positions have to be maintained. First, the human will has to be free, otherwise the problem has no sense. What does the freedom of the human mind consist of in relation to the question of a way of life? It consists of being responsible to oneself, i.e., responsible to oneself for what one elects to do. Secondly, this gives rise in particular to the position that existentialists hold about codes of morals and other codes. If a person passively accepts the code of morals taught to him by his parents or his teachers, or a code given to him by his religion, or a code simply of his group or society, then for an existentialist, he is not acting from his own true self but in accordance with something imposed upon him from without. Hence, existentialist freedom consists in acting in accordance with one's own personality. This does not, however, necessarily mean giving up all codes of behavior adopted by society or other people, because one may freely choose to adopt those. However, one is unfree, insofar as one has simply acquiesced in them rather than chosen them. It comes, as it were, as a corollary that it is "bad faith" to act in accordance with the precept of another. In short, one could put it that the emphasis lies on integrity of the personality.

To take an example from Sartre. During World War II a young man might have had a conflict over whether to join the resistance movement against the Germans or look after his aged and ailing mother. He would have felt an understandable pull in both those directions. It might well be that if we knew this man well, we might realize that he was not free in an existentialist sense and be able to tell very well what decision he would take, and with different people the answer might be different. In the case of somebody with existentialist freedom the issue would be open. One could not tell in advance which course of action the young man would elect to follow, and he would choose, in accordance with his personality rather than with what he considered was a duty imposed either by the state or by social custom.

This example leads to a further point, namely, that in a situation of freedom there is anxiety. In acquiescing in a code adopted from others, anxiety in the extreme cases would be nonexistent, because, so to speak, the choice is taken for one by the code. But the existentialist has to have his heart wrung by the process of reaching a decision. Anxiety is, so to speak, measured by the "gap" between the problem and the decision and action.

It is perhaps worth noticing a particular feature of this philosophy. It is sometimes charged with being a philosophy of irresponsibility, because it appears to be a philosophy of subjectivism. That is to say, a person would act on his own ideas, irrespective of an objective right or wrong. Anything goes. But the philosophy does not, in fact, advocate acting in accordance with personal purely selfish desires in complete disregard of other people. Acting in this way would arise only if this was in fact the code adopted by one's personality. In persons of any real maturity, however, it is part of one's make-up to have relations towards, and adopt an attitude about, other people, which may include concern for them, and this will enter into part of the process of deliberation. Hence, the philosophy could reasonably claim to be a philosophy of the highest responsibility.

Thus, one might say that existentialism is epitomized by the philosophy of Polonius "To thine own self be true", and this may take us back to the Greeks, in particular to Socrates whose doctrine "Know thyself" was surely not simply an epistemological demand but a maxim to enable one to act in the most exemplary manner.

We can now see that this strand, concerned with the way of life, has run through philosophy from the earliest times to the present. It has been overtly a minor strand; most work on philosophy has been concerned with other things. But it is quite noticeably there. And it is difficult to see why it should not have just as much right to be there as any other approach to philosophy. It is surely concerned with the human problem of living that exercises nearly all human beings at some time or other in their lives, and for this there are no generally accepted guide lines, though there are those various codes claiming to provide guidelines on the part of some of the religions.

I would conjecture that philosophers more than most people are imbued with a need to come to terms with problems of this sort, but that this tendency gets submerged in the philosophy of the schools, and is not in evidence in many forms of philosophizing that take place. Nonetheless, if we look between the lines of the philosophizing of great philosophers, even those who ostensibly have been concerned only with great metaphysical questions, and who would appear to have nothing to do with the way of life, we may be able to discern even here a common tendency to be trying to grapple with some such problem. At this point I shall simply illustrate the possibility very briefly and therefore dogmatically. The philosopher, Bradley, who was an Anglo-Hegelian at the turn of the 20th century, produced one of the most abstract philosophies that has ever existed, centring on a logical principle about the nature of relationship. What the philosophy amounts to is this, that everything isolated in any degree from the entire whole constituting the universe is by such isolation rendered partially false; the truth lies only in the whole. This metaphysical theory certainly seems remote from anything to do with life. When the question of evil comes in, we can at once see the application to life. Evil is seen to be evil only when isolated from the whole of which it is a part. In other words what is supposedly evil is not really evil when seen in its setting in the whole. Now if this is correct it is clear that one at least of the main sources of Bradley's approach to philosophy was to come to terms with the problem of evil, which, indeed, has oppressed so many people. It would seem that Bradley was unable to tolerate the existence of evil and had to invent a metaphysic which was such that evil would fundamentally be seen not to exist. And, indeed, such an intellectual device is a reminder of the ancient philosopher who tried to abolish the problem of death by a logical trick.

Whether or not, however, this conjecture about metaphysics applies in part or generally, it is clear that there is a well developed tradition of philosophy as a way of life. One can see how difficult it is to understand what philosophy is about, when it can concern such very different things as metascience, metaphysics, and philosophy of life.

CHAPTER VIII

Mode(8): Evaluation of Modes of Philosophy

MODE (1)   METASCIENCE

DEDUCTIVE LOGIC "has arrived"; indeed it "arrived" under Aristotle. It gets results which can satisfy public scrutiny. It is the only philosophical subject to have done so. So much so, that it has become transplanted, in some universities, to the Mathematics Department. Not that logic has no difficulties—so has mathematics—but the doubt surrounding them is of an althogether different order from the doubt that permeates all other philosophy. In my opinion, it hardly belongs to philosophy any more, but, tradition apart, it touches on philosophical problems at a few—only a few—points (many contemporary philosophers, eminent ones, hold, however, that deductive logic underlies all philosophy).

Metascience (commonly and perhaps conveniently, if wrongly, called methodology, scientific method, inductive logic) has, I think, gone at least some way in this direction. It is still highly controversial. But it is a clearly discernible field, one knows what one is trying to do, the procedures are publicly intelligible; it possesses theorems, or gets results, though these form two rival systems, each of which satisfies the public scrutiny of its own public, and neither of which has as yet come out on top. Such a situation is unlike the morass of philosophy; it is perhaps like the position of optics when controversy persisted about whether light consisted of waves or corpuscles, or the position of the concept of probability when there is doubt, even after centuries of accurate application, whether it was a frequency or what-not, or the position of the theory of heat when there was much dispute about whether it consists of one fluid or two. The area of doubt in such a scientific case is on an altogether different level from that of philosophy, where the simplest thing you say may be wildly wrong, where you try to build on a quicksand because you think (maybe wrongly) that your only alternative, water, would give less support.

The controversial aspect here is straightforward enough. Metascience traditionally meant the logic of inference from particular premisses to a general conclusion (which might be certain or probable).[1] This has been opposed since 1934 by the theory of testability, which refers to a hypothetico-deductive framework, the testing of hypotheses by attempted refutation, and the denial that induction is possible.[1]

Inductive logic has been highly developed and transformed by Carnap and his school. It is a highly coherent system (even if not completely so), whether or not it is correct.[2] It has something of the character that a mathematician feels at home with.

The theory of testability has been largely[3] invented by Popper.[4] It, too, is a highly coherent (even if not completely so) system, whether or not it is correct. It lacks the character that is of mathematical appeal, but at some levels it clicks exactly with the thinking of theoretical scientists of the highest eminence, e.g. in physics and biology.

It has recently been brought out by Lakatos that there is a difference of aim : Carnap's to justify scientific conclusions after the fact; Popper's to provide a theory of the (logical) structure of discovery. It should not, however, be supposed that the two systems are concerned with non-overlapping areas and that each has its own job to do; they conflict fundamentally.

Both systems are developed to an advanced degree. That is to say, one knows pretty well where one is with them. Both may be susceptible of improvement in their well-worked out parts by tinkering here and there or clarifying some minor point; but radical redevelopment of the central parts is hardly to be envisaged.[4]

I will state my opinion for what it is worth (for I do not object to holding opinions in philosophy, only in not seeing the other side of the case). I think that Popper's theory, within the limits he set himself, is highly successful; I do not think Carnap's is; I think "inductive logic" would disappear in a generation with the passing of his immediate followers, were it not for the power Lakatos has pointed out, that research programmes have to protect false theories, to which I would add that the opposition created by a better theory (as I take Popper's to be) acts like an antibiotic and develops a resistant strain of the theory at bay. Popper's theory answers to science as I know it—and also, though not a justificationist theory, copes with the problem of justification. Further, Popper's theory, if properly understood by social scientists and seriously utilized, is to my mind one of the most essential tools required for the development of the social sciences.

I do not think there is any real doubt that metascience has a distinct field, an application, and a useful, though modest, role.

To accept the virtues of metascience—as also to accept the virtues of logic—may indeed influence one's attitude towards other modes of philosophy, but, except in extreme cases, it is neutral with regard to them, i.e. it is left open to adopt any position towards them.

MODE (2) EPISTEMOLOGY

I have portrayed epistemology, to begin with, as a like activity to metascience though with a different object of scrutiny—not scientific knowledge and its ingredients but non-scientific knowledge and its ingredients. Epistemology is concerned very broadly with man's intellectual relation to matter or the world. So, in this role, epistemology is "metacognition".

No doubt metascience is metacognition; but it is a trivial decision whether to include metascience within metacognition or hive it off. More convenient, I think, to hive it off, terminologically, provided this does not lead us to forget that metascience is a species of the wider metacognition. We must not be prevented from holding that metascience can be used to solve or throw light on some problems of metacognition (*i.e.*, that the study of science might help us with epistemology), or the other way round. Although some philosophers would like metascience to swallow up epistemology, others epistemology to swallow up metascience, all such matters must be kept open, even if we adopt a seemingly non-neutral terminology.

But I have urged that metascience and metacognition are fundamentally different in a certain respect over their main areas, even if one were successfully used to solve the problems of the other. Indeed the epistomologist mostly sits in the third row, considering truth, knowledge, and rationality.

If metascience is well along the road to respectability, metacognition is not. There is no commanding epistemological system, like Popper's or Carnap's in metascience, with a clear set of theorems, which produces order in its field and which, whether one agrees with it or not, is open to public scrutiny. There is but a motley collection of approaches, unintelligible outside their home schools, perhaps reminiscent of the situation that prevailed in the early days of the study of electricity.

A physicist or a historian, dipping into a work of epistemology, unaided in his selection, might well be dismayed.

This does not mean that metacognition is futile or unimportant. It does mean that (even after centuries or millenia) there is still a need to formulate its problems. It might indeed make our professional journals less uninteresting if some issues constituted a forum devoted to the task of formulation. Formulation is very difficult; but it is no more than very difficult; it should yield to systematic hard work with the considerable intelligence that is available (and some consider usually wasted by being channelled towards originality—gambits of the utmost unimportance). Formulation needs to be neutral with respect to known theories, and needs to show why there is a problem.

In my view there are genuine problems in metacognition: *e.g.*, the problem of perception, the problem of truth, the problem of the origin of knowledge.

It is not so obvious whether such problems are "important", or so important as those of metascience, in the sense of having repercussions outside themselves. It happens that Tarski's theory of truth does have this kind of significance; but the repercussion is peculiar—it enables us to find proofs of theorems by means of meta-mathematics that cannot be proved by means of mathematics itself. If we should solve the problem of perception, it is not clear that this could do anything for us beyond solving the problem of perception. But it would be nice to do that.

So long as a problem is genuine, the fact that its area is a morass and revolting to a tidy intellect which can endure only success and cannot live with failure should not be taken to mean that the subject is futile; rather should it be regarded as a challenge to a pioneer.

MODE (3) THE EMBEDDED ONTOLOGY OF SCIENCE

This tells us what the universe is basically made up of. The contents asserted are not assured by reason; they are the commitments of well-tried scientific theories. They are "well proved" like a well proved man—who may unexpectedly fail in an hour of need. The ontology lives off the theories: so long as the theories are corroborated, the ontology survives. When the theories are overthrown, the ontology may be put in a museum, or it may be adopted by the new regime.

The situation of the embedded ontology is not pleasing to one's hankering after rationality, in the cut and dried form in which everything would be susceptible of a definite answer. But at least it does not contravene rationality, in that the scientist does not have to *adopt* an embedded ontology *as an article of faith*. This mode of philosophizing, or form of metaphysics, is thus not wholly likable intellectually, but we know where we are with it.

MODE (4) PARASCIENTIFIC ONTOLOGY

What is to be gained by rising questions about the infinite divisibility of matter, the finiteness of space, the existence of a vital force, before we have scientific theories that might carry answers?

i) It is a natural propensity to wonder about such matters, for whatever reason, whether because of the aura of paradox or the implications supposed or real about man's place in the universe.

ii) Before the discovery of relevant scientific theories we have non-scientific theories that lead to conclusions about them. Thus behind vitalism is the notion that everything that works is made to work by something. Again, since we meet no boundaries, space appears to us an endless container. Such answers are incorrect or "stupid" only when they are the product of theories long given up. It should be noted, however, that they are not stupid in their context. The theory that the earth is flat, once so hard to overcome, now not even a target for ridicule, was not stupid—in fact if anything was stupid or mad, it was the idea that the earth is round, given the background knowledge of the time.

iii) Before we have a scientific method of answering such questions, we may well believe that other methods can be used or found, such as the essentialistic method of reflection on the essence of life or the essence of space.

iv) If, however, we hold that there is no method of obtaining correct answers in advance of discovering appropriate scientific theories—and this in itself is a policy, belief, or epistemological principle that might prove fallible—then indeed discussion seems pointless.

v) But we always need to keep unsolved problems in the forefront of our minds, to remind us where we are trying to go.

vi) And discussion may conceivably lead to the conception of a framework, point of view, ontology, Weltanschauung, within which an appropriate new theory may be discovered. I do not think this is the usual course of events, but I think it is possible and has even occurred. The discontinuous notion of matter in quantum mechanics may be an example.

vii) Discussion may bring out weaknesses in existing ontologies of science, and thus promote a critical attitude towards existing empirical theories. Landé, for example, has persistently done this for many years with quantum mechanics. That his work in this area evokes little response from many working physicists, who at times even spurn it, reflects only the splitmindedness of mankind's rather backward state of knowledge and education.

In short, the most significant grounds for airing these questions are the possibility of detecting flaws even in empirical theories, the possibility of fostering a situation promoting new empirical theories, and preserving our scientific perspective.

Moreover, for those who adopt a cosmological philosophy, such questions may have an acutely relevant bearing.

MODE (5) COSMOLOGICAL ONTOLOGY

Although the "in groups" of this century would have no truck with *studying the world,* this ancient propensity is represented more widely than might be imagined from a perusal of learned journals and Ph.D. titles. McTaggart, almost unread, was possibly as fine a philosopher as any in the seventeenth century—a Spinoza born three hundred years too late. Whitehead, occasionally read, was concerned equally with the depths. Bergson saw the cosmos in a new way. And all of these philosophers made time an integral part of their thought. Perhaps Alexander, once much read, now almost never, should be added, even if he failed to achieve the grand manner which came easily to the others. Croce's target was not the cosmos. But Husserl, who was much more influential than the others, himself aimed, by means of epistemology and the nature of experiencing the world, to penetrate into and reveal the nature of the cosmos; though it is not for this reason, in the main, that Husserl is studied.

Although the approach is apparently not in tune with the twentieth century, one cannot of course tell whether it will have a comeback. Popper has introduced the notion of a "third world", which would have been acceptable to Parmemides, Plato, and Hegel. Strawson is said to be outlining, in his new "descriptive metaphysics", a certain structure the cosmos must have. But the comeback has not come far.

At all events, the cosmological mode has had a long innings from the first known philosopher of the western world, Thales, who said that water constituted the nature of the cosmos, through a long line of Greeks occupied with the permanent and the changeable, to Plato who held that the cosmos consisted of the changeable or low-grade environment of man and of the permanent or perfect archetypes beyond our mortal reach; from Descartes who depicted the cosmos as constituted of two substances, mind and matter (with a third substance, God, outside) to Kant who saw the cosmos as a combination of three entities, a chaos (as in various creation myths), a primordial (though human) mind-stuff (substituting for the prime mover of the myths), and their product, the environmental world of man; and thence to Hegel and the Hegelians (or semi-Helegians) who saw the world as a complex structure of abstract components of mind.

It is philosophy of this genre that has (occasionally) captured poets and that has (often) evoked the contempt of scientists. Are philosophers of this genre inspired to visions ordinary geniuses cannot comprehend, or are they pretentious madmen? (Or both?)

One could of course take the line that this sort of philosophy can be left to "them as likes it". But I do not think one should opt out like that; and I think one can do something to come to grips with it. I would make the following points.

i) However esoteric any such system may be, there are always some people who understand it. A highly intellectual person may, these days, be "educated" to understand only his own field, and possibly only his own corner of it ("It is not my period/area, old man"), but such an intellect ought to be able, and I believe actually is able, to understand anything put in front of him, if he takes the necessary trouble to do so. It is an interesting challenge to find out what an expert in some cosmological ontology understands by it (or what sort of undertaking is involved).

ii) Some such systems may possibly have been constructed by the mad. I think it is certain that most of them were not. In general, the great philosophers who gave birth to them did much other work that was sane, and I get no flavour, as a rule, of a pretentious inflated ego (such as one does sometimes get from the more unintelligent kind of cranks or from intelligent cranks who do not bother to master their subject). Such philosophers were making a heroic attempt to come to intellectual terms with the world or whatever it was they were trying to do; these men were mental giants. One must make a serious attempt to understand their endeavour.

iii) Cosmological philosophy poses for us a problem of rationality—of which more in later chapters—of how to find out whether such a system is true or false. This problem is widely swept under the carpet because it cannot apparently be solved. That, however, is precisely the reason why it is an interesting, and perhaps even important, problem.

iv) I feel with Hamlet—"What a piece of work is man". What sort of creature is it that has achieved such a unique creation as cosmological ontology? Whether you regard it as a monstrosity, a white elephant, the ultimate map of the universe, or the ultimate mirror of man, one cannot but be awestruck at the single-minded intensity of the undertaking, as one may be at the Serapeum.

v) If this arises about man in the singular, it also arises about man's social structure: if social structure did not contribute to the development of cosmological ontology (though I believe it did), at least it was permissive. Can something be learnt, therefore, about social structure from cosmological ontology?

vi) And what is the role of cosmological ontology in the life of a man?

vii) And what is the role of cosmological ontology in society? At least it is worth raising the question of its role (on functionalist lines) and whether it has one.

viii) These are all questions to do with the nature, structure, and function of cosmological ontology, and our attitudes towards it. There is also the question of its theoretical utility. This concerns not the question whether it succeeds in telling us anything about the universe, but whether it assists us in any way in our other theoretical enquiries.

I do not think it does. (This opinion could be proved wrong by an example.) Here I can add only the wishy-washy remark that to study it broadens the mind (that is to say, broadens the minds of those whose minds can be broadened in this way, not all minds). But this is a high value. Thus, as I have assessed the matter, cosmological ontology is simply "for them as likes it"—an allocation, however, not now meant as a "liberal" dismissal, but one to be granted only after a serious attempt has been made to live with it.

ix) However I have one further addendum, different in kind from the above which are hardly contentious, for it is a speculation about the nature and aim of cosmological ontology to be developed later. I think cosmological ontology is the attempt to discover man's place in the universe.

It will, I hope, be clear to the reader that, while I do not think truth can be reached by means of it, I am attributing many merits to traditional metaphysics; indeed, I am treating it with a seriousness and sympathy but little accorded to it by philosophers in this century.

MODE (6)   META-ONTOLOGICAL NEGATIVISM

The initial phase of twentieth century philosophy, consisting of logical analysis in England, under Russell, Moore, and Broad was in intention negativistic. There was undoubtedly a tough negativistic aim towards vague, pretentious, or wildly unrealistic modes of thought, and there were deliberate attempts to sweep away dead wood. But the strong hope was entertained that live wood with (modest) new growth would result.

This aim was not reflected in the logical positivism into which the movement passed. Logical positivism mounted an almost unparalleled onslaught on all positive results in philosophy.

Logical positivism is now 'officially out".

Logical positivism has done some harm of no inconsiderable extent. Not only did it obviously cramp philosophical thinking, but it even had an adverse effect on science. For it led to a generation of positivistic physicists who refused to allow the admissibility of certain questions in the foundations of physics (see Agassi, 1964). It has been a major factor in side-tracking the social sciences into a groove along which no significant results could be obtained—with the result that we have been passing through a period reminiscent of the middle ages in which high-grade intellect worked assiduously and achieved nothing.

Although a total failure as regards specific aims, it should be recognised that logical positivism *did* constitute a worthy attempt to grapple seriously with the question of what could be known. It *did* attempt to handle this in a rational manner. It *did* attempt to get philosophy to have its feet upon the ground. It *did* oppose the a priori omniscience of old-time philosophy (even though in a negative sense it tried to do exactly the same thing). It could fairly be said to have attempted to provide a rational account of what may be believed.

In short, the medicine of logical positivism apparently effectively killed off all the infection prostrating philosophy, but the medicine was prussic acid, not penicillin, and killed the patient as well.

We have seen that this movement turned into linguistic philosophy, concerned with the ordinary use of language. And we have seen that this became wholly permissive. Semantic meta-ontology can permit any ontology.

The over-riding effect of this approach is that it contains no philosophical content. Anything can be said and therefore no claim is made. Any ontology is permitted, and there is no way of making a selection. Although this seems nice and liberal, it is a loose liberalism allowing that anything goes.

There was a small amount of writing in this area with a significant and interesting thesis. But there are very very few language analysts of whom this may be said. Those who concerned themselves simply with rebuttal questions raised by others, and those who were concerned simply to allow anything to be said, have produced a growing mound of linguistic analysis, which seems to constitute a declining and devitalized phase of this philosophy. Devitalization sank into inanition, no claims were made, the only activity was use-watching, and the mode of philosophizing became more and more obviously vacuous. The philosophy is virtually dead as a position, though numbers of philosophers continue to practise language analysis in some measure.

The difference between logical positivism and linguistic philosophy can be described like this. If linguistic philosophy is taken really seriously it amounts to the same thing as logical positivism, or logical positivism in a slightly more linguistic dress. Insofar as language analysis is not just a repetition of logical positivism it turns out to be vacuous. So the only really significant phase in the whole of this movement, in the sense of having a definite thesis, was that of logical positivism, and this thesis was that the epistemological problem of meaning is solved by the principle of verifiability and that questions of metaphysics are liquidated by its ontological negativism. In that way the debunking of philosophy was for a short while complete and such as has never been seen on so great a scale in the entire history of philosophy.

MODE (7)   PHILOSOPHY AS A WAY OF LIFE

If we see metascience, Mode (1), and embedded ontology, Mode (3), as being reasonably concrete studies constituting the philosophy of science, and if we see epistemology, Mode (2), and cosmological ontology, which is the hard core of metaphysics, Mode (5), as studies not understandable to a scientist, constituting the centre of philosophy, and if we see para-scientific ontology, Mode (4), as a cross between Modes (3) and (5), some questions resembling those of (3), others being more like those of (5), then in sum we have two radically disparate conceptions, whatever their common ground or mutual influence, namely philosophy of science and the study of knowing and being. If we take meta-ontological negativism, Mode (6), to be a species of Mode (2) that denies the existence of (5), we hardly have a different category of approach, though negation as a special cultivation may seem to have a character of its own—yet someone who does nothing but put down weed-killer and never plants anything is still a kind of gardener. To our two fundamentally disparate approaches, however, we must add a third, which is Mode (7), philosophy as a way of life—or as a former colleague, Professor Oli Gates, so neatly put it, the ideas we live by, or rather the style set by the ideas.

But the "way of life" presupposes many things. To work out a way of life is impossible without coming to terms with questions, such as "what is it all for?", or the possibility of a future life, or the possibility that life is essentially absurd, and questions about the nature of human nature, what is man, what is the source of evil, is there a fixed relation between good and evil, and the like. Thus one has to consider what is man, what is the place of man in the universe, how does one conceive the relation of a man to other human beings. (And many of these questions presuppose that one has given oneself at least tentative answers to some of the great enduring cosmologico-ontological questions.)

I do not find it at all surprising that philosophers of science, students of knowing and being, and metawayfarers—or meta-anthropologists—lack mutual communication.

FOOTNOTES

[1] A very small number of philosophers have tried to extend the denotation of "induction" to include the hypothetico-deductive theory. This is an abuse of the right to extend the coverage of words, for the new theory was introduced not as a *new form* of induction but in opposition to it.

[2] For a sympathetic attempt to sift the matter, see Lakatos (1968).

[3] To make allowance for the possibility that it can be discerned in Pierce or for seeds of it in Fisher.

[4] Lest some readers expect a Popperian work it might be useful to say that, though I am not a partisan Popperian, I think his falsifiability theory of empirical content is a major achievement which I accept. My further views on the nature of science develop in a different direction from Popper's, which affects the way one draws the line in solving his demarcation problem. Moreover, most of the ideas in this book, while not perhaps opposed to his philosophy, would probably be uncongenial to him.

REFERENCES

Agassi, Joseph (1964), "The Nature of Scientific Problems and their Roots in Metaphysics", *The Critical Approach to Science and Philosophy*, New York, 189–211.
Lakatos, Imre (1968), "Changes in the Problem of Inductive Logic", *The Problem of Inductive Logic*, Ed. Lakatos, Amsterdam, 315–417.

Part II

WEEDING AND PRUNING

CHAPTER IX

The Problems of Proof and Disproof

OF OUR seven Modes, (1), metascience, and (3), the embedded ontology of science, are susceptible of a publicly ascertainable and understandable method of treatment; results in these fields could be as objectively acceptable in something approaching the way that most parts of logic are. (4), the mongrel parascientific ontology would be dealt with according to the approach adopted, by whatever means are used in (3) or (5). (6), meta-ontological negativism, would be subsumed under (2). And (7), way of life, is in a class on its own. This leaves us with (2) epistemology and (5) cosmological ontology (or the central kind of metaphysics). Hence we are in effect concerned, so far as the problem of proof and disproof are concerned, with epistemology and metaphysics.

It is notorious that no position has been given a proof convincing outside the ranks of its immediate supporters. In other words proof in philosophy has been a total failure. Can we ever hope to obtain proof? Let us review the various modes of proof that have been tried.

INTUITION AND ESSENCE

The oldest method of trying to obtain philosophical knowledge about the world, seen or unseen, was the method of *intuition*; its aim was to intuit *essences*; and, so far as proof was concerned, the method was regarded as self-guaranteeing. Thus you intuited the nature of man as being "rational animal". This approach lasted more than 2,000 years. It has turned up in new forms in modern times. Thus with Descartes we find it under the form of innate ideas and natural light, it reappears in Kant in its original form (together with a subtle expansion), and it assumed a new form in Husserl's phenomenology, in which essences are obtained by a new method (still, a sophisticated version of intuition).

Results of intuition have been found to conflict. No way of deciding such a conflict has been thought of. And even if it were, the very fact of unending conflict shows that the method is not self-guaranteeing and not reliable.

DEDUCTION AND INDUCTION
(ANALYTIC AND EMPIRICAL)

Deduction also is thousands of years old. It produces reliable conclusions, if valid, only if they are derived from true premises. How are these to be obtained, i.e. known to be true? The method of deduction was naturally hooked on to that of intuition of essences, and dropped out when the latter dropped out—it is retained, of course, as an auxiliary though not as a way of getting successful results. Induction arose as an alternative method of getting results. Here it was believed that a self-guaranteed starting-point existed, namely pure observation. This has failed mainly because induction is not a valid process, or if you like not a logic at all. More sophisticatedly, it would be held by some that there is no self-guaranteeing observation, i.e. no wholly reliable observation to start from, and by others even that there is no such thing as a pure observation.

This approach is paralleled, though not in a basically different way, by the distinction between analytic and empirical propositions and the attempt to build up knowledge with certainty upon one or other or both of them.

Induction arose later than deduction and might seem to be independent of the notion of an essence. But it is reasonable to suppose that the observational starting point of induction manifests the idea of an essential and self-guaranteeing truth.

SYNTHETIC A PRIORI AND TRANSCENDENTAL

Kant made an attempt, even if quite wrong, which required genius, to circumvent these difficulties by inventing the synthetic *a priori* proposition, a new form of proposition which would be self-guaranteeing. It had no success and little following.

Coupled with it is the notion of an *essential presupposition,* known as *transcendental,* required in order to have knowledge at all (to which in Kant's philosophy there was the additional requirement that some features of our knowledge of the world would have to be deducible from this transcendental knowledge, i.e. there would be a two-way process of presupposition working up to the transcendental and down again to the starting-point). The method of carrying this out was also known as transcendental. But it all hinged on the validity of the notion of the synthetic *a priori.* A magnificent failure. (It has never been *proved* untenable; the position is absence of success and disillusionment).

DIALECTIC

Faced with deficiencies, as he saw them, in Kant's method, Hegel invented his famous dialect (different from Plato's and also from the colloquial sense current today in America of give-and-take interchange and argument).

Although there have been many Hegelians, the method has never been accepted by others, because they cannot accept a method that embodies contradiction, because it seems as if any result may be obtained or, what is (dialectically!) the same thing, no result obtained, and because on close inspection it is unintelligible to them. So, although it has not been refuted, it does not achieve results in a way that is acclaimed by a sufficient section of the philosophical world.

SEMANTIC PHILOSOPHY

Twentieth century logical empiricism has taken a variety of forms imbued with pragmatism: verifiability, dissolution of problems and meaningless conceptions, and proof by paradigm case.

Pragmatism attempted to solve problems by interpreting truth and meaning in accordance with the actions you deem appropriate to a problem. Thus that the sun goes round the Earth, despite Copernicus, is true if you stand steadily on your feet and do not feel yourself tilting in the course of the day. It is widely considered that the pragmatist theory of truth is an evasion and also that it presupposes truth in a different sense and therefore is no solution at all.

The positivist method of verifiability and its successor in linguistic philosophy are methods of showing that certain statements are meaningless. The former has been acknowledged to fail in this, the latter claims some success. But the latter has provided a positive aspect of method in the argument from the paradigm case. According to this the use of a paradigm expression in language implies that it can be successfully used and therefore that what it stands for exists in the world (one might call this a *linguistic ontological argument*). Thus, we cannot be absolute sceptics and doubt everything, i.e. doubt all knowledge, because this would conflict with the use we make of the word "knowledge" typically or in paradigm cases and be incompatible with our ever managing to learn the use of the word. Or, we cannot doubt that we sometimes exercise choice—otherwise or we should have no paradigm use of this expression and could never have learnt it.

There are several short answers to this. (i) What the argument proves, if it proves the existence of something (as it probably does), is not the philosophical objective sought; at most what would be established would be knowledge or free choice denoting some phenomenological experience but not the states of affairs underlying these. (ii) The argument, if it proves anything, must assume that a use is a paradigm, apparently on an essentialistic intuitionist basis. The argument from this paradigm case has been attacked by Watkins (1957); however it is not even universally accepted within the linguistic school.

That ends my list of traditional methods. Now one more.

CONJECTURE AND REFUTATION

Popper's theory of metascience is that the one general method of science is hypothetico-deductive, the aim being to test hypotheses by trying to find conclusions from them that might be false; this is given a broader scope as conjecture and refutation.

It is an epistemology of falliblism.

Thus it makes no attempt to offer proof.

I believe it is of the closest relevance to philosophy, for I have extended the use of the idea, even if this has meant going beyond Popper's theory of refutability restricted to empirical content, and have shown in chapter 10 that even philosophical ideas can be tested by scientific theories (though not by observation), i.e. the embedded ontology of science, but the method can also be used on parascientific ontology, and even on cosmological ontology. But, not providing proof, his method is irrelevant to the question of philosophical proof.

COMMENT ON THE QUESTION OF PROOF

This lightning sketch of methods should be more or less uncontroversial and be enough to bring out to those with some background that no satisfactory method of proof in philosophy has been found, and therefore no cause for optimism about achieving positive results in philosophy. Such a conclusion is trite and can only be expected because we know that results of universal acclaim have not been achieved. This is not to say no proof ever will be found. I do not think it will, but I do not think there is any way of proving this. I shall provide a way of indirectly undermining such a possibility. But the whole scene might be completely altered by a new, totally unexpected and unforeseeable idea.

DISPROOF

Since one fails with proof—in practice though not in principle—one turns sometime or other to consider disproof. This turns out to be as interesting as my excursion into proof is dull. The main discussion of it will be in the next chapter. Here, however, it is appropriate to consider minor methods of refutation which have been attempted or which are near the traditional approach. They do not apply widely, let alone universally. Like the traditional methods of proof these tend to be unexciting, but I shall put them, like those of proof, in brief compass. They are, after all, of some little interest and worth noting.

i) The first is the method of self-contradiction. One might suppose that one could run self-contradiction to earth in the work of great philosophers and great systems, but if this were the case, then surely these contradictions would have appeared long ago. Very clever critics have been examining the great systems of philosophy for generations and centuries and almost no agreed contradictions have turned up. Now and then the accusation of self-contradiction is made, but it is not a very common accusation. An example is to be found, I think, in Leibniz. He held that monads were wholly and completely independent of each other; secondly, God pre-established a harmony of corresponding events between different monads; and thirdly, God was a monad. From which three propositions, it follows that God interfered with independent monads. A rarity is to be found in Locke's account of an abstract general triangle which was said to be isoceles, scalene, right-angled, equiangular, and all and none of these at once.

ii) The second is empirical refutation by observation. It might come as a surprise that this method can be used at all. Full-blooded metaphysics would not stoop to anything connected with observation. None the less, the realistic theory of perception, which involves that sense-data are part of the surface of the object you are looking at, is commonly refuted by pressing the eyeball and getting a double image, which shows that these images cannot both be part of the surface of the physical object. Here is an observation that is generally taken to constitute a refutation. I would be hard put to it to provide another example in philosophy.

iii) There is what I will call the fallacy of Repeating the Question. An example will bring out what is meant. There is an old essentialistic version of the theory of inductive reasoning, which is that an inductive generalization is known to be true because it connects the essence of the subject with the essence of the predicate. You do not find much about this in modern works, mainly because this kind of doctrine has not been fashionable or even interesting to most philosophers for a great many years. The last person I know of to have written about it in a logic book was Joseph who was an Aristotelian. The idea was that the essence of a swan would be connected with the essence white, and therefore you could trust the generalization, "All swans are white", because of the intrinsic connection of the essences, swaniness and whiteness. But in order to achieve this end, one must begin with the observation of a swan that is white, and then pass from the observation of the swan to the essence of a swan, and finally in order to achieve the desired result, one would have to have the inductive generalization holding good that the observation of the swan was universally and necessarily connected with the essence of the swan. Which is the problem of induction again. So it seems to me that what happens, in this alleged solution of the problem of induction, is to raise the question once more, exactly the same question, at a slightly different point. And this seems to me to be as invalid as the classical fallacies, such as that of begging the question, and I call it the fallacy of *repeating the question*.

This kind of fallacy is of a little more interest, because it is a little more widespread, than the first two. Another example concerns the controversy between idealism and materialism. Presumably subjective idealism arose because there was a belief that there could be no relation between two utterly unlike entities such as mind and matter. Therefore it had to be supposed that matter was not really matter but was mentalistic in some way. So the dualistic difficulty was overcome by a monistic reduction treating the two entities as essentially of the same sort. Let us say that matter equals a kind of disguised mind. Then for the idealist it becomes conceivable that this mentalistic matter should be relatable to mind. But you have then on your hands the problem of understanding the relation between matter and its disguise which would seem to raise the same problem all over again. And you can apply the same criticism to materialism if you treat the mind as kind of an ethereal matter.

We may formulate the fallacy, or the refutation, as follows:

Consider a metaphyical position (M) designed to meet a problem-situation containing a difficulty or a question Q. If M necessarily leads to Q, then in answering the question, M raises the same question again. Then M is untenable: M repeats the question.

iv) Let us take another example, which rests upon what may be called the fallacy of *begging the denial*. In the doctrine of occasionalism as usually interpreted, it was regarded as inconceivable that mind and matter should be related because the two entities were so unlike. In particular they could not be related by the relation of interaction, i.e.

there could be no causal relation between mind and matter or mind and body. The device was therefore used that an intermediary occurred consisting of the agency of God. According to the doctrine, on the occasion when I will to raise my arm, God ensures that my arm actually rises. It does not take a great amount of perspicacity to see that God, i.e. another mental entity, is now acting on my physical body. Therefore there is a relationship between a mind and my body, which was presumed inconceivable. So the occasionalist solution would seem to presuppose the relation that it actually denied.

We may formulate the fallacy, or refutation, as follows:

Consider a metaphysical position, M, designed to meet a problem-situation ostensibly containing a factor, F, that is regarded as inconceivable. If M contains F, M assumes the possibility of a factor presumed to be impossible. Then M is untenable: M begs the denial.

Examples of (iii) and (iv) are forms of solution depending on the idea of a *tertium quid*. So there is a certain field of application of this sort of fallacy.

COMMENT

These methods of disproof are more successful than any of the methods of proof ever proposed. Nonetheless they do not apply universally, or even to the most important forms of metaphysics. Thus the central problem of disproof remains with us.

REFERENCES

[1] Watkins, J. W. N. (1957), "Farewell to the Paradigm-Case Argument", *Analysis* **18**, 25–33.

CHAPTER X

On The Refutability of Metaphysics

A PROBLEM OF RATIONAL DISBELIEF

WHAT I wish to open up is a sub-problem of the problem of rationality. Most of us who think of ourselves as rational men would like to be able to give reasonable reasons for the things we believe. What is much less explored is the opposite problem, regarding the things we do not believe, of being able to find reasonable reasons against the things we disbelieve. The problem arises because so many systems of philosophy are put on the shelf without being firmly refuted. Consider, for example, the system of Spinoza or of Berkeley or of Kant. It is the dominant outlook in the Anglo-American philosophical world to regard most of these philosophies as outdated and as saying very little that can be taken seriously. There may be justice in this view : quite possibly there are very few living issues in many of these philosophers. But one must take them seriously if for no other reason than that there is no standard refutation of them. But if you look back on attempts to discuss historical philosophies, it is extraordinary how little agreement there is to be found on what is wrong with them. We all know that there is no agreement about positive contributions to philosophy, but there is equally little agreement on what shall be rejected and how. It seems to me very curious that there should be no way of settling these matters. In view of this I have cast around for various methods by which metaphysical views, if they should be false, might be rejected. That, in short is my problem.

SYNTHETIC A PRIORI METAPHYSICS

IF YOU cast your mind back over the great philosophies of the past, to consider how you might refute them, you are bound to consider the notion of a synthetic a priori proposition, upon which the whole Kantian philosophy was built; and the question must arise whether the notion of such propositions can be refuted.

A synthetic proposition is a priori if, though synthetic, it is necessarily true (or true independently of all experience).

Examples of supposedly synthetic a priori propositions may be taken from Kant himself. Thus causality was a category that applied to the world universally and necessarily. Kant also had some rather unfortunate but still rather instructive examples such as that two straight lines cannot enclose a space. For when he gives examples that we know are not true, this does not encourage us to place much confidence in the concept of the synthetic a priori proposition. Incidentally, I think it was a pity that he used the example of two straight lines not enclosing a space; if he had been bolder and said that one straight line cannot enclose a space it would have been more striking, seeing that in elliptic geometry one straight line can enclose a space.

To try to get some clear idea of what this very curious kind of proposition is, let us remember that a synthetic a priori proposition is not analytical, is not just a tautology. A tautology is a proposition that is true of all possible worlds. But although a synthetic a priori proposition is not tautological it is necessary. Thus it meant a proposition that is true, not of all logically possible worlds, but, I suggest, in all possible worlds of a certain sort, namely of all "conceivable" worlds. The difference in scope may be shown like this. A tautology contains no information, but a synthetic a priori proposition does or is intended to do so. This, of course, is a stumbling block; practically no modern logician of any school could swallow the possibility of an a priori proposition that was other than analytical; and the synthetic a priori proposition is just this. It is worth turning this the other way round, even if it helps only a little, to see what would happen if you tried to deny a synthetic a priori proposition. The denial would be a proposition that is false, and necessarily false, without being self-contradictory. And this is very curious.

The notion of a synthetic a priori proposition is particularly important because it may well be central to most metaphysics. Although Kant introduced the idea of a synthetic a priori proposition only rather late in the history of philosophy, the idea, or its equivalent, can be detected much earlier. There are in particular two ancestors of the idea that I should like to mention. One is the doctrine of innate ideas in Descartes. It is to some extent obscure just what an innate idea really was in Descartes. Nonetheless certain features stand out. An innate idea is characterized as something that is clear and distinct and gives you necessary truth. But it also provided truth about reality, and hence was not simply tautologous; for innate ideas were not intended to be vacuous ideas that were uninformative about the world. So you get the same two characteristics in connection with innate ideas in Descartes as you get with the synthetic a priori in Kant. More interesting, perhaps, is the idea of an essence in Aristotle. Though he put it in terms of "real definition", an essence was something that you contemplated in order to find out real knowledge about the world. If you wanted to find out about man, you would first of all ascertain what is the essence of man. The essence of man was said to be rationality and animality; and this would be your major premiss. Then, by deductive procedures of logic, you would arrive at other properties. Thus one could put Aristotle's view of scientific procedure like this : you do not have to build upon experience; you need impeccable logic, and a perfectly sound manner of ascertaining essences of things; given the essences, to be stated in the major premiss, apply impeccable logic, and you would derive necessary properties of things. In this way you learn about the universe.[1] The point to note about this is that the properties of the essence were necessary (and therefore of course universal), but also provided information about the world. These two characteristics of necessity and information-content lead me to suppose that the old idea of an essence is something that can and must be the same as the idea of a synthetic a priori proposition, and expressible by means of such a proposition, and therefore that the Kantian doctrine of synthetic a priori propositions represents something that is well-nigh as old as philosophy.

My surmise is that really metaphysical metaphysics always turns on such propositions.

A THEORY OF THE SYNTHETIC A PRIORI

Be that as it may, we have to consider how we might handle these things. For this purpose, I would propose the following : that a synthetic a priori proposition has a universe of discourse, which so far from exhausting the entire universe, is limited to what is regarded as "conceivable", and that this restriction is due to some limiting property that is taken to characterise the universe of discourse; such a property excludes a certain domain from discourse; moreover the excluded domain is kept outside our intellectual vision, because "inconceivable". An example I shall begin with comes from the Kantian distinction between phenomena and things-in-themselves. Kant's theory was that the only world that you can know is the world of experience. It is a short step to disregard the rest of the world so that the whole world comes to mean simply the world you know. The domain of things-in-themselves does not count in our experience, and becomes excluded from the universe of discourse. This world that you know is the world that is subject to the categories of causality and so on. Now if you make a restriction, excluding the domain of things-in-themselves, then you can do it in such a way that a category like causality will necessarily apply to the whole of the rest. If that is so, then the synthetic a priori proposition, to do with causality, is necessarily true of all phenomena or must in fact hold of all phenomena.

Now if we look more widely and try to see whether this idea has been employed elsewhere, I think we can find other examples of it. Consider Hegel, for instance. Though he is notoriously difficult to discuss, nonetheless one can fairly say that the Hegelian philosophy contains centrally the proposition that the real is rational. What does this tell us? That the real excludes the irrational; the irrational is not part of the real world. In that case, any proposition that is true of rational things holds for the whole world, and therefore has the look of being synthetic a priori, because it excludes the domain of the irrational, which may plausibly seem not to exist.

Take a different sort of example altogether. Supposing you are born colour-blind, so that you can see only black and white. You might very well suppose that is was a necessary truth that colours are divisible into black and white. Or take a much more mundane example such as this: we may easily suppose that all rabbits are long-eared. If a new animal appeared, which might be a rabbit with short ears, a controversy could develop, perhaps among biologists, about whether this was a rabbit or not. Some might maintain it could not be a rabbit because it is synthetic a priori that rabbits are long-eared.

We may, if we wish, refer to the notion of the synthetic a priori proposition as the principle of "synthetic a priori exclusion". It is exemplified by the plausible exclusion of that other field of things-in-themselves we know nothing about.

What I am trying to bring out, by means of this device of analyzing the synthetic a priori proposition, is this. If a supposed example might by chance be true, then in particular it might so happen (though some of us do not believe it) that causation is a universal category, for it might so happen that everything in the universe without any exclusion is subject to laws of cause and effect. In that case, then this proposition would be factually true. Hence if one of these propositions might be true, then of course there could be no way by which you could ever refute them in principle. You might be able if you are lucky to refute one or two of the specified members, but you could not refute all of them in principle if any one of them could be contingently true.

Thus the first point I want to bring out about them is that any of them might be empirically true. This is part of the reason why they carry some air of plausibility. Next if you consider a supposed synthetic a priori proposition, it is always possible that somebody will be able to devise an area to which it does not apply. And if you can devise one you have a satisfactory refutation. For example, supposing you hold that energy must always be a positive quantity, which might sound reasonable enough, and that this was synthetic a priori. Then you would not be receptive to the possibility of a counter-example. And yet, of course, Dirac did in fact postulate the existence of negative energy, leading to the discovery of the positron. This refutation of the idea that energy has to be essentially positive is, of course, highly imaginative. Moreover you find such a counter-example only when you are lucky. The fact of imagination, not to mention the luck required to find an area to which a synthetic a priori proposition fails to apply, readily explains why we regard such a possibility as inconceivable, and why the proposition seems necessary.

An interesting feature comes out here, that it is possible to broaden the scope of enquiries by deliberately trying to deny what appear to be universal necessary truths. An example that naturally comes to mind is the standard "truth" of Euclidean geometry which I referred to before, namely that it was maintained that the Euclidean axioms were universally necessary and true. One can sit down deliberately, as in the end mathematicians did, to try to see whether one could find an alternative or find an area in which the "truths" do not hold. In this connection, I should like to mention another example. A synthetic proposition that was denied a priori, was that of the spontaneous creation of matter out of nothing; but it has appeared in contemporary scientific cosmology, put forward by Kapp, Bondi, Gold, and Hoyle. This was a serviceable theory up to a point, in that it did some explanatory work, so it cannot be thrown out on the grounds that the idea does not make sense. If it could solve a problem, then the idea was good. A similar though stronger example concerns the spontaneous breakdown of radium atoms, which involves the idea of spontaneous destruction of matter. These theories violate the idea that matter cannot come out of nothing and cannot be destroyed. And most thinkers for thousands of years had held that these were necessary truths. Again, we can see that a synthetic a priori proposition can be denied effectively, but only when we can produce a testable theory that denies it.

Now to turn to synthetic a priori propositions in connection with metaphysics. If it is true that all metaphysical metaphysics centred on these things, then I suggest that we have a method of handling metaphysical questions. There has been an idea, of course, for a very long time, which Hume and logical positivists have had in common, that there exists a principle yielding a method of relegating all metaphysics to the flames. That is well known. And it is also known that it cannot be done: there is no principle of drawing the line or inserting a wedge between metaphysics that is nonsensical or false and science that is not.[1] Now if the foregoing theory of synthetic a priori propositions is correct, we can see why this is so. The reason is that anyone might happen by luck to hit on a synthetic a priori proposition that happened to be true without excluding part of the universe from its scope. Hence a piece of metaphysics might by chance be true, and therefore would not be nonsensical. The question then arises, what should you do? I suggest that the procedure is to try to find the boundary line that renders it such a proposition, and then challenge the boundary—which means being able to invent something on the other side of the boundary.[2] This will usually prove too difficult because it may require that one should have a new scientific theory which one cannot invent on the spur of the moment.

The consequences of the foregoing theory of the nature of the synthetic a priori proposition are thus: any supposed example might be empirically true, hence such propositions are always plausible, and are never refutable in principle; on the other hand, individual counter-examples can sometimes be found, hence no such proposition can be necessarily true—a synthetic a priori candidate cannot be shown to be necessarily false or necessarily true. In particular the Humean or logical positivist general method of liquidating such propositions is impossible, though a method of modest challenge can be provided. The method of challenge, when no counter-example is actually found, leaves them unrefuted but shows that they are necessarily unprovable so that no conclusions that might be based upon them are thereby reliable.

THE EMBEDDED ONTOLOGY OF SCIENCE

Let us now turn to a specific method of refutation, which I happened to light upon, (Wisdom, 1963, 1972) that relates to a different form of metaphysics altogether. Let us recapitulate Mode (3) described earlier, in order to discuss it in connection with refutation. It is well known that in Popperian methodology the aim of a scientist or experimentalist or methodologist is to consider the refutability of scientific theories. And the method dealt with by Popper in his first work was to find empirical refutations i.e., factual observations, that would refute a theory. Now Popper never suggested that refutation by observation was the only method of refutation; he was also concerned with criticism of theories in general; but it was refutation by observation that he developed a theory of. I noticed, however, that one can go further, and, in line with his broader idea of criticism, can devise a different method of refutation for certain statements to which the method of refutation by observation does not apply. Now if you have a theory that is testable, tested, and corroborated, and that theory has a logical consequence, you have to accept that consequence; and if it is incompatible with the former theory, the former one has to be rejected. In particular, quantum physics, which is testable, tested, and corroborated, has a consequence that energy may exist only at discrete levels (possess only eigenvalues). This contradicts the consequence about continuous energy-levels I have drawn from classical physics; therefore quantum physics refutes this statement from classical physics. The statement is not, Popperwise, observation-refutable; *it is theory-refutable.*

Now this is not an absolute refutation, because after all we might have to give up quantum physics. In which case the refutation would go. But this is really not very detrimental to the purpose in hand, for our purpose is not to find absolute refutations. Even such apparently absolute things as contradictions may be found to be wrongly ascribed, because we misconstrue a theory or its symbolism may have been too vague. Again, even an observation-refutation of a theory is not absolute, because we may find that the observation was at fault (Popper, 1959). It is true that refutation by means of observation is in a slightly stronger position than refutation by means of a theory; but that does not produce a difference of principle. The point is that, so long as we do accept quantum physics, in the rational sense that it is tested, testable, and corroborated, that is to say, so long as it has not been refuted, then we have to accept its logical consequences, and that means that we have to deny something that is incompatible with its logical consequences (in this case we have to deny the classical proposition that energy exists with continuous values).[3]

But are we dealing with metaphysics? Certainly to say that energy exists at all levels (or only has discrete values) is to say something about the "furniture of the earth". We are therefore dealing with what I will call the "embedded ontology of science". Other examples, however, which seem more metaphysical, such as the idea of absolute space in Newtonian mechanics, may help better.

This idea is no part of the empirical content of Newtonian theory in the sense that whenever you carry out any calculation or try to prove any theorem in the system you never write down the hypothesis that space is absolute. So in this sense there is a piece of metaphysical framework, or even metaphysical warp and weft, different from the empirical theory. Nonetheless the idea of absolute space in Newtonian mechanics is refuted by the theory of general relativity; for it is a consequence of this theory that space is non-absolute. And here you have a perfectly good metaphysical hypothesis, namely that of absolute space, refuted, not by an observation, but by a theory. And the doctrine of absolute space is surely metaphysical in some sense. And it is perhaps the sort of metaphysics that scientists should indulge in, the sort that is and probably must be indispensible to science.

METAPHYSICS OF INADEQUATE SPECIFICATION VACUOUS POSTULATION

If metaphysical metaphysics is full-blooded metaphysics, there is also a milk-and-water metaphysics, which hinges not on the synthetic a priori proposition but on inadequate specification of basic notions and their relations. Parturiunt montes . . . The resulting cosmological vision may be described as an "ontology of unspecified make-up".

Such a position may be illustrated by Berkley's cosmology. His problem was to explain the existence of sense-perceptions. We are not concerned with the very acute and subtle inferences that he made in the body of his work and the valid attacks he made on other philosophers, but only with his overall solution. His position was that a postulated entity, called God, with very few properties such as omnipotence and perfection specified, explains the existence of the perceptions that we have, by causing these perceptions in us or manifesting them to us as a language by which we read of God. This explanation is like an *ad hoc* hypothesis because the only evidence for it is the sensory experiences to be explained; there is no independent evidence for it. Further we are given practically no specification of the entity involved, and practically no specification of the machinery by which the effect is brought about, or by which the deduction is made, in short by which the explanation does its work. This is what I am describing as inadequate specification. The point about it is that there is no way of refuting such a doctrine because it is essentially too vague to be discussed. One cannot say that no claim at all is made because one or two specifications or properties of God are mentioned, and some process of causation also; but there is insufficient detail given to identify the object, and insufficient detail given about the chain of deduction by which the explanatory concept explains by a causal process our sense-perceptions. So there is only a very partial claim. I would summarize the position by saying that there are, in this Berkeleian solution, bits and pieces out of which a theory might be propounded, but which are only bits and pieces not really hewn into shape; you can hardly refute the position because you have hardly got a claim; and if you have a very mild claim, too weak to specify to any significant extent, then you have almost nothing to answer.

There is, however, something more to it. The vacuous claim is "vacuous" in relation to the post-Copernican tradition. What it asserts is an effect wrought in the absence of a specifiable process, i.e., omnipotently. Thus the issue could be subsumed under that of magical versus non-magical explanation, and magic would be a form of the synthetic a priori.

TYPES OF METAPHYSICS

Earlier, we saw that a central form of metaphysics consisted of the embedded ontology of science. We also found a different form of it in cosmological ontology; this being the basic form of metaphysics in philosophy.

It may suffice to discriminate these two as basic types. Parascientific ontology lies uneasily between them, and it is didactically convenient to differentiate it, but it hardly constitutes a fundamentally different type.

The kind just described, the ontology of unspecified make-up, again hardly merits a separate category. But it is influential, for it is characteristic of the ontological views of the world taken up by a few fine intellects like Berkeley[4] and by numbers of ordinary people who can hardly articulate their belief at all. Its power lies in its vagueness and the lack of a standard type of refutation. Here I have suggested that its "refutation" lies in its making virtually no assertion. But we could perhaps strengthen this rebuttal. Such claim as is made by the ontology of inadequate specification—and it is admitted to make some claim however slight—is purely structural in the sense that it is not linked concretely with any functional manifestation, i.e., nothing ensues. Now a claim about a functional manifestation, where something ensues, is a serious claim because refutable; and a postulated structure that manifests itself thus is likewise serious because refutable; but without a functional manifestation, a structural ontology, weak or strong, is not discussable.[5] It is not serious philosophy, or simply not serious, to say that there may exist in the universe an X ($X =$ unicorn, a monster, a jabberwockie, etc.). Since this is a mode of thinking that still can animate good minds, I think it has to be reckoned a type of metaphysic. But I do not propose to discuss it further.

For my purposes the two really significant types are embedded ontology and cosmological ontology. The former shows itself in the functional manifestations of science, and has its raison d'être in science. The latter has a wholly different source or sources.

The preceding investigation of the notion of the synthetic a priori relates to the latter. Further is is, I think, fairly obvious that cosmological ontology must be synthetic a priori.

Thus metaphysics in all its forms is unprovable; a refutation of a full-blooded metaphysic (or cosmological ontology) *may* be found from time to time, depending on the discovery of a new empirical theory, testable, tested, and corroborated; but this is a matter of chance, there is no systematic way of setting about effecting a refutation.

Now let me take one or two other examples of problems from the history of philosophy that can be handled in a similar manner. There is a very interesting question about whether matter is infinitely divisible or not. I think it is very reasonable on the part of mankind to wonder about such a question. Unfortunately philosophers find it less interesting than they used to, and it has become unfashionable. What sort of question it may be is hard to characterize. It looks like the sort of thing people might have called the philosophy of nature; it differs from metascience in that it is not a second-order subject; and it is not a subject of scientific inquiry. It is considered by the philosopher in his arm-chair directly concerning himself with the real world. And there are other questions of the same sort, e.g., whether space is infinite or not. It happens that philosophers have not got very far with such questions; but I think we can now understand why. Philosophers have produced logical antimonies about them and have got nowhere with resolving these. But an interesting fact is that there are hypothetical answers to some of these questions to be got from modern physical theory. General relativity gives an answer to one of them and quantum mechanics gives an answer to another. Thus one answer would be that matter is not infinitely divisible, because in quantum mechanics matter must have a certain minimum size or ceases to be matter (in terms of the ordinary conception). And in the case of the infinity versus finitude of space, general relativity requires that space-time should be finite (although you meet no boundary no matter how far you move in space-time). These two answers are consequences of scientific theories, though the consequences themselves are not directly checkable. So, in these cases of philosophical investigations of nature, philosophers have had to wait for answers depending on results of science.

FOOTNOTES

[1]Church (1946) torpedoed the main formulation of the principle of verifiability by showing that this in fact admitted all metaphysical statements as verifiable. I (Wisdom 1963) tried to show that the matter was not one of formulation, but that any principle driving such a wedge is equivalent to a synthetic a priori proposition; this will be found in the next chapter.

[2]This is the same in spirit (though put forward here for a different purpose) as the metascientific principle of dropping restrictions, introduced by Kapp (1960), which he used to derive a number of results in physics.

[3]I would like to mention one or two bizarre examples of ideas that can be refuted by this method. One might suppose that things like values were outside the sphere of refutability altogether. But consider preclassical physics, before Galileo. In the days of Aristotelian physics, or of the theory of impetus, it was common doctrine accepted by all that the earth was not only the center of the universe, but was the center of the universe because the dignity of man required it to be so. And another idea was that the heavenly bodies had to be round, because that was the perfect shape. Now these value judgments, so far as I know, actually entered into the body of the theory, i.e. you could not carry out the deductions or explanations in Aristotelian physics or in the physics of impetus, without making use of these value-judgments. If this is so, then the refutation of these systems of physics would carry refutations of these value-judgments as well, because the refuting theories entail that the earth is not the center and that orbits are not necessarily circular.

[4]This was the only criticism of his philosophy I gave in my book on Berkeley (Wisdom, 1952); so far as I am aware, it had not been made before.

[5]Locke's theory that substance, which can hardly be said to be specified at all when described as an "unknown somewhat", provides a base for our perceptions; it is structurally just the same as Berkeley's. Other parallels are to be found in occasionalism and Kant's theory of the thing-in-itself.

REFERENCES

Church, A. (1946), Review of A. J. Ayer's *Language, Truth and Logic*, in *J. Symb. Log.* **14**, 53.

Kapp, R. O. (1960), *Towards a Unified Cosmology*, London, Ch. 2.

Popper, K. R. (1959), *The Logic of Scientific Discovery*, London, 104.

——————— (1963), *The Open Society and its Enemies*, Vol. II, London, Ch. 11, pp. 9–12.

Wisdom, J. O. (1953), *The Unconscious Origin of Berkeley's Philosophy*, London, 28.

——————— (1963), "Metamorphoses of the Verifiability Theory of Meaning", *Mind*, **72**, 335.

——————— (1963), "The Refutability of 'Irrefutable' Laws", *Brit. J. Philos. Sc.*, **13**, 303.

——————— (1972), "Scientific Theory: Empirical Content, Ontology, and Weltanschauung", *Philosophy and Phenomenological Research*.

CHAPTER XI

The Refutation of Logical Positivism

1) IT may be flogging a dead horse to question further the verifiability theory of meaning, because there are no longer any logical positivists. I will take this risk because, although I do not believe in the reincarnation of souls, I am not so sure when it comes to the re-incarnation of dead horses. Depositivisation has, of course, changed things a little, but when a reform has been adopted, especially tacitly, the status quo is often reestablished, albeit in a manner in which it is not always recognised. The point is significant because a certain more modern doctrine is perhaps, a re-incarnation, with a new look, of the principle of verifiability.

I am not concerned here with the problem of the formulation of the principle; it will suffice for my purpose that verifiability is a requirement that in some way or other drives a wedge between meaningful and meaningless statements. The preliminary question I am concerned with is whether verifiability is a necessary or a sufficient condition to determine meaning, in order to lead up to a reductio ad absurdum argument to show that no such wedge is possible.

2) About one part of the content of the principle, however, it is essential to be definite. Was its function merely to guarantee (or deny) that a statement *has* a meaning, i.e. to show whether or not a meaning *exists*, or was its function to specify *what* the meaning is? The latter is the more extreme doctrine, and it was this that the earlier logical positivists intended. Now it is obvious that the more extreme version entails the less extreme; i.e. if it is true that a verification tells us the meaning of a statement, then it ipso facto guarantees that the statement has a meaning.

It is with the milder, the entailed principle, which is all that was implied in the later days of positivism, that I am concerned here. And my question now is this: is the possibility of a verification to be considered as a *sufficient* or as a *necessary* condition for a statement to have a meaning (for the existence of a meaning of a statement)? In a characteristic and simple sort of case, the possibility of a verification is

D

sufficient to show that a statement has a meaning : thus the statement, "There is a book on the mantelpiece in the next room", if you can verify it, that is, go into the next room and take a look, certainly has a meaning. Thus verifiability is, at any rate, a *sufficient* condition for a statement to have a meaning.

3) The mere idea of sufficiency has a practical merit which should not pass unnoticed. This merit, which is extraneous to the theory and does not entail it, is simply that when one is confronted with a statement that is difficult to understand or whose meaning is obscure, or even when one is doubtful whether the statement has any meaning at all, then one can ask for verifications. Answers to this request may, and often do, enable one to see what the statement was intended to mean. Thus one might be confronted with the following statement : "A slowing up of vital processes in the organism is producing increased longevity." In such a case one might be floundering until one got answers to the request for verification. But of course a device for enabling one to hit upon the meaning of a statement does not necessarily imply that the device contains the meaning or is a necessary way of arriving at the meaning. This has been aptly put by a well known philosopher, "I used at one time to say that, in order to get clear how a certain sentence is used, it was a good idea to ask oneself the question : How would one try to verify such an assertion? But that's just one way of getting clear about the use of a word or sentence. . . . Some people have turned this suggestion about asking for the verification into a dogma. . . ."[1] In case it should be thought the philosopher just quoted was a reactionary against the whole movement of analytical and positivist philosophy, it should be mentioned that the remarks are reported as having been made by Wittgenstein.

4) It is easy to show that the positivistic thesis was much more than the claim that the possibility of a verification is a *sufficient* condition for a statement to have a meaning; the thesis amounted in effect to the claim that the possibility of a verification is not merely sufficient but is also necessary. In a characteristic type of case this is plausible. Consider the well known example, "There are mountains on the other side of the moon". The thesis was that a verification (going to the moon and taking a look) could in principle be effected. The thesis was further that without the possibility of such a verification the statement would be meaningless; that is to say, a verification of this sort would be a *necessary* condition for a statement to have a meaning; in other words it was tautological that the statement to be meaningful must be verifiable. This is plausible, because a mountain that was in principle invisible would

be something beyond the comprehension even of some non-positivist philosophers; in other words, the meaning of the word "mountain" would include that it should refer to something capable of being seen.

5) With regard to statements other than those that are analytical it was taken for granted that no form of verification other than an observation was known or even conceivable.

6) Hence the required conclusion was obtained that *verifiability was a necessary condition for the meaningfulness of any kind of non-analytic statement.*

7) There were, of course, other necessary conditions that need hardly detain us long: that a statement had to be formed in accordance with correct syntax and had to embody the appropriate designation-expressions; but these two conditions, though necessary, were not sufficient for a statement to have a meaning. Clearly, a statement might be well formed in accordance with these two requirements, and still not have a meaning. Thus, "The dog's bark sounded either green or loud" might be correctly formed syntactically, according to the rules of some syntax, e.g. those of English, and yet the statement might be meaningless. In order that the statement should have a meaning, it would be necessary, as well, that a relevant observation should be capable of being made. But these syntactic (v. semantic) considerations may be left on one side simply by speaking not of a statement having to be verified, but of a *well-formed* statement having to be verified (unless we restrict the word "statement" to what is well-formed). Thus the theory was that for a well-formed statement to have a meaning, it was not only sufficient but also necessary that it should be verifiable. In this paper I am concerned only with meaninglessness that is not attributable to violation of syntax.

8) Before considering the question of necessity, a distinction must be drawn. A given statement can yield an observation-statement only in one or other of two ways: (i) where the observation-statement is part of the content of the given statement or an instance of it—that is where the verification might be said to be immediate—and (ii) where the observation-statement must be deduced. I wish to consider the latter situation, which is typical for a theoretical statement. (I follow the fairly usual practice of distinguishing these two cases, i.e. generalisations and more abstract theories, but logically they both involve deduction: an instance of a generalisation is strictly a consequence of that generalisation together with an initial condition.)

Suppose such a well-formed statement is meaningless, then no verification of it exists; hence no verification-statement is deducible from it. Now in order to make a deduction from a theory, an essential requirement is that the theory should be combined with an initial condition, otherwise no deduction of an observation-statement is possible.

9) Consider the general theory of relativity announced in 1915. One test known for it concerned the calculation of the motion of the perihelion of Mercury. If there had been no such planet, or if Mercury had not been so close to the sun, this test would not have existed. Another test was also thought of later—that light-rays should be attracted by matter to a calculable extent which it is possible to measure only when there is a total solar eclipse. (The third test also could be carried out only in the same conditions.) No one might have recognised the relevance of these initial conditions, but this would not have affected their relevance. And—quite a real possibility—no one might have been able to use them, to deduce a test from them, but this would not have shown them to be unusable. (A striking example from Newton's time, when the inverse square law was being considered, was the inability of his contemporaries to draw a deduction from it.) Further, and this is the most important point, if the earth had happened to possess no moon, no such eclipse could occur. We could have had a satisfactory theory, though not capable of being known to be satisfactory because of having no means of testing it. Hence that the theory was untestable in practice does not imply that it was untestable in principle. It would have been testable in principle because someone might have thought of the possibility of deducing the bending of a light-ray during a total eclipse if an eclipse were to occur. No one might have been able to think of a hypothetical test; but it would have been illegitimate to lay down that none could be thought of.

10) This example brings out (i) that suitable initial conditions might exist but be unrecognised, but this would not render the theory untestable; (ii) that suitable initial conditions might exist and be recognised as suitable, and yet no one could carry out the requisite deduction, which again would not show the theory to be untestable; and (iii) that there might be no suitable initial conditions capable of yielding a test, but again the theory could not be regarded as untestable on this account.

The only possibility left to consider is that there might be *in principle* no suitable initial conditions capable of yielding a test. This gives the following criterion: *for a theory to be unverifiable it is necessary that there is no possible set of initial conditions enabling a verification to be deduced.*

11) By concentrating on generalisations positivists have made the verifiability-claim satisfiable, because generalisations typically have instances and must therefore have verifications. But a theory, like general

relativity, does not have instances, and, until someone thinks of a possible deduction of an observation-situation, no one can tell whether or not any such deduction is possible. The verifiability-criterion cannot help towards this end, and it therefore fails to provide a priori knowledge of exactly which statements are meaningful and which meaningless.

12) The presupposition that no initial conditions exist suitable for a certain purpose could be established neither analytically nor empirically. To establish it would be on the same level as establishing the principle of verifiability itself, except in one respect: whereas the principle of verifiability can look reasonable, the presupposition looks wholly untenable.

Thus, as it might be put, *the principle of unverifiability presupposes a principle of no initial conditions*, which looks so preposterous that possibly no one would try to defend it; and possibly no one would have taken the principle of unverifiability seriously if its presupposition had been appreciated. But unplausibility is not a refutation; let us therefore examine the question whether it can be refuted.

13) Let T be a theory and, if possible, let it be unverifiable; and let I_n be any set of any possible states of affairs, i.e. initial conditions true in some possible world. Since T is unverifiable, no possible observation can be deduced from the premisses T, I_n (for any n), provided it does not follow from I_n alone. Now consider all false observation-statements "O_m" (for any m). The principle of verifiability asserts both that the inference with premisses T, I_n (for any n) and conclusion O_m (for any m) is invalid and also that the inference with these premisses and conclusion $\sim O_m$ (for any m) is invalid, provided neither O_m nor $\sim O_m$ follow from I_n alone (for any m, n). For the inference to be invalid, a counter-example must exist, *i.e.* an inference of the same logical form with true premisses and false conclusion.[3] Since O_m (for any m) is false and I_n (for any n) is true in some possible world, it follows that, for counter-example to exist, there must be a theory (at least one) of the same logical form as T that is true in some possible world.

In short, given a theory T that is unverifiable, there must be a true theory, in some possible world, of the same logical form as T.

This argument may be put more informally thus. If T is an unverifiable theory, no possible observation that is not deducible from initial conditions alone can follow from T in conjunction with any initial conditions, i.e. the inference is invalid. Hence a counter-example exists, or possible world, that renders the premisses true but renders the conclusion false. Thus, in order that T should be unverifiable, there must exist a possible world in which T is true and therefore is verified.

Would logical positivists have been prepared to accept this conclusion in order to maintain the principle of verifiability? If so, it would be at the following price. The situation bears some resemblance to that concerning the existential import of propositions if null classes are excluded, where the existence of anything can be proved : in order to create a true theory all that is required is to write down an unverifiable (though well-formed) theoretical statement. Though this procedure gives no way of identifying a true theory, it guarantees the existence of an infinity of true theories.

I take either the conclusion of § 10 or that just obtained to be a reductio ad absurdum of the verifiability theory of meaning.

14) The rôle of verifiability differs markedly from the rôle of testability in a scientific context; testability requires that an observation-statement should be deducible, and this of course lends a certain plausibility to the theory of verifiability simply insofar as both require an observation-statement to be deducible; but a basic difference shows up at once. If an observation-statement is not at present deducible, then a statement is not at present testable, but this does not imply that no initial conditions of a suitable kind exist. It implies only that they are not known, and therefore that the statement is not at present a part of science. This does not prevent the statement from being meaningful, and from entering at a later stage into the corpus of science, should a suitable initial condition turn up. Moreover, the statement, if treated as meaningful, may be worked at to see if it can be made testable. It has a pre-scientific character.

15) I have not been concerned with the difficulty of formulating the theory of verifiability, but it is well known that its original formulations were too narrow, that is too stringent, and made it impossible to preserve many scientific statements as meaningful, and that the later formulations have been too wide, that is too weak, and have admitted back all the metaphysical ideas that had been considered undesirable. No formulation has been found that is neither too narrow nor too wide but just right. Here I have been concerned to show the untenability of any principle, apart from all difficulties of formulation, that is designed to divide theories into meaningful and meaningless according to whether or not deductive consequences can be drawn. The present argument would seem to apply no matter what improvements are made in the formulation of the verifiability-principle.

FOOTNOTES

[1]Cited by Passmore (1957).

[2]Here I follow the theory of validity deriving from Tarski, that an inference is valid if and only if no counter-example exists. The inference with premisses "All men are mortal" and "Socrates is mortal" and conclusion "Socrates is a man" can be shown to be invalid by constructing a counter-example, obtained, e.g. by substituting "Xanthippe" for "Socrates". (See Tarski, 1956; Popper, 1947).

REFERENCES

Passmore, John (1957), *A Hundred Years of Philosophy*, London, 371.
Popper, K. R. (1947), "Logic without Assumptions", *Proc. Arist. Soc.*, **47**, 251.
Tarski, A. (1956), *Logic, Semantics, and Metamathematics*, Oxford, 409.

CHAPTER XII

The Refutation of Semantic Ontology

16) The principle of verifiability has been generally abandoned and there has grown up a procedure about words and statements having a use. It could be said that there was an evolution from one to the other, because the procedure of verification ("What do you do to verify?") is easily given a metalinguistic form ("What do you do with a statement; how do you use it?"). It is a question of some importance whether the aim of the verifiability-principle, namely of liquidating unwanted statements such as those of metaphysics, survives in association with the new procedure.

Let us consider the relation between "verifiable" and "having a use". It would probably not be questioned that if a statement is verifiable then it has a use. But how about the converse, i.e. that, if a statement has a use, then it *must* be verifiable? On this alternative, the new principle of "having a use" must have exactly the same range of reference as that of verifiability.

As regards the question of formulation, if that of the verifiability-criterion is too narrow, then its equivalent in terms of "having a use" is too narrow also. Likewise, if the verifiability criterion is too wide. Hence, "the use of" or "having a use" would have to be placed in between the narrow and the wide formulations of the verifiability-criterion, but since no formulation for the latter has been found or appears likely to be possible, it seems unlikely that a formulation can be found for "having a use". If the problem of formulation were tackled, it can be expected to resurrect the untenable criterion of the verifiability-principle.

More generally, since we have found that it is impossible to drive a wedge characterised by verifiability between the meaningful and the meaningless where deduction is required, it seems likely that it is equally impossible to drive a wedge characterised by "having a use".

It is not suggested that anyone has explicitly maintained that if a statement has a use it must be verifiable; but since this could readily be presupposed, it is worth noting its consequences.[1]

90

17) We have now to consider the alternative possibility, that, though a verifiable statement has a use, a statement can have a use *without* being verifiable. There would seem to be no objection in principle to this possibility. The use of "the use of" involved may enable confusions of many kinds to be brought to light. Whether without some restrictive qualification it is a criterion of anything, and therefore of any philosophical interest is another matter, and one that will not be discussed here. What is relevant is to distinguish the use of "the use of" which is not qualified by any restriction from one that is qualified by some restriction. One possible restriction would be to proscribe technical or scientific phrases; but this, of course, would be arbitrary and would liquidate science. It is not necessary to suppose, however strongly appearances may sometimes suggest it, that such a proscription has been intended by language analysts. They have been opposed to needless technicalities, e.g. where there is an equivalent in the ordinary use of language, and they have been concerned to check up on technicalities that have somewhat similar counterparts in the ordinary use; but the great emphasis on ordinary usage could have a raison d'être that does not involve the total liquidation in principle of all technicalities in philosophy. For the use of "having a use" under discussion provides, as it were, a working model against which philosophical assertions can be measured : a philosophical statement when interpreted in terms of the model is accepted. Assuming that a philosophical statement is not misinterpreted so as to square with the model, the model is *sufficient* to guarantee it. But, without an additional assumption, the model is *not necessary* as a guarantee. The model would, however, be necessary if, for example, uses other than ordinary uses were to be for some reason proscribed, and in particular if such uses were to be regarded as meaningless. But then the model would become a criterion equivalent to verifiability driving a wedge between the meaningful and the meaningless and would be open to the objections previously mentioned.

It would seem that one of the main aims of the method of "having a use" is to provide a sure base to which to refer philosophical statements. Whether it involves or is free of the restriction just described depends upon how it is handled. If a philosopher utilised the restriction unwittingly, his model would be a re-incarnation of logical positivism. Free of the restriction the model is in order but whether it has a bearing on philosophy may be open to dispute.

18) There would seem to be one other main rôle to be found for "the use of", to do with category-mistakes. This doctrine and his celebrated main argument for it, as put forward by Ryle in his *The Concept of*

Mind, are intuitively highly plausible; but they are nonetheless open to doubt, so that it is necessary to enquire into them further.

The doctrine of category-mistakes may be put as follows. You see men in uniform passing you, and in seeing the men you see the regiment. If you look for something additional to the men in the way you might look for a flag, you will look for it in vain.

It is important to distinguish the bare bones of the doctrine from consequences that might be taken to be part of the doctrine itself. Thus one consequence might be that there could be no inference from the men to the regiment; another might be that there could be no causal relationship between them; another that no statement whatever can be made about both except one about composition; another that the absence or presence of category-mistakes determines whether a statement is meaningful or meaningless. (It is not to be assumed that every one of these possible consequences has been maintained by someone.)

What sort of mistake is made? It is held to be one of counting wrongly: to say that there are so many men, and that the regiment is one more object, is to speak wrongly. A regiment cannot be counted as an object in addition to the men composing it: for instance, the context of the march-past indicates that the regiment, as an organisation of men, is not to be counted numerically along with men. To do so would be a mistake; and the mistake would seem to consist of confusing an organisation with its elements (or with similar elements).

19) What underlies the mistake? Does it consist in speaking meaninglessly or in something else? Three accounts of it may be considered.

One is that, whatever else an organisation may be, it as at least a class (an organised class) of its elements. Hence to count the regiment as one more object in addition to its men would be to treat a class as a member of itself. Then, apparently, we should have a category-mistake; and it would be meaningless to count the regiment as well as its men.

On this account the theory of category-mistakes would drive a wedge between meaningful and meaningless statements.

For this account to hold, it is necessary to presuppose either Russell's theory of classes and theory of types or some other that renders it meaningless to speak of a class being a member of itself; for in some systems, e.g. Quine's, it is not meaningless to speak of a class thus. Hence this approach would not lead to the required conclusion. However, I do not think that language analysts had Russell's paradox in mind as a prime consideration.

Another account of the confusion would be that the idea of an organisation (or theory of its nature) and the idea of its elements (or theory of their nature) have some incompatible empirical consequences. For instance, a regiment has a tradition but no memory; a man has a memory but no tradition; a regiment has persons as its elements, a man has not. But only some of the consequences are incompatible. For instance, both a regiment and its men may have certain inanimate possessions, one having flags and the other having uniforms. What is a mistake is to confuse the two ideas when the context concerns the incompatible empirical consequences. When the context concerns empirical consequences that are compatible (or the aspects of a regiment and its men that are compatible), no confusion arises.

This provides an account of a definite mistake, and one that is commonly regarded as one. It is basically about the incompatible aspects of two things.

According to the foregoing account, two concepts might be of different categories in one context but they might not be in another. The third account would deny this and go further than the second, holding that if two concepts are of different categories in one context they are in all others. For instance, in "This regiment has a flag" 'having a flag' is of a different category from "having a uniform" in "This soldier has a uniform". And even in the case of "This company has never surrendered" and "This soldier has never surrendered", 'has never surrendered' would be of a different category in each statement.

The difference comes to this: on one view, a category-mistake exists only in some contexts, and the mistake stems from treating the organisation as numerically on the same footing as its elements, while no mistake arises in contexts other than those of counting; on the other view, a category-mistake exists in all contexts, and the mistake arises if the organisation is treated on the same footing as its elements in any context and not merely where counting is involved, perhaps because there is always a covert (when it is not overt) reference to counting.

20) For the present argument it makes no significant difference which of these two accounts is adopted. I will consider only the second and stronger one, partly because it is probably the one language analysts have in mind, and partly to give my argument the maximum task; but partly because I think the stronger account the correct one. It seems to consist of two assertions. One is—as with the weaker account—that an organisation is not to be counted as an individual. The other seems to me to be—and this is not part of the weaker account—that an organisation operates or is affected through an individual or individuals. Thus "This company surrendered" means that one man (the captain) used his institutional authority to order his men to surrender (which they did). This account seems to be unobjectionable. But it also seems to me

not to have certain philosophical consequences usually attributed to it. Thus the mere substitution of one category for another in a given meaningful statement, as the above example shows, does not automatically make it meaningless so that no principle exists here for driving a wedge between the meaningful and meaningless. But if this escapes notice, as I think it sometimes has, the doctrine might be used, as I think it sometimes has, to drive such a wedge—in which case it would be a re-incarnation of the principle of verifiability.

One of the most important possible consequences of the doctrine that seems dubious is that causal relations between an organisation and its elements are excluded by it. To show that this is not so, consider "The police arrested a spy" and "A policeman arrested a spy", which involve different categories. According to Ryle's procedure, for instance, in being arrested by a policeman the spy is arrested by the police. Now a policeman can be arrested by the police. Hence, even if "policeman" and "police" are of different category, the organisation (police) can have an effect upon its own elements (policemen). The doctrine of category-mistakes concentrates on showing that an organisation operates through an individual; and the conclusion it aims at is that an organisation cannot be said to operate upon an individual. But this does not follow; an organisation might operate both through and upon an individual. Thus even the stronger account of category-mistakes is ineffective, for example, against the idea of mind-body interaction.

Hence, unless some other account of the confusion between an organisation and its elements exists, the doctrine of category-mistakes either fails to reach its objective, because in its weaker form it is too weak to hit philosophical doctrines such as mind-body interaction, and in its stronger form it gives the impression of effectiveness by constituting a criterion of what is meaningful and meaningless—and thus a re-incarnation of the principle of verifiability.

Perhaps we can now understand the plausibility of the doctrine in the light of the interpretation that is mild but ineffective, and understand its apparent effectiveness in the light of the interpretation that is radical in form.

21) It is important to recognise that the method of "the use of" is not intended to embody a universal principle : that is to say, it would be held by most and perhaps all language analysts that there is a variety of uses of "and use of". Hence it might well be that in some applications it does drive a wedge between meaningful and meaningless statements, whereas in others it does not. Should this be so, its use in one set of applications is a target of the argument against the wedge; while its

use in the other, though unobjectionable is of questionable value to philosophy.

22) The previous chapter aimed at showing that for a theory to be meaningful, according to the principle of verifiability, it is not merely *sufficient* but also *necessary* that a verification should be deducible; and hence at showing that, for a statement to be unverifiable, it is necessary that no initial conditions exist enabling an observation-statement to be deduced.

This chapter has examined the use of "having a use" and brought out certain dilemmas, leaving the choice of horn to those who wish to choose one. The general dilemma is that the principle of "the use of" either reduces to the principle of verifiability, or, if used without the restriction that what has a use is verifiable, fails apparently to hit the philosophical doctrines supposedly under attack. The particular dilemma concerns one of the most important applications of "the use of", to do with category-mistakes. Here again the use of "the use of" either reduces to a criterion distinguishing meaningful and meaningless statements, or else, amounts to a correct theory of a certain sort of confusion (organization and members) but this confusion though of some importance, cannot provide a basis, for example, for undermining philosophical theories such as mind-body interaction.

It would seem that, even though the innocuous horn is sometimes chosen or perhaps always intended, the extreme horn comes perhaps unwittingly to be adopted. If this should be so, the principle of verifiability, although given up, would make its presence felt, and the use of "the use of" would amount to a re-incarnation of the spirit of logical positivism.

FOOTNOTES

[1] Since I first wrote this I noticed that Ayer (1960) links verifiability and "having a use", and indeed he takes them to be fully equivalent, for he considers that "having a use" implies "being verifiable":

The point of talking about "use" emerges only when we go on to consider how we are supposed to determine what a given sentence states; and it is here that the principle of vertification once more comes in. For the answer is that to specify the use of a sentence, in this sense, is to describe the situations to which it is applied; in other words to describe the situations, the states of affairs, by which the statement it expresses would be verified.

REFERENCES

Ayer, A. J. (1960), *Philosophy and Language*, Inaugural Lecture, Oxford, p. 23.

CHAPTER XIII

Evaluation of Refutations and Residues

IN CHAPTER 10, I have offered a refutation of the possibility of knowledge synthetic a priori in Chapters 11 and 12 I have offered a refutation of logical positivism and of linguistic philosophy, i.e. of empirical knowledge. If metaphysics and empiricism are untenable, what is left?

The position is not unlike that in which Kant found himself two hundred years ago. Kant awoke to find that analytic knowledge was empty and empirical knowledge unprovable—which torpedoes all philosophy from Descartes and Locke to Leibniz or Wolff and Hume. To save philosophy from the impasse he introduced a new conception of knowledge, synthetic a priori.

This notion did not, however, save philosophy. Certainly it dominated philosophy until replaced by twentieth-century empiricism-cum-analysis whether in its phase of logical analysis, the principle of verifiability, or knowledge as linguistic use. We have been invited to reject knowledge as synthetic a priori and accept knowledge as experientially constructible. But if this is vacuous we are virtually back to Kant's problem. Instead of trying to invent a new philosophical salvation, I propose to scan what we have got, and without propping it up, enquire what we can do with it.

We may hive off metascience, Mode (1), as a separate discipline, the study of scientific procedure, just as logic has become hived off since *Principia Mathematica* became established.

Mode (3), scientific ontology, may also be hived off as an uncertain, though fundamental, part of the study of science.

Mode (4), parascientific ontology, may in the present context be taken with Mode (5), cosmological ontology, as constituting classical metaphysics. Here my contention is that, apart from a few milk and water efforts that make virtually no assertion, all the great metaphysical endeavours were rooted in the notion of knowledge synthetic a priori, and therefore that no metaphysical claim can be proved, although any one such claim might happen to be true.

Mode (2), epistemology, shares some of the definiteness of Mode (1) with some of the inconclusiveness of Mode (5).

Mode (6), meta-ontological negativism, is bankrupt as a position (though some of its arguments may occasionally be useful).

Modes (1) and (2) are obviously germane to our knowledge of the universe; they require no defence. Mode (3), however inconclusive, is an inescapable part of science, and its contentions merit discussion even though we know we can never establish them, and even though we know that most of them are probably false, and, further, even though we know that we can obtain no general method of refutation of those that are false, but only occasionally light on a disproof of the odd one.

Merging (4) with (5), we are confronted with cosmological ontology, the great questions that have provided the greatest challenge over two and a half thousand years. They cannot be proved; they do not, or do not often, help science; they can only occasionally be refuted. Some of the questions in this area are in a sense a dead letter, but some are living issues. What are they?

The group consisting of universals, essences, and categories is of significance, at least because many people put forward answers to social problems that presuppose an unproved position taken up with regard to these questions (thus a view of contraception may be based on an assumption about essences).

Likewise significant are the problems of mind and matter, of mind and body (or of substance), at the very least because of their bearing on medicine.

The problems of determinism and of the relation between the past and the future (or whether the future is full, empty, or partially full) are vital to our knowledge of what it is open to us to plan.

The question of a physical nexus between events is an unsolved one, which lost its interest because it appeared to be intractable; it is clearly linked with that of determinism.

Then there is the queer question of Being: why is there a universe at all, rather than nothing? We cannot fully understand our universe and ourselves unless we can answer this.

How questions of this sort relate to man and society will be the subject-matter of later chapters. Here some brief comments will be made on the issues themselves (though each could be the subject of a book).

UNIVERSALS, ESSENCES, AND CATEGORIES

The problem of universals, which began in the days of Greek thought, persisted as one of the central questions in the philosophy of the Middle Ages, and it is still present in contemporary philosophy, though in modified form. Before trying to understand modifications of the problem, it is wise to recall its initial form; for whatever answer we may obtain using sophisticated modern distinctions, we shall nonetheless want to understand how our solution relates to the original problem. The original question was: Is a universal a word, or a conception in the mind, or an essence in a natural object?

The twentieth century has been noticibly nominalistic, that is to say, contemporary philosophers have favoured placing the universal in the word, or rather equating universals with words. One of the powerful reasons behind this attempt has lain in the fact that nominalism works so beautifully in mathematics and logic that it was tempting to try to extend nominalism over the entire field. Intuitively it is easy to see a weakness in this, for nominalism stands a reasonable chance of being applicable only in areas where the subject matter consists of artifices formed by the human mind. This would explain why nominalism fares very well in abstract fields such as mathematics and logic. But a doubt arises in the case of real things (as opposed to abstractions) in the universe. Universals, which characterize more than one thing, seem to be, in some way or another, a real part of a real universe. Moreover, to persist with nominalism would imply that in the universe, considered purely physically without human beings, no two material objects would share any characteristic whatever.

The power of nominalism lay in the weakness that some have found in what was traditionally called "realism" but which would be better known by Popper's word "essentialism". In a nutshell, the weakness was that, if a universal was part of the world, then the world contained a greater number of things than the number of actual particulars that you could count. Moreover there is a very famous argument introduced by Plato which still retains full power: namely, if Plato and Socrates both shared the universal *humanity,* this at once gave rise to problems of the relationship between Plato and humanity on the one hand, and humanity and Socrates, on the other. One has given an account of universals in the world at the expense of raising another problem essentially reproducing the same difficulty. Clearly the conception that Plato was criticizing, and the point of view from which he criticized it, hinged on the notion that the two particulars and the universal itself constituted three things.

However, since nominalism did not afford a satisfactory solution and, in fact, commanded but scanty following over a period of two thousand years, many philosophers fell back on conceptualism. The latter endows a universal with a more genuine universality than is possible if the universal is identified with a mere word, without, however, adding to the number of actual entities in the universe. Conceptualism thus avoids particularizing universals. In fact universals were regarded as constituting not the contents of the universe but a way of looking at it.

Conceptualism suffers from one of the difficulties of nominalism : namely that, in the physical universe without human beings, it would still be the case that no two material objects would share the same universal or would have anything in common. If a universal is a conception only, and therefore privately in the mind of one person, it would not be communicable to another person; universals can function only if the same conception exists in the mind of another person to whom the communication might be made, and if a linkage between the two conceptions can be effected. Moreover, while conceptualism would rid us of the difficulty involved in ascribing reality to universals in the world, we should do so at the price of ascribing reality to universals in human minds; and here essentially the same problem would break out once again.

The controversy that ensued lasted for two thousand years with some philosophers taking up one stand and others taking up another. Sometimes one school was more influential, sometimes another. The issue was never resolved and the reason for this is clear : that the weaknesses inherent in all three positions are so great.

What does appear to be clear is that if the universe is to be described as containing universals in some way or other, this must be such that they are not essences. It is still an unsolved question whether it is possible to construe a universal in such a way that it is part of the universe yet not an essence : and if it should be possible it is also an open possibility that such a conception would embrace some features of conceptualism and of nominalism without taking over much from these, or, more specifically, without falling foul of the overwhelming difficulties that these two positions suffer from.

If indeed philosophy has made any advances at all during the past two thousand five hundred years, one result that may count as such an achievement would be the fallaciousness of the concept of essence. The first great attack in modern times on the concept of essence occurred in Berkeley and was followed up by Hume. This is not to say that there were no percursors at all. One might hold, for instance, that the first great anti-essentialist was Heraclitus and one might perhaps add Gorgias. However, anti-essentialism was forgotten for a long period and was revived only in the present century. However vacuous the greater part of twentieth century schools of philosophical analysis may have been, they have the merit of embodying a major onslaught against essentialism (a feature it would share with its arch opponent Popper).

Two aspects of twentieth century philosophy should be mentioned in connection with universals. One concerns Ryle's (1949) theory of category mistakes. According to Ryle's treatment of category mistakes, when a company of soldiers passes by you would count 120 soldiers, but you do not count the company itself as the 121st object marching past. The company is of a different category from the soldiers that compose it. Ryle's argument is, in fact, an argument against the essentialistic interpretation of a universal. Nonetheless Ryle, while he does not commit himself to a view about universals in this context, does say that in the process of seeing the soldiers pass you ipso facto see the company pass. He is therefore subscribing to the view that the universal is somewhere in the world. One should, however, only attribute such a view to him with caution or with qualification, because he would, no doubt, hold, with conceptualists, that the company was a way of looking at the soldiers; and he would, no doubt, hold, with the nominalists, that the marching of the company depended on the use of the word "company". This amounts to saying that Ryle was not in this context concerned to solve the problem of universals and did not add up the various features of his category restrictions into an integrated theory.

The other feature that calls for comment is the well known results that come from Russell's work on the foundations of mathematics. Here he discovered that if you assemble a number of objects into a class, then the class itself could not be related to its members, either as one of them, or even as not one of them. This famous paradox of classes has made for great difficulties in logic; however, in this context we are concerned with its relation to the problem of universals. Attempts have been made to interpret the universal as the class of all particulars that resemble one another. At first blush this would seem to be a new theory of universals. different from the classical Greek or mediaeval theories. But if so, it has its own peculiar difficulty, for the universal can be neither an entity like the things that share it nor, paradoxically, can it be one among these. One would wonder what other theory this could be. Critics were quick to realize that, if a universal is a class of entities that resemble one another, there is the connecting bond of resemblance, and this would seem to be a universal in a different sense, for it is not in its turn a class. Hence the class interpretation of a universal would presuppose a universal of some different sort, and reopen the old classical question.

What is the significance of any such question about universals? Clearly one goal that philosophers were after was to find out what sort of things make up the world or, as Berkeley put it, constituted the furniture of the earth. Although we are still without a definitive answer, the question is one for which we have every right to try to find an answer.

In the course of considering the problem of universals, we have incidentally noted that the notion of an essence has been repudiated. What are the reasons for this? Is there a cast-iron argument? (Isn't the third man argument an argument against *equating* universals and essences, rather than an argument simply against essences?)

One very powerful argument is Plato's own against the third man outlined above: namely that Plato and Socrates are two men, while humanity would seem to be a sort of third man, by virtue of which Socrates and Plato are both men but only intrinsically observed as leaders of argument. Another argument would be the Berkeleian contention to the effect that all attempts to characterize an essence must fail because all characteristics turn out to be non-essential. Gravely undermining to essentialism, though not a philosophical argument, is the result of Darwin's theory of evolution according to which species are not essentially distinct. To these should be added the novel position brought forward by Ryle in introducing his conception of the category-mistake. As indicated above, this argument constitutes an attack on the notion of essence. I would add finally, that the notion of an essence is equivalent to a synthetic a priori proposition, as brought out in Chapter 10, the upshot of which is that no such notion can be established.

But it is, I think, clear that whether we are philosophizing with the Greeks, with the scholastics, or with Ryle, in terms of categories, we are even in the last case concerned with what the universe consists of.

MIND AND MATTER; MIND AND BODY

The great problem of mind and matter was most important in the period from Descartes to Hegel, though, of course, it was also discussed by the Greeks. It has not been prominent in twentieth century philosophy. The problem may come back if natural science should reach a stage of trying to develop a unifying theory of a much more general character than that of Einstein. To illustrate unification in science: the physics of Kepler and of Galileo became unified in the celestial mechanics of Newton. Electricity and magnetism became unified in the electro-dynamics of Maxwell. Einstein died without having successfully unified the theories of gravitation and electro-magnetics. There is still no overall unifying theory of all branches of physics. Likewise, it is obvious that the social sciences have almost no unifying theories.

Several social sciences are pursued in departments without even a local unifying theory. But the time may come when there will be such a unifying theory of the social sciences; and it may be then that a future Einstein will spend his life seeking unifying mind and matter theories, and achieve a unifying theory of the social sciences and of physics together.

Hundreds of years earlier before this problem had aroused the interest of several schools of philosophers, beginning with Descartes, extending over perhaps 250 years, there were no relevant scientific tools, nor did they have any remotely adequate scientific theories. All they could do was use pure reason, with such scientific ideas as were available, such as the notion of conservation of motion. Out of this they created their difficulties and their naive solutions. There is no purpose to be served in the present context by going into the details of the ideas that arose, interesting though they are; what is worth noticing is that philosophers were struck by the immense disparity between the world of mind and the world of matter and were utterly defeated by the question of how these areas could be related to one another. At least those philosophers knew a great question when they saw one.

Closely allied with this question is that of the relation of mind to body. That is to say, not mind in general, but a given person's mind and its relation to the body that the mind animates. This question inherits difficulties that beset the general question of the relation between mind and matter. However, it has a significance all its own and in recent years has become an important question since psychosomatic medicine has become an accepted idea in the medical world and even a domain of popular knowledge.

The question is one of vital theoretical and practical significance. Before the relationship is in the least understood, the various parties involved, whether doctors or philosophers, assume attitudes to the question; indeed, they often fly their flag with a courage unjustified by the evidence at hand. Their attitudes manifest themselves in practical action; for one doctor will approach a patient with the attitude that the mental stress from which a person is suffering must be fundamentally reducible to bodily factors, while another may hold it is not thus reducible and must be considered as a reality in its own right—and these attitudes govern the treatment prescribed. This is a prime example of practical importance, for instance, for the middle-aged business executive with a coronary thrombosis; when the treatment he gets from his doctor may turn on a philosophical view, the patient's fate may hang on an ancient but unsolved philosophical problem.

In this case the problem does indeed touch on the fundamental make-up of the world in the sense that it is concerned with whether the mind can make fundamental alterations in the body, and it also concerns how institutionalized professions, like the medical, may operate.

DETERMINISM

The ancient problem of determinism is still with us, though not so widely discussed as one might expect. It is clearly related to man's view of what the universe is composed of and how it functions. The key question is whether this historical train of events, the passage of time, can take place in only one way. The significance of this is largely either individual or social. Several theories concern the question: is an individual free to effect a change in his own life or not? Others concern societies, the issue being whether the progress of society must pursue a certain course, or whether the future is open. Such matters are involved as whether it is open to mankind to plan; whether it is possible to exercise any control over the enormous cloud of social difficulties besetting mankind in the twentieth century.

Perhaps the lack of contemporary interest in the abstract problem of determinism is due to the fact that many people seem to feel that there is bound to be some way around the difficulty of determinism: with the presumed upshot that if the problem is worked out philosophically it will make no difference to any practical problem. Thus if it should turn out to be provable that freedom, in some real sense, is possible, that will only cohere with what we have always tended to believe, so we shall go on with our inherent tendency to plan. Alternatively, if it should be provable that determinism holds, in the sense that no freedom for human individuals or society is possible, mankind in all probability will blindly struggle on. In other words, the issue seems to be viewed as a scholastic one.

PROBLEM OF THE FUTURE

The past is felt to be as real as the present, in the sense that the assertion that Queen Anne died in 1714 is every bit as true as the assertion that the sun is shining outside my window this morning, and the past event is just as real as the present one. But the future? If you are a determinist, the future is in a similar position to that of the past: it is as "full" as the past is. If you are not a complete determinist, the future is either "empty" or "partially filled"; so there may be no future facts for some assertions to correspond to, and the future is not fully real in the way the past is. The problem (genuine for some philosophers, pseudo for others) is whether the future is "full", "partially filled", or "empty".

PROBLEM OF A PHYSICAL NEXUS

This problem is perhaps a sub-problem of the problem of determinism. If determinism is true, or indeed if there are causal laws at all, it would seem that there must be some physical linkage between events to which a causal relationship is attributed. In the twentieth century this notion is taken to be a myth and there is widespread agreement in philosophy that there is no physical nexus at all, i.e. that there exists only what I have elsewhere called a de facto regularity (Wisdom, 1946, 1952). It is easy to see, as I think I have shown, that this notion of de facto regularity is quite unworkable. The problem arises, however, of finding any kind of alternative at all, let alone a reliable alternative. The only kind of nexus philosophers recognize as valid is a logical necessity. It is accepted by practically all that there could not be a logical necessity between events, and further that there can be no empirical evidence for such a nexus. And this throws us back once again on the notion that a physical nexus can only be a synthetic a priori proposition, which as argued in Chapter 10, can never be proved. Or it throws us back on a subjective bond originating in our minds which we ascribe to phenomena; and this would guarantee the illusion of order in the world. The only alternative to de facto regularity are variants of a logical or physical or subjective necessity which are inapplicable, unprovable, or fail to do what is required. We shall have to agree with idealists in finding in causation more than regularity and with empiricists in denying that what is additional is logical, physical, or subjective.

The dilemma leads me, however, to make the following suggestion :

The dilemma arises from the fact that the causal nexus must either be one of a necessary connection or one of de facto regularity; but necessary connection, of the physical kind, would seem to be a myth; while de facto regularity would allow anything to happen after anything and would therefore be inadequate to explain such orderliness as exists. In an infinitely extensible universe, however, it is 100 per cent probable that a volume in space and time, large to us but infinitely small in relation to the rest, exists characterized by orderliness as a chance effect. In other words, we should have the impression of a law of orderliness persisting and ubiquitous in our "universe" which would in reality be but a random effect in an isolated pocket of the universe as a whole. For this to solve the problem of natural necessity, we should have to test the hypothesis that most of the universe is lawless or without order. But even the untested conjecture is enough to show the causal nexus does not have to be either one of the necessary connection or one of de facto regularity throughout the entire universe.

Although offering a solution, my primary objective is not the solution as such, but to draw attention to the basic need that such a problem represents. It reflects the puzzlement of mankind about the make-up of a universe in which there is orderliness, causation, some things governed by other things, while lacking any clue how all this comes to be. We are without the knowledge of whether the things connected are intimately bound up, or loosely bound up, or have virtually no relation with one another—virtually a capricious relationship. If we are to try to apply the notion of causation to ourselves—as individuals in a society, we are bound to be deeply concerned with the nature of these bonds of the causal nexus.

BEING

This is the most bizarre of all philosophical questions and hardly arises in contemporary philosophical books or papers at all. There is one very good reason: that nobody has anything to say about it. It is a question that attracts beginners. Just because we feel helpless before such a problem, we should not relegate it to the dustbin as nonsense. It is better to acknowledge that we can make no contribution to it, but to admit that it is a fundamental question, perhaps the most fundamental question of all. If one can preserve one's youthful sense of curiosity, and look around the world including the classical starry heavens, and if one realizes that the cosmological argument is not viable because it is based on an infinite regress, one is faced with the question, why is there anything at all? Correlative to this is the question whether non-Being exists, i.e. whether non-Being is included in Being. In the past it was only theological cosmologies and philosophies such as Hegel's that have even attempted to deal with it, but in recent times it appears in existentialism at the hands of Heidegger. The repercussions of such a question on man and society would seem to be much more remote than with the other questions just described. In the present context I do not propose to offer any comment.

ACHIEVEMENTS OF PHILOSOPHY

Since there is a widespread sense among non-philosophers and also among philosophers that in the course of its two-and-a-half-thousand years of existence it has made no progress, I venture to give the following list of achievements (even if strikingly negative):

1) Knowledge in general is not obtainable by Reason alone (though it is in certain narrowly defined fields).

2) There are no essences (except artificially contrived ones, e.g. in mathematics or logic).

3) No knowledge is based on pure experience or pure observation.

4) There are no synthetic a priori truths.

5) No well-formed statements (other than self-contradictions) are false or meaningless a priori.

6) The theory of category-mistakes has the function of arbitrarily rubbing out ontologies.

7) All empirical knowledge is fallible.

REFERENCES

Ryle, Gilbert (1949), *The Concept of Mind*, London.
Wisdom, J. O. (1946), *Causation and the Foundations of Science*, Paris.
———————— (1952), *Foundations of Inference in Natural Science*, London, Ch. 17.

Part III

WHAT ARE PHILOSOPHERS' GOALS?

CHAPTER XIV

The Problem of Philosophers' Goals

A STRANGELY puzzling phenomenon arises in an unexpected quarter, namely areas of philosophy with which one happens to be most familiar such as the thought of some philosopher whose work has long engaged one's interest and attention. The situation is this: a celebrated philosopher, say, occupies the centre of the philosophical stage of the education of an undergraduate and of a teacher, and is well known through his works, which are perhaps lucid and well understood; there exist in addition numerous good commentaries; and there may also be helpful histories of philosophy which do, on occasion, bring out features not made plain by the other two sources. It may even be that one has even been teaching this philosopher for a number of years without encountering any major difficulty in the interpretation of his views, and one may have had a correct intuitive comprehension of the place of his philosophy and, roughly, what he was out to maintain. Nonetheless, if one then begins to reflect on that philosopher's overall goal, one may find that one's intuitive comprehension of the work as a whole does not provide a ready, far less a sure answer. One begins to realize that the philosopher had a number of important questions to raise, quite apart from a number of less important ones, but that the relationship between some of these more important questions is obscure. It could be, of course, that he was concerned simply with a handful of disparate questions which had no special relationship to one another, but initially, one may approach the philosopher with the sense that he had some goals which were more overriding than others and that there was some perspective into which these might be fitted. What is strange is that a matter of this sort should be, in fact, so difficult to sort out. And it is also strange that it is possible to expound over the length of an entire book the work of a philosopher or to teach his work to students over an entire course without being able to answer such a question. Yet if it cannot be answered readily and accurately, there is at least a presumption that something about the philosophy has eluded one, in other words, that the philosopher has not yet been properly understood.

Having taken some trouble to carry out this exercise with several philosophers of different schools, I have come to at least a preliminary conclusion, that the goals of a philosopher can be ordered in a series, as it were, of mountain tops: though one peak is important in itself, it also is a means of access to the next and the next, thence to the next and possibly last one. In other words, it would appear that there are different levels of goals.

In sorting this out, I have distinguished for convenience, several levels, the first four of which are: *subsidiary, subordinate, penultimate,* and *ultimate* goals. It is fairly easy to catalogue the preliminary goals. This is merely a matter of sifting out minor questions. This is not to say, of course, that the result of such a weeding out is beyond dispute, but that there would not be very much tendency to raise disputes about this level. It has been reasonably easy to rank the preliminary goals in some sort of order of more important and less important. A rough order is possible in which one is not committed to being completely correct about which of two adjacent goals should take precedence, but in which one should be sure that a goal allotted to place three really does take precedence over one put in place seven. Moreover it should be possible to see that those lower down in the ranking scale should be explicable or understandable in terms of those nearer the top. When we have divided these preliminary goals, then, into a top and bottom set such that the top set are the goals of the bottom set, then we concentrate on the top set to skim off it a level to constitute the penulimate goals. Here again there is, of course, room for disagreement, but in most cases there would probably not be much.

The penultimate goals may number from, say two to four. Real difficulty arises over the last step in the series of arranging these in an accurate ranking order so as to isolate the ultimate goal itself.

Further, when a real difficulty of this sort arises, it carries with it a peculiar problem; for the matter would seem to be one susceptible of investigation and solution, yet it is not at all easy to say how one might go about settling it.

The procedure generally speaking is to ask which goal leans on the other, or requires the other to be settled in order to be susceptible of solution itself, i.e. if G_2 stands in the way of G_1, it is less ultimate. Again if G_2 is a particularized form of G_1, it may not have to be dealt with in advance, but it is generally less fundamental than G_1; nonetheless it need not be, for the interest in the more general problem can be that it affords a means of solving the particular form. These relationships are obvious enough, but it is not always possible to apply them unequivocally. There can be a reason why the solution of G_1 is required for the solution of G₂ and at the same time another reason why the solution of G_2 is required for the solution of G_1. In such an impasse, there is left the recourse of seeking further consequences that G_1 or G_2 might explain.

To illustrate the situation very briefly, one does not have to have recourse to a very difficult case such as that of Hegel, for whom it may be a matter of considerable difficulty to state even his preliminary goals; nor does one even have to have recourse to, for example, Kant, whose overall aim has, from time to time, been a matter of dispute. But we can find the problem arising in such an ostensibly simple case as that of Descartes. Yet, as I will venture to suggest, we are far from understanding what was Descartes' ultimate goal.

In the next few chapters I shall attempt to illustrate this from a group of markedly different philosophers.

However, when one has attained even preliminary answers to the question raised, that is, attained a *perspective* on the philosopher's goals, and a tentative hypothesis about which the ultimate goal was, a further curious point then obtrudes. For the question arises, why did the philosopher attempt to reach this ultimate goal. In other words, having isolated what it is, it ceases to be self-evident why it should be a rock-bottom affair. This situation may be illustrated very briefly though at this stage not sufficiently to be convincing. Supposing the ultimate goal of a philosopher is certain knowledge. At first glance this seems a high and desirable thing and natural to every philosopher to want; but the question can be raised, what is so important about it that a great thinker would spend his life on finding a philosophy to underpin certain knowledge. This question has led me to postulate a further level, namely an extra-philosophical goal.

Expressed otherwise, the ultimate goal may seem to be an expression of a way of coping with an extra-philosophical goal. This is particularly apparent in the controversy arising over the relationship between Kant's three *Critiques*: it is a matter of dispute whether Kant was fundamentally concerned with basic knowledge which he then applied or whether he simply needed it to help him up the road to uncover perhaps the nature of the good. We can see that this controversy is a question of ranking goals. And the nub of the question becomes apparent, on considering the ultimate goal of some philosopher, if we ask: Why does he have this goal?

Some might prefer to put the extra-philosophical goal along with the ultimate goal, the two together constituting the basic philosophy of the author. This is simply a matter of convenience, of the ends to be served by the classification.

Allowance should, moreover, be made for the possibility of there

being more than one ultimate goal, which are not merely companion
goals. If two goals are unconnected, such a situation could mean only
that the philosopher pursuing them has two components of his life unrelated to one another; but it could mean they both subserve the extra-
philosophical goal—and we might be able to find out which, only after
locating the extra-philosophical goal. Connected with this is the possibility of change of goals. Subsidiary, subordinate, and even penultimate
goals may change considerably, though they could generally be replaced
by others leading to the same ultimate goal. I would expect the ultimate
goal to change but rarely, and when it did I would expect the replacement to continue to subserve the extra-philosophical goal. Change of
the latter would indicate a character upheaval.

The framework adopted here attributes to extra-philosophical goals
an outstanding role, that of determining in some way the prior goals
like a teleological cause. "But", to quote a comment by Dr Hattiangadi,

these extra-philosophical goals are not necessarily determinative of the *style* of a man's
research . . . he might have attacked his problem in different ways . . . the par-
ticularity of a man's work, the way he dealt with his ideas . . . are dictated by the
internal logic of ideas, even though the process may well give the man great extra-
philosophical satisfaction.

This variability in a man's style is in conformity with the present framework because its variations will all exude the same personal features
indicative of the same extra-philosophical goal; the internal logic, important though it is as a determinant of an investigation, is not the only
factor and does not preclude its being presented in a personal way
indicative of the same extra-philosophical goal.

By extra-philosophical goal is not meant an unconscious goal in any
deep sense. The philosopher might be more or less aware of it. By way of
illustration, consider a philosopher who has devoted nearly all of his
most prominent works to questions of logical application. We may find
that in some small, little-known work, he made a somewhat cursory
application to the question of public versus private self-interest. It might
be that this was his ultimate goal even though he spent his active
academic life exploring other questions. It might well be also that the
extra-philosophical goal arose from a deep-seated sense that, in some
situation of conflict, he habitually found himself at a loss, and found
this an overwhelmingly distressing situation, and never attained the sense
that he had done justice either to society or to himself. And it is conceivable that he might be very well aware of this. On the other hand
it could be that he would devote much work to this problem, and yet
be oblivious of its connection with his more routine professional investiga-

tions of, say, logical applications. In this case it would form part of what Freud called the preconscious.

Underlying such a philosophical goal or, if you like, preconscious goal, it seems inescapable that there are fully unconscious goals of a sort I have tried to bring to light in presenting psycho-analytic investigations of Berkeley, Schopenhauer, and Descartes. Such unconscious goals would concern fundamental psychological conflict and the philosophies stemming from them would be what I have called *unconscious auto-biographies* (Wisdom, 1947).

Now it seems to me further that the extra-philosophical goals, if readily susceptible of being interpreted, are concerned with a way of life.

My aim in disentangling these levels of goals is that they may help us to evaluate the reality of the problems occupying a philosopher's attention. It may help us to do something towards translating his more personal problems into the more covert problems they conceal. In this way we may hope to see what are apparently purely academic problems of metaphysics as roundabout ways of trying to handle deep-seated problems of vital concern to the individual person, and possibly even problems of society.

It is perhaps not without significance that one of the most zealously objective of all philosophers, Descartes, should have raised the question in one of his dreams *quod vitae sectabor iter*? (What path shall I pursue?).

REFERENCES

Wisdom, J. O. (1947), *The Metamorphosis of Philosophy*, Cairo.

CHAPTER XV

Of the Optimists:
Descartes, Spinoza, Leibniz, Berkeley, and Kant

1 OF DESCARTES

DESCARTES IS A particularly interesting figure for a number of reasons. He was one of the founders of modern philosophy, or more exactly, he was *the* founder of one of the main strands of modern philosophy, and in so being, he introduced new ways of thought after the middle ages. Coupled with that, however, as has now become widely understood, and despite appearances to the contrary, he retained a great deal of the conceptualization of the middle ages and part of the way then customary of seeing the world. Descartes' canvas was nothing if not broad. He took the whole world as his subject and occupied himself with the most central problems of his day. On the other hand, his standard of argumentation was not nearly so high as certain other philosophers, such as Berkeley and Hume, who might well be regarded as less interesting.

There is an important complication. We have to recall that Descartes was not simply a philosopher in the modern classroom sense. Nowadays we have faculties which are separate from one another—the Faculty of Science, the Faculty of English, the Faculty of Philosophy—and this has led to a kind of trades-union restriction: You are not to participate in the other man's job if you want to remain academically respectable (this is, of course, breaking down with the growth of interdisciplinary activities); on the whole if you are a philosopher you must do a logical job or a philosophical job, but if you want to mix in a bit of science with it, or need to do so because of the problem you are engaged in, then this is not really doing philosophy. Such an outlook used not to prevail. It is quite a new tradition, going back only to the last century. In former times, when a philosopher was concerned with a problem, he did not mind using any discipline that would help him. Descartes wanted to understand the universe, the universe of matter, the universe of mind, man, animals, and so on, so he used mathematics and physics as well as a more narrowly philosophical approach. He was a great mathematician, indeed introduced, or rather was the discoverer of, one of the greatest ideas in modern mathematics. He was an outstanding, perhaps even a great, physicist. If we overstress these aspects of Descartes, we may end up by thinking that philosophy was just a hobby on the side, as it sometimes seems to be with scientists, especially when they get old. The main mistake, however, that needs combatting is the idea that philosophy was a subject on its own, detached from the rest. Not at all. Descartes was fundamentally a philosopher, but in a very broad sense, concerned with the overall problem of understanding the world as a whole. Instead of falling for the old mistake of taking Descartes the philosopher to be the author of the *Meditations,* which is a metaphysical work making virtually no use of science, we have to see Descartes as concerned with basic problems about the universe which, though philosophical, might require mathematics, physics, or philosophy for their solution. Thus, if Descartes's physics had a good deal to say about the nature of the physical universe, there would also be additional questions to be answered about the fundamental stuff of that universe, on which physics as such threw no light but without which physics would not be complete. Moreover, despite impressions to the contrary, there were a great many sceptical thinkers around and if they threw light on some of the findings of science, or indeed even of philosophy, it was necessary for Descartes to answer them if challenged on matters of principle concerning the reasonings he used, whether in the sciences or in his more narrowly philosophical work. So it was natural for him to go into the problem of knowledge and look for a method of knowledge that could be regarded as certain. This need is, of course, what he sought to satisfy when he introduced his famous cogito—I think; therefore, I am—as one of his basic principles of philosophy with which he hoped to obtain other results of importance. A more detailed account of the structure and contents of Descartes' philosophy is not needed here because it is very well known and readily accessible. The present enquiry has a different objective.

One of the most curious features of the philosophy of Descartes is this: Despite its extraordinary clarity of presentation, the breadth of the canvas, the absence of scarcely relevant minutiate, it is not clear what was for him the most central problem of all. It is to me a matter of some astonishment that one can read Descartes, feel at ease with his writing, be confident perhaps for many years that one has understood him correctly, even down to matters of some detail as well as in broad outline. One may even have "taught" him reasonably successfully, and yet one may wake up to the fact that there is something central to his

E

position that has eluded one. Do you think you know what his central problem was? Do you think there could be any serious doubt about it?

Let us make a quick sketch of what is taken to be his official philosophy. Perhaps no knowledge at all is reliable, for it is just possible that we may be taken in by an evil demon. So let us try to doubt everything that we possibly can and see if there is anything left that cannot conceivably be doubted. The one thing that the philosopher finds he cannot doubt is that he himself exists, for in doubting his own existence he confirms it. But how are we to proceed further to obtain results that can be guaranteed? Descartes needs a criterion of truth which he bases on a principle of clear and distinct ideas, which will be self-guaranteeing, and provide a form of truth that could not be denied. How then apply them to obtaining consequences about the universe? Descartes' tactic is to prove the existence of God, and of a perfectly good God, who will not allow him to be deceived. He concludes that it is most improbable the external world should be a chimera or dream, thence that the external world probably exists.

The above is the commonplace of Descartes' philosophy, and one assuredly should not overlook it, for it contains factors that were most important to him, but it is hard to believe that the conclusion about the reality of the external world was his central aim. If he was arguing against the sceptics, his treatment of the external world might have been an exercise or application of his philosophizing, and his principles of certainty with which he begins might constitute the central content.

In order to investigate Descartes' goals, I propose to list a large number of those questions that were of concern to him and to try to sort them out. The first selection will consist of what I am calling "subsidiary goals".

SUBSIDIARY GOALS

The nature of explanation

The idea of describing the world mathematically

The principle of conservation (whether conservation of motion, energy, or matter)

That animals are machines

The immortality of the soul

Our knowledge of the external world

Deceptiveness of the senses

The deductive conception of knowledge

Freedom of the will

Evil

Error

Appearance and reality

Conservation of reality

Determinism[1]

Some of these are overtly subsidiary, such as the idea of describing the world mathematically, and the deductive conception of knowledge which was adopted to arrive at certainty. Likewise the principle of conservation of reality, which was taken from the middle ages, was used to such ends as providing a proof of the existence of God. Others, such as the belief that animals are machines, formed part of the way one saw the world with God at its head, but it could hardly rank in significance with the nature of man. The deceptiveness of the senses was not so much a basic question as something that triggered one off; it was not that the senses were of concern but the fact that they played into the hands of the sceptics; and the same holds true of several similar issues. The freedom of the will, so far as it interested Descartes, was simply parasitic on a rational understanding of the world. And immortality, again so far as it interested him, was something that made no sense without the existence of God and was not in doubt if God exists.

It is evident both that we are reaching more central considerations, and we approach highly important problems that have not yet been listed above.

SUBORDINATE GOALS

> Truth and innate ideas
> Rationality
> God
> Physics

I have bracketed truth and innate ideas together; they are not, of course, the same thing. Innate ideas constituted the most important means of access to truth. The truth was the entire raison d'être of innate ideas. Rationality is virtually equivalent to the problem of truth.

It might be thought that truth was a natural candidate for being an ultimate goal. But, in view of the great challenge from the sceptics at the time, it seems inescapable that truth was demanded as a means of countering the sceptics so that the problem of scepticism and its cognates would have been more fundamental.

It is desirable to add a cautionary word about the role played by the existence of God in Descartes' philosophy. Descartes was a religious man, so far as I have been able to judge, and he was not hypocritical in the way that has sometimes been suggested. In other words, he believed in God sincerely but the existence of God played no significant role in his philosophy, apart from one fundamental point. The role played was indispensable, but not absolutely central—we lack words designating orders of importance to indicate the different rungs of a ladder near the top; Descartes needed to prove the existence of God in order to guarantee important results, notably the probability that the external world exists. The point is, however, that the existence of God in this context was simply a means to an end, not an end in itself. The conception that God may have played a role in his life is another matter. The contention here is that so far as his philosophy was concerned, the existence of God was a subordinate concern, that is, subordinate in relation to more ultimate questions. Otherwise expressed, I am drawing a distinction between a subordinate level of basic questions and more ultimate questions. The study of physics loomed large for Descartes in his enquiry into the nature of the world. But in the end physics was clearly concerned only with corporeal objects, and the conservation principles suggested that physical forces could not impinge on the mind, which therefore formed a world apart. Thus, physics would be subordinate to the problem of mind and matter or of substance.

I turn, therefore, to my final list, which is much more difficult to sort out. Because of this, I have not attempted to forestall the answer to be proposed. Whereas in the earlier listings I have been reasonably confident that there would be little to dispute, at this point I am quite unsure about my tentative solution or ranking. And this will serve to underline the question I have raised about the difficulty of specifying what Descartes' main goal really was. I therefore list a combination of two levels to be separated out later, if this should be possible.

PENULTIMATE AND ULTIMATE GOALS

> Scepticism versus certain knowledge
> Substance
> Mind and matter
> The mind-body problem

As regards the first pair, the problem of scepticism versus knowledge is that Descartes wanted to find means of obtaining knowledge that was absolutely reliable in order to be able to beat down the sceptics. One might urge, however, that rationality amounts to much the same thing; for the problem of rationality raises the question: How can a rational man justify his beliefs and how can he do it with certainty? The latter formulation is perhaps more general than that of certain knowledge, in that one could raise the question of rationality apart from a sceptical challenge. But in view of the sceptical challenge of the period, we may leave rationality alongside truth and take the problem of scepticism to be the representative problem.

Now, if we take the other pair, mind and matter on the one hand and mind and body on the other, we really have a distinction between two fields of application. It is the same problem with mind and body as it is with mind and matter. The common problem is the one of relationship; and the answer, whatever it is, is the same for Descartes in both cases, at least in broad terms. In the case of the mind-body problem, it happens to be just a special form of matter that is concentrated to form one's body. Otherwise expressed, it is the same problem of substance in both cases.

It might, however, be argued that the problem of substance was the more fundamental because the more abstract, and there is a long tradition in the history of philosophy of taking the problem of substance to be the Cartesian problem. In my view this tradition is correct, but that does not necessarily mean that the problem of substance is somehow more ultimate. It is simply the form of expression the more concrete problem assumed with Descartes. There is not much difference of level between these two; and it will be convenient to allow the mind-body problem to do duty for the problem of mind and matter and for the problem of substance.

I have now come nearly to the end of the task of ranking Descartes' questions in a perspective forming a pyramid. If the penultimate goals included truth and innate ideas, and rationality, we have left:

ULTIMATE GOALS?

Scepticism
The mind-body problem

An unanswered question concerns two fundamental problems, scepticism on the one hand and the mind-body problem on the other. Which of these is penultimate and which is to crown the pyramid as the ultimate problem?

It is easy to reach an answer if we follow the obvious line. That the mind-body problem was penultimate may easily be maintained on the grounds that the problem just constitutes a blemish on the map of man's knowledge; so long as this remains unsolved the problem of knowledge itself is at stake, for there must naturally be doubt about the certainty of our knowledge, if a major problem cannot be made to yield, or so at least the intellectuals of the time might well have thought. Further, if you were confronted with a very recalcitrant problem like the mind-body problem which nobody could solve, how could you be a rational man? The sceptics would be able only too easily to show you that you were believing in relations between two domains, like mind and body, which you could not justify at all. Thus the problem of mind and body was one simply to be mopped up in the service of the problem of scepticism, which would then occupy the position of being the ultimate problem.

This is straightforward. But we should look to see whether it is possible to construct the situation the other way around. At first sight, this would seem to be impossible. If we consider the question, "Why does anyone want to obtain knowledge that is certain?", it seems, at first sight, to be self-answering; for philosophers at all ages, and indeed all students of any kind of knowledge, would have liked to have obtained knowledge that was certain. How, then, could the problem of knowledge be otherwise than ultimate? However, it has transpired in the twentieth century that we seem to get along quite well with knowledge that is conjectural, and, indeed, it is so widely held as to be conceivably universally held, though this is probably not so, that certain knowledge is impossible in principle and conjectural knowledge is in principle the only knowledge possible, that we can begin to entertain seriously the idea that perhaps certain knowledge need not have been an ultimate requirement. In any case, we *can* raise the question, *"Why* do we need knowledge that is certain?" "For what?"

But if the problem of scepticism was not the ultimate problem, then the mind-body problem would have been, and the problem of scepticism would have been near the centre of the stage solely in order to help philosophers tackle the mind-body problem. If the mind-body problem was really the one that made philosophers tick in that period, then how were they to tackle it, Only after they had got an instrument strong enough to tackle it with, namely an instrument of perfect knowledge.

The disparateness of mind and body, the prevailing conceptions of them as utterly incommensurable, raises a problem which appears to have escaped notice, the problem of communication between person and person. If I want to communicate with you, my mind will require some connection with my body, whether by speech, writing, gesture, or the like. This would necessitate that my mind should act on my body in the first place, which, if mind and body are disparate substances, is impossible. But if achieved, then at least our bodies can touch even though our minds cannot. But then there is a chasm between your body and your mind, as there is between mine. Hence mind-body incommensurability renders communication between person and person in **principle impossible.**

Now, if we accept this conclusion, we may hazard the conjecture that this problem lay at the root of Descartes' philosophy; i.e. the impossibility of communication was manifested through the medium of mind-body incommensurability (or disparateness of substances).

The perspective proposed then is that the pyramid is crowned with the mind-body problem as the ultimate goal.[2] And the problem of communication between person and person would be an *extra-philosophical* goal.

In an earlier chapter, I have suggested that innate ideas constituted an equivalent of the synthetic a priori proposition, and indicated that the central forms of metaphysics at all times presumably hinged on a synthetic a priori proposition. If this should be so, then it should be possible to render a philosopher or a philosopher's general theory, by means of one or two central synthetic a priori propositions. The task therefore faces us of formulating these to represent Descartes' philosophy.

One of his central procedural axioms was, "Whatever I can conceive of, clearly and distinctly, is true." This I think could be rendered by, "A priori principles suffice to prove ultimate truths."

So much for the procedure. Now for content. The problem of substance might be rendered, "How can we reveal the relatedness of all things, or more particularly, of independent, infinite substances?" Likewise, "How can we solve the relation of mind to body?"

Now, these last questions of content cannot be formulated in terms of answers supplied by Descartes, because he never reached a solution and he provided no philosophical theory. The most we can do, therefore, is to combine his principle of method with the content he hoped to achieve in something like the following form, "By means of a priori principles we can solve the problem of scepticism or the problem of the mind-body relationship."

2 OF SPINOZA

If we compare Spinoza's problems with those of Descartes and make a list of those in Spinoza, we find that, of the first 14 that I have compiled for Descartes and described as subsidiary, the first 7 are not really of concern to Spinoza. This leaves the second 7 of these subsidiary problems. Let us turn briefly to them.

Firstly, there is the problem of freedom of the will. This interested Spinoza and he gave a specific answer to it, namely, that a man's will is free when he understands and accepts the eternal necessity of determinism. It generates the significant notion of *rational resignation*.

Secondly, he is interested in the problem of evil in a notable way. For one gets the impression from his writing of a moral flavour to his work that seems to be absent in Descartes. With Spinoza it ranked much higher among significant problems.

Thirdly, error is a matter of concern to him, as with Descartes. This, I think, is clearly of subsidiary importance, and can be seen to be so without much discussion, because error simply constitutes a paradox in being part of a manifestation of God.

Fourthly, there is a question of appearance and reality. This question, again, is absorbed in the wider question of the relation of substances.

Fifthly, there is the deductive conception of knowledge. Now important though this was to Spinoza, and surely he laid more emphasis on it than did Descartes, it was important simply as a means to an end, namely knowledge and certainty. He knew of no other form of knowledge of high standing; that was the standard model of knowledge handed down the ages from the time of Euclid and Archimedes. Thus important though it was, it was subsidiary, for, after all, the deductive procedure was simply a means to an end.

Sixthly comes the conservation of reality. Here again, this is a principle, as in Descartes, inherited from the middle ages, without which Spinoza could not give a causal account of the changes composing the two manifestations of God, namely matter and mind. In short, it was a principle for working out one of his ideas, but not in itself a main goal.

Seventhly, and lastly, there is determinism. Like Descartes, Spinoza was a determinist, but determinism for all such thinkers was an ingredient of rationality, for their outlook apparently was that one could not have rationality without a completely orderly system, unless there was the relation of determinism rigourously connecting causes and effects. Otherwise, there would be some degree of indeterminism or disorder or even chaos, and hence incomplete rationality.

As with Descartes, however, I want to point out that all of these features were important for Spinoza, but nonetheless, most of them were subsidary. And this has already been made clear in the case of some of them. It remains to comment only on evil and freedom of the will. As with determinism, it is natural to suppose that, if there were freedom of the will, in any libertarian sense that really excluded determinism, an irrational ingredient would come in to the universe, for mind could interfere with natural processes in an indeterminate, even haphazard way, and this would be counter to rationality. So here again, there seems to be no difficulty. Evil would seem, perhaps, to be the only problem in this domain which might seem to be of more central importance. However, I think it is not difficult to see that evil is of importance, mainly, and perhaps wholly, because it appears to be incompatible with the omnipotence and perfection of God; it would therefore be more central than the subsidiary questions but subordinate to the problem of the existence of God. Perhaps error should be put with it.

Let us leave these subsidiary problems now and turn to those that may be more central but still subordinate. These seem to be exactly those to be found in Descartes. Namely, (i) truth, or rationality, and (ii) the existence of God. Thus we have:

SUBORDINATE GOALS

Truth or intuitive ideas
Rationality

We may therefore proceed straightaway to the candidates for penultimate and ultimate positions. In the case of Descartes I made the mind-body problem do duty for the mind-matter problem, since in the context the two amount to much the same thing. Descartes did discuss both, but with slightly more emphasis on one than on the other. In the case of Spinoza, his overt discussion is not focussed on the mind-body relationship but on the mind-matter relationship and this loomed extremely large. So in his case I will take the mind-matter problem as doing duty for the two.

As regards the nature of knowledge, namely "where we get it" and "what it is that it is composed of", Descartes' answer is that there is self-evident truth and that it is characterized by consisting of innate ideas which are clear and distinct. Spinoza had exactly the same conception of self-evident truth, consisting of innate ideas (to which he gave a different name, intuitive knowledge), and, though he does not underline this point, they would be characterizable as clear and distinct. Descartes looked upon the certainty of innate ideas with an element of doubt until he had gone on to prove the existence of God, who being perfect, would not decieve him; and then he was in a position to trust his conclusions about the nature of knowledge. Though the structure may be somewhat different in Spinoza, Spinoza also used the existence of God, which he tried to establish fairly early on in his array of theorems, to underpin his position about substance. This means that with Spinoza, as with Descartes, the role of God, though of primary importance, was not quite ultimate. Thus, as with Descartes, God initially plays a slightly subordinate role in Spinoza; the problem of the existence of God is brought in, not at the beginning, but fairly early, in order to support the development of his ontology. Now Spinoza was a more religious man than Descartes; both were believers, Spinoza devout, Descartes probably more intellectualistic about the belief. Thus there is no question of their trying to denigrate the conception of God. It is simply a case of establishing what his role was in their system of ideas. Possibly the simplest way to express it would be this: If we have a ladder with a number of rungs from the bottom to the top, and if we rank the various problems that they were concerned with in ascending order of importance, the problem of God is so important that it is near the top of the ladder. In fact, it would seem to be on the third rung from the top, though not the very top, while many others are in a descending order of importance below those three rungs. Thus, I count this problem as primary, though no more, in both their systems.

Nonetheless, God plays a second role in the philosophy of Spinoza which it did *not* play in that of Descartes, for God also figured as a still more significant goal. Spinoza explicitly says that the goal of life is the "intellectual love of God". Whatever difficulties commentators may have in explaining what he meant by this, it is clear that he meant God to be at or near the centre of his system and a primary goal to be reached by a philosophical avenue. And this was not the case in Descartes. The difference is well recognised, for Spinoza has been widely accepted as a deeply religious man and has been called the "God intoxicated man".

In Descartes we are left with two problems that are candidates for the ultimate positions. With Spinoza there appeared to be several possibilities: mind and matter (subsuming mind and body); God in relation to man; evil; freedom or rational resignation.

Let us consider the question of certain knowledge of God. Since God is explicitly stated by him to be primary, whereas with Descartes this would appear not to have been so, the purpose of certain knowledge could be interpreted as having one purpose, namely, to provide a means by which the intellect could have knowledge of God. If Spinoza is interpreted in this way then the intellectual love of God clearly means the communication between an individual and God by means of a rational channel. Hence, it would seem that the goal of certain knowledge falls below that of God, which is penultimate or ultimate, whereas in Descartes it remains a question of dispute up to the very end whether knowledge and certainty are ultimate or penultimate.

Assuming this position, we have now to ask whether the problem of God or the mind-matter problem is the more ultimate.

It is very easy to interpret this along the lines that the solution of the mind-matter problem is penultimate because we have to solve this in order to obtain access to God, the ultimate, by the intellectual causal linkage with God through understanding the two manifestations, mind and matter, that he displays.

This perspective of the two problems makes excellent sense. It is not easy to find any argument against it. Nonetheless, it is worth considering whether it is possible to view the perspective the other way round.

Supposing God is penultimate and that the intellectual communion with God is designed to lead to a proper understanding of the relation of mind to matter. Could this possibly have any cogency?

As with Descartes it remains true that Spinoza was faced with a Cartesian split between mind and body, even though he does not discuss the mind-body problem, and therefore he may have been faced with the same problem of how to establish the existence of communication between persons. It could have been a real problem. Let us, however, look at a further aspect of it. Given the Cartesian position of mind and matter, mind as thinking substance and matter as extended substance are so isolated as to have nothing in common between them. Spinoza went to the most extraordinary lengths in an intellectual, philosophical way to link these two disparate substances, even going to the length of identifying them in a certain sense, regarding them as different manifestations of one substance, so that the two manifestations of the same substance contained exact parallels to each other. One might think that he could hardly have gone to such peculiar lengths of such an unplausible kind, if there was no inordinate need to solve the problem at any cost, even at the cost of rationality. One is reminded of the incredible length the Roman philosopher was prepared to go to, in order to come to terms with the problem of death, hoodwinking himself by saying that "when we are here death is not" and that "when death is here we are not". Both Spinoza and the Roman appear to have tried to liquidate an overwhelming problem by logical guile. This suggests to me that the need by no means tells us whether *that* problem was ultimate or whether it was the king-pin of some *other* problem that was ultimate.

If this is true it creates a further question, as with Descartes : we are left without understanding why these two ultimate problems were pressing. On the interpretation I have suggested, Descartes had to solve the mind-body problem above all else. With Spinoza it was the mind-matter problem, but underlying it was perhaps the mind-body problem. If so, the question would be why this is so, and the answer I am putting forward in both cases is that there was a difficulty in communication between persons.

Now this would lie beyond the ultimate problem, and would constitute an extra-philosophical problem.

To try to settle this issue, let us see where the other top problems exert their weight. The ideal of rational resignation has a clear place in a scheme with God at the centre; it has no discernible place in communication between men. And, as regards evil, Spinoza's conception of it was of an incomplete perspective, apparently partially detracting from the perfection of God, through not being seen to be a necessary element in the deterministic whole. Here, too, the issue has a clear place in relation to God though not, as Spinoza handles it, in relation to men.

Hence it would seem that the ultimate goal was communication between man and God, to which the questions of rational resignation and of evil are directly subservient; and that the problems of rationality and of mind and matter or of substance are penultimate.

Thus we have :

PENULTIMATE GOALS	ULTIMATE GOALS
Truth and intuitive ideas	God in relation to man
Rationality	Freedom or rational resignation
Evil	
The problem of mind and matter	

On this construction, the ultimate goal of communication between man and God (the intellectual love of God) is a conception of The Good which involves the idealized human sentiment of rational resignation.

This goal, however, carries with it as a corollary communication between person and person, for all persons as well as all other objects are necessary components of the whole which is God.

It is, moreover, difficult to avoid the possibility that such a portrayal of The Good coupled with resignation and tranquillity is indicative of a coming to terms with the deepest disappointment and loss that life can offer. The dignity and completeness of the acceptance would seem to rule out an extra-philosophical goal (for the kind of goal that was extra-philosophical for Descartes fell within the philosophical sphere for Spinoza as part of the ultimate goal).

If we raise the question of the synthetic a priori basis of Spinoza's philosophy, it is evident that, as with Descartes, the method consisted of an a priori principle that sufficed to prove ultimate truths, and the content consisted penultimately of the interrelatedness of all things, in particular of mind and matter, an interrelatedness that constituted God, and ultimately of the consequence that man could attain unto a knowledge of God.

This construction depicts Spinoza's philosophy as a way of life : it would seem to stem from the extra-philosophical goal of communication i.e. communion between spirits.

3 OF LEIBNIZ

For Leibniz the foundation stone is the monad. It has the following properties: (i) It has no separable parts, as matter has; it is "organic". (ii) Its existence is not caused by anything nor can it disappear by decay. (iii) But it can begin and end by creation and annihilation. (iv) It cannot be acted upon by anything outside itself—it has no windows, by which anything could come in or go out. (v) Monads are distinguishable if their properties are distinguishable. (vi) The monad undergoes continuous change. (vii) This is due to "appetition" or unconscious striving. (viii) Some monads, namely souls, have the capacity for introspection.

God is the Senior Monad, whose existence is established by rational means alone, without the use of any empirical element. In spite of the self-dependence of monads, they are maintained by "continual fulgurations of the Divinity from moment to moment" (*Monadology*, 1714, 47). Of all the possible combinations of monads which might form universes, some only are "compossible", so that there is no inherent contradiction or incompatibility between the monads. Of the compossible universes God chooses the best, and upon this he bestows existence.

Seeing that monads are isolated from one another, they can enter into a system only by having relations with all others. They do this by reflecting everything that occurs in every other; each is a living mirror of the universe;

every body is sensitive to everything which is happening in the universe, so much so that one who saw everything could read in each body what is happening or what will happen, by observing in the present the things that are distant in time as well as in space. (*Monadology*, 61).

Thus there is a parallelism between what takes place in one part of the universe and another. But, since a monad may not introspect every internal occurrence, there must be "minute perceptions", i.e. unconscious occurrences.

How is the parallelism or co-ordination between monads accounted for? This comes about because God laid down a *pre-established harmony* (actually there are three forms of pre-established harmony in Leibniz: between monads, as here, between mechanism and telcology, and between the physical order and the moral order). This harmonizes the relation between body and soul:

Under this system, bodies act as though, *per impossibile*, there were no souls; and souls act as if there were no bodies, and both act as if each influenced the other. (*Monadology*, 81).

This is illustrated by the famous simile of two clocks that keep in perfect time with each other, though there is no connecting mechanism, because God has set them and adjusted them to keep together. It may be noticed that there is no difference between choosing a compossible world and imposing a pre-established harmony upon a possible world—these are just different ways of saying the same thing.

The universe contains no dead matter; everything is a monad of one sort or another; there is a continuous chain of living things—plants, animals, entelechies, souls, God. In keeping with the absence of birth, organic bodies are always produced from seeds, which existed in a state of *preformation* (there was such a state of both the body and the soul before conception); similarly there is no immortality in a personal sense.

Because souls mirror God, human beings enter into a society of citizens in the City of God. Relative to what is below the soul, minds or rational souls are little gods, made in the image of God, and having in them some glimmering of light (*New System*, 1695; Morris, 1934, 100). And the knowledge of God is a beatific vision (*On the Ultimate Origin of Things*, 1967; Morris, 1934, 40). While it is true that there appear to be evils, we may be assured that they contribute to the greater good of those who suffer them. Thus everything in the universe is a necessary good, or, as Bradley put it everything in it is a necessary evil.

Leibniz would have subscribed to almost all of the fourteen subsidiary questions listed for Descartes. The sole exception would be the attempt to describe the world mathematically. Strangely enough, for one of the greatest of matematicians, Leibniz does not seem, at least in the works known to us, to have been interested in this project. Two others should be added: the question of relational space, and the infinitude of the world. On the other hand, like Spinoza, one of the questions, namely that of evil, should be taken out of this list and imported into that of central goals. This list is slightly different from that of Descartes and of Spinoza.

SUBORDINATE GOALS

Truth and innate ideas in the
form of an a priori principle
A principle of continuity
God

Leibniz transformed the idea of innate ideas, making the conception much more articulate than it had been either with Descartes or Spinoza. As a result of his work in formal logic, he developed explicitly the notions of an analytic proposition and of a self-contradiction and, moreover, he used these explicitly in his philosophical argumentation. But in addition he virtually transformed Aristotelian logic into a metaphysic, which he did by incorporating into it his famous principle of sufficient reason. Now it is fairly obvious that this principle is synthetic a priori, but discriminations between different kinds of a priori propositions had not yet been made. So, it is scarcely possible to pin Leibniz down on whether the principle of sufficient reason was analytic or synthetic. He certainly would have regarded it as a priori and would probably have sensed some difference of kind between it and analytic propositions and the principle of self-contradiction, or in his terms, the principles of identity and contradiction. But if it was a priori, that would be enough for his purposes. He would probably not have realized that one kind of a priori proposition is not capable of being proved with the ease of another, namely, that there is no agreed way of proving a synthetic a priori, as contrasted with an analytic a priori proposition. It would seem, therefore, that Leibniz's position was that the principle of sufficient reason was guaranteed a priori and therefore could be part of logic. With such a logic, he was, of course, in a powerful position because, with the synthetic element built in, he would be in a position to arrive at metaphysical results.

The principle of continuity, while not out of keeping with the philosophies of Descartes and Spinoza, was certainly implicit there. Leibniz made it explicit and put it to very considerable use. In fact, he made three large-scale applications of the principle. He applied it to the external world to the effect that there is everywhere continuity between part and part. He applied it to the mind-body problem to the effect that there is no gulf between mind and body, and he applied it to perception to obviate a dualism between objects of the external world and our perception of them. The principle of continuity was mainly a working principle, very basic, though not an end in itself. It served the purpose of the theory of monads with which Leibniz constructed his picture of the world.

The existence of God plays a role in Leibniz, somewhat analogous to the role it played in Descartes. That is to say, important as the question was in its own right, its function in the philosophy was to preserve the continuity prevailing everywhere in the world or underpin what Leibniz regarded as various pre-established harmonies. The existence of God had one further and most important function, namely to ensure that the universe was put together in a "compossible" way (that is to say, that all the pieces fitted together in a consistent way) which was also the best possible. To this we shall return. As with Descartes, the conception of God played no further role in the philosophy of Leibniz of the kind that made God central for Spinoza. Thus, important as the question was in its own right, it did not reappear as a penultimate or ultimate goal save insofar as God was part of the ultimate system. To these we now turn.

PENULTIMATE AND ULTIMATE GOALS

Scepticism versus certain knowledge
Rationality
The mind-body problem
The problem of mind and matter
The problem of substance
The problem of perception
"The best of all possible worlds" and
the problem of evil
Immortality
A colony of souls

It seems hardly necessary to argue that the questions of scepticism and rationality are penultimate and have to do simply with furnishing a firm base with which to handle the other goals.

Likewise, it seems very evident that the four problems, that of mind-body, that of mind and matter, that of substance, and that of perception, all have to do with the continuity or inter-linkage of all things constituting the world. But while this inter-linkage was equally to be found in Spinoza, it served a different purpose in the two philosophers. With Spinoza, it was to ensure a path by which man could know God. With Leibniz, it was to ensure the mirroring relationship between all monads, which was such that every monad reflected every occurrence in every other monad in existence. Since monads were essentially souls, whether fully human souls or minute forms of them, as with all other natural objects, this result ensured that the world was a collection of inter-connected souls. And this latter conception seems to come out of Leibniz undisguised as an ultimate goal.

But the notion of the best of all possible worlds does also seem to have been an ultimate goal. If Leibniz, like Spinoza, was overwhelmed by the problem of evil, and, because of his determinism also like Spinoza, concluded that evil was a necessary evil, then he was confronted with the fundamental problem of evil, namely how to square evil as a necessary ingredient in the world under the dominion of an omnipotent and perfectly good God. And this problem Leibniz attempted to resolve by arguing that a perfectly good world would be, in effect, inconsistent with itself, and that the only compossible world was one that contained some evil. But, because God was perfectly good, out of the possible worlds that are compossible, God would naturally choose the best; hence, this would be the best of all possible worlds.

Immortality would simply have been an ingredient of these two goals.

We may now separate the penultimate and ultimate goals:

PENULTIMATE GOALS	ULTIMATE GOALS
Scepticism versus certain knowledge	"The best of all possible worlds" and the problem of evil
Rationality	Immortality
The mind-body problem	A colony of souls
The problem of mind and matter	
The problem of substance	
The problem of perception	

It seems plain, moreover, that these ultimate goals may be compounded into the synthetic a priori proposition, "this world is the best of all possible colonies of souls".

GENERAL REMARKS

In attempting to sort out the goals of a group of philosophies with a strong family resemblance to one another, it is not, of course, part of the project to criticize such philosophies logically or philosophically. One point may, however, be made. Descartes ended up his philosophy without giving an answer. He had none to offer, so he did not offer one. This is surely to be respected and put him ahead of Spinoza and Leibniz. Spinoza and Leibniz provided answers, but their arguments for attaining them, while for the most part well forged, at certain key points have more the look of forgery. But, indeed, Descartes himself indulged in a bit of this in his well-known circular argument where he established the validity of clear and distinct ideas in order to prove the existence of God, and proved the existence of God in order to justify the validity of clear and distinct ideas. This charge should be made explicit though it is not necessarily to be levelled as a moral charge. It is virtually certain, for example, that Spinoza's integrity was unquestionable, so the reasonable presumption is that he took himself in. The point, however, should be noted because it helps to underline the preposterous nature of their solutions, and it raises the interesting question of how men of such magnificent intellect could have taken themselves in at times by such bad argument.

To turn now to the theme of an extra-philosophical goal, the suggestion was made earlier that Descartes had a problem about personal communication and that the extra-philosophical goal entertained by him, whether consciously or not, was to assure himself by philosophical means of the reliability of communication between human beings. While it might be possible to peddle this thesis for Spinoza, it seems to me that although it is probably in some degree true, it is subordinate to another goal; and his chief goal on this account would seem to be communication between him and God. Still, even in this form, we can see that the need to overcome human isolation was paramount. And with Leibniz the thesis suggested for Descartes is overt, but with Spinoza and Leibniz the goal was ultimate and not extra-philosophical, as it appears to have been for Descartes.

4   OF BERKELEY

In the sense in which the occasionalists, Spinoza, and Leibniz, were Cartesians, so also was Berkeley a Cartesian. Partly because of the countries of his origin and residence, the language in which he wrote, and his close discussion of Locke, together with the detailed attention he gave to matters of perceptual experience, Berkeley has been habitually treated as a British empiricist. He has, it is true, been treated as a very odd sort of empiricist because, in fact, he has for two centuries been interpreted as a subjective idealist. Detailed research on the two texts of Berkeley by Luce and Jessop, in the period before World War II, revealed that this is not the case. Berkeley was no subjective idealist. He repudiated the conception of matter that had reigned from Aristotle through the middle ages to Locke, and this, no doubt, served to render his philosophy apparently subjectivist. But, although he gave an "immaterialist" interpretation of the physical world, he did so by making it objective and God-centred. Thus, Berkeley's philosophy was nothing if not a priori. Since Berkeley has been traditionally interpreted as a subjective idealist, or more sharply as a solipsist, this cannot be countered without reconstructing his philosophy in the light of the researches of Luce and Jessop. And since this interpretation of Berkeley's philosophy is far from widely known, I propose to recount the main steps briefly.

1) What we are aware of in sense perception basically are "sensory-ideas", such as the greenness of an apple or its sweetness and so on. The apple itself is a collection of such sensory ideas and may be thought of as a "thing-idea".

Sensory ideas, such as great and small, are relative and, therefore, exist only in the mind. This holds also even of a thing-idea, for when I refer to a table in the next room this means that *if* I were in the next room, I *should* perceive it. This interpretation of the nature of things unperceived is known as phenomenalism, a position prominent in the twentieth century but invented by Berkeley. It implies that things cannot exist outside the minds that perceive them. Their *esse* is *percipi*. Berkeley considered further that the view that natural objects can exist unperceived is a fallacy stemming from Locke's doctrine of abstract general ideas, and Berkeley added some further arguments to show that things-ideas exist only in the mind. It should be added, however, that an *esse* does not depend narrowly on being actually rendered by *esse* is *percipi posse*.

2) What he succeeded in showing in this way is that thing-ideas depend on the possibility of being perceived, but this means that perceiving is an indispensible condition for the existence of thing-ideas. There is nothing in his argument to show, nor did he wish to maintain, that perceiving was a sufficient condition. Unfortunately, for purposes of clarity, Berkeley never made plain this distinction between necessary and sufficient conditions. But grounds are to be found in Berkeley to show that perceiving is not, in fact, a sufficient condition; for where ideas of the imagination are concerned, perceiving is a sufficient condition, but where ordinary thing-ideas are concerned, they are not under the domination of the percipient's will or imagination, so that they differ in a marked way from ideas of the imagination. Hence, some further condition is required for their existence.

3) Now begins Berkeley's great attack on the conception of matter. In this, he induces a great number of cogent, precise, and accurate arguments to attack this conception. He shows that matter cannot be an additional factor requisite for the existence of thing-ideas.

4) The only possible remaining factor that might contribute to the production of thing-ideas is, therefore, spirit. Berkeley's next task, therefore, is to establish the existence of other spirits. He maintains that we have *notions* of spirits or finite persons. Unlike matter, which was inert, persons are active. He held that we have a notion of a person as co-ordinating the sensory ideas we have of the body.

If, then, other persons can be inferred or known, then thing-ideas can have a stable existence in the mind of some other created spirit. But other persons can no more create objective thing-ideas than he can; therefore, the additional cause or condition required for thing-ideas does not lie in any finite mind.

5) Hence, the only remaining possibility is that thing-ideas subsist in the mind of some eternal spirit. Berkeley, therefore, has to establish the existence of God. To this end, he produces three strange but interesting arguments. One is that God can be found pervading the harmony or coordination of the world. Another is that he can be cognizant of God in the same way as he is of other finite persons. And the third is that God is a necessary presupposition of thing-ideas.

6) For a number of reasons it seems plain that God does not perceive thing-ideas, though this has been the classical interpretation of Berkeley, leading to the view that he was an idealist. For, in order to get out of the difficulty of solipsism in which thing-ideas would depend solely upon being perceived by one person, he had, by some tour de force, to give stability and objectivity to thing-ideas by placing them in the mind of God. It therefore seemed that if finite persons were not perceiving a thing-idea, the thing-idea would be a perception in the mind of God. But in fact, the correct interpretation of Berkeley would seem to be that God *causes* thing-ideas. This is a vital feature of the reconstruction of his thought.

7) We are now in a position to link the basic conceptions of his work. We saw that a perception was not a sufficient condition for the existence of a thing-idea. What is necessary, over and above this, is that the thing-idea should be caused by God. But if it is caused by God, the question must arise how it can then be dependent on the perception of a finite person. The answer is that these two propositions can be very simply combined by the theory that what is caused by God is not an abstract perception-in-itself, so to speak, but the perception that exists in the finite mind. Otherwise expressed, God might be said to imprint perceptions upon the finite mind.

8) Because of the inertness of thing-ideas, natural objects cannot be causes. Moreover, they are the opposite of this, they are effects caused by God and by God alone. Otherwise expressed, we are not to expect to find in the world dynamic material causes producing effects, but to find only two events related by regular recurrence, maintained in their regularity by God. Thus, the causal efficacy is taken out of the realm of thing-ideas and located in God. Otherwise expressed, thing-ideas are not causes but are signs of causes, and the thing signified is the cause, which lies in God.

This enables Berkeley to interpret the world, and the regularities constituting its laws of nature, as a *language* by which mankind can read the underlying processes of the author of nature. Thus, Berkeley regards the percepts of nature as constituting a divine language by which we can read of the ways of God. This position, which has long been called immaterialism, can be more explicitly described as theocentric phenomenalism. According to this, a thing-idea is a possibility of perception and the possibility is actualized in the minds of finite persons by being caused by God.

10) The subsidiary problem arises about two people seeing the same thing. What does this mean in Berkeley's philosophy? A possible answer could be constructed on the lines of supposing that God imprints upon different people the perception of a series of perceptual ideas conveying to a common source.

It is plain that on this interpretation of Berkeley's philosophy what he is portraying is no mere chimera. It is even possible to give an account of the existence of the world before human beings arose. This would be done in terms of the thing-ideas that would have been imprinted upon a human being by God if the human being had been around.

Whereas it is usual to think of Berkeley as a very subtle philosopher, arguing with incredible skill for something that could not possibly be true, to do with the mind-dependence of objects in the natural world, we can see, on the contrary, that his philosophy contains this as a highly important ingredient, that is to say, as a subsidiary goal. Moreover, the denial of matter loomed very large and constituted a penultimate goal, but the ultimate goal was to underpin the God of the Anglican church. Although in this regard his philosophy is thin, we may attempt a synthetic a priori representation of it in the form: "Perceptual objects, both in themselves and in orderly relation to one another, according to the laws of nature, constitute a language of nature in which we can read of the laws of nature instituted by God."

This resembles a synthetic a priori proposition as it might be found in other philosophers, though the resemblance is only superficial. It can hardly be credited with this status because it is, after all, only a metaphor.

Reverting to the place we have suggested for Berkeley in the history of philosophy, we may note not only the great extent of the parallels between him and Malebranche as brought to light by Luce, culminating in the Malebranchean conception that we see all things in God (though Berkeley would have put a slightly different construction on this from Malebranche), or in the Pauline notion, which Berkeley himself preferred, of interpreting God as "him in whom we live and move and

have our being". However, in addition to the linkage with the occasiona
ists,the re is the even less known linkage with Leibniz: for what is
effect the basis of Berkeley's philosophy is a world consisting of Go
and the collection of all finite spirits; and this is equivalent to a lar
slice of the world of Leibnizian monads, i.e. those monads that a
complex enough to constitute human souls and the supreme mona
which is God.

5 OF KANT

Kant starts off his three great *Critiques* with a great problem explicit
stated : How is knowledge, typified by Newtonian science, possible? H
problem arose because he had assumed that analytic principles we
sufficient to provide the basis of knowledge until he was confronted wit
the devastating sceptical attack by Hume. Kant's solution lay in co
structing a new conception of knowledge altogether, at least so far
explicit formulation went, rooted in the notion of a synthetic a prio
proposition. This invention enabled him to have a priori certaint
coupled with a content that otherwise might be supposed to come fro
experience alone and thus be undemonstrable. The conclusion he reache
by this method was that the human understanding consisted of univers
and necessary frameworks or moulds with which it inexorably interprete
all experience. Experience had to conform to these universal and nece
sary moulds of the human understanding because experience was co
structed by these moulds so as to conform. Kant's solution solved h
problem : How is knowledge possible?

But there was a sting in the tail. The solution provided certainty
knowledge within the realms of perceptual experience (and, of cours
mathematics and logic) but not outside. By the very nature of th
solution, the raw material of the world, or the raw material that woul
enter into experience as structured by the mind, could not itself b
structured by the mind and therefore could not be understood by th
mind or known in any way at all. Kant's brilliant solution ipso fact
barred part of the universe from human enquiry. About that realm ov
knowledge is and must be entirely silent.

Such a limitation on the extent of human knowledge would not hav
mattered had it not been that Kant was concerned with fundament
issues that could not be resolved within his new conception of th
structure of knowledge. Notably, the problems of God, freedom, an
immortality could not be handled by the moulds of the human unde
standing, nor could such conceptions as the good or judgments of tast
or beauty.

Kant attempted to get around this difficulty by approaching these problems differently. Since they could not be handled by means of the moulds of human understanding, he had to introduce a different sort of framework in accordance with which he treated conceptions such as God as "ideals of reason", with the status of postulates. Within this framework, Kant developed a system of ethics in which human beings are to be treated as ends always and never used as a means only, and a theory of taste, beauty, and teleology in which man is portrayed in his transcendental aspect as an end in himself.

I do not propose to enter into a matter that has long been the subject of controversy among historical scholars, whether Kant was fundamentally concerned with the problem of knowledge, and then applied it to see what could be done about the other problems which, important as they were, would have to take what was coming to them, for better or for worse; or whether he was concerned with the problem of knowledge in a subordinate way only to make sure of being able to handle these further and quite vital problems. It will suffice for my purpose to point out that after achieving his brilliant solution on the problem of knowledge, Kant allowed himself to be ensnared, as other great philosophers before him had been, by procedures whose validity could not stand the full light of day. The fact that he did this is evidence that, even if the goals to do with man were not the ultimate ones towards which his examination of knowledge was directed, yet they were of overriding importance to him. Why stoop to a slippery argument over something that does not matter? Add to this that Kant avowedly sought to understand man's place in the universe, and that he arrived at an image of man, qua man, consisting of Understanding, Reason, Will, and Judgment (all of them transcendental).

It seems reasonably sure, therefore, that his notion of the kingdom of ends and the dignity of man was an ultimate goal of his philosophy.

And in this respect he would seem to have been striving for a community of persons and communication between them, along with his predecessors considered above.

FOOTNOTES

[1] The last seven in the right-hand column are also in Spinoza; the first seven on the left are not.

[2] This conclusion does not conflict with the masterly historical scholarship in Popkin's work on scepticism, insofar as scepticism played a very great role. One may raise the question of what the sceptics were fundamentally sceptical about—was it personal communication?

CHAPTER XVI

Of the Pessimists:
Hume, Schopenhauer, and Bradley

1 OF HUME

HUME WAS concerned, as was Berkeley, to build up our knowledg
of the external world upon sensory ideas, as I have called them in co
nection with Berkeley, or impressions, as Hume called them. He us
many of the same arguments as Berkeley and, indeed, acknowledg
using some of Berkeley's. But he applied them in such a way as to rea
a conclusion that was the exact opposite of Berkeley's, by, in fa
turning Berkeley's arguments against one, or perhaps, two, of the latte
fundamental assumptions. That is to say, Hume used Berkeleian arg
ments to show not only that matter does not exist, but that minds do n
exist either, at least in anything like the ordinary sense. More specificall
Berkeley's notion of a person, by which one could be aware of the e
istence of another person through the order and arrangement of t
sensory-ideas of his body, was for Hume just as nonsensical as the co
ception of matter.

In Berkeley, sensory ideas were seen to go together to form a thin
idea such as an apple. The principle involved was hardly articulate
but Hume made it explicit and he enunciated three principles by whi
the relationship between ideas could be built up, namely by resemblanc
contiguity, and causation.

Given complexes of ideas built up in this way to form the subje
matter of our immediate experience, Hume then faces his initial proble
which is:

To enquire what is the nature of that evidence which assures us of any real existen
and matter of fact beyond the present testimony of our senses or the records of o
memory.

Hume continues by claiming that the only way of gaining knowledg
beyond the immediate present is by the relation of causation. Thus,
I wish to know how experience can teach us that a phenomenon whi

has occurred in the past will be repeated in the future, as for example with the famous question: "How do we know that the sun will rise tomorrow?", Hume answers that we operate on the principle that where we have similar natural objects we expect similar effects to follow from them. In short, we have experienced a constant conjunction of events in the past and we adopt the principle:

That instances of which we have no experience must resemble those of which we have had experience.

Hume contends boldly that this principle is a passage from the past to the future which cannot be justified. He holds, moreover, that the linkage is effected by custom or habit. It is interesting to note that, like Berkeley, he distinguishes between experiences that are imagined and those that are, so to speak, real, and distinguishes them in the same way, but this leads him to postulate a pre-established harmony between the actual course of nature and the succession of our ideas. At this stage, then, the world consists of a course of nature, which we wot of, that produces impressions upon us corresponding to it.

Now since the structure of knowledge so far is based upon the notion of necessary connection, Hume has to investigate this. He develops the theme by making one of the most famous innovations in his philosophy: he denies that there is any necessity by which a particular cause has a particular effect; for him this knowledge could be provided only by experience. But, he points out, no amount of repetition of constant conjunction of impressions could lead to the idea of a necessary connection.

The connection, therefore, he concludes, is effected by a principle that unites the cause and effect in the imagination and this principle is one of custom or habit, mainly the habit of expecting the same conjunctions to occur in the future as we have experienced in the past.

That is Hume's theory on the nature of the causal relation.

In the course of developing this, he has denied that experience can produce the idea of necessary connection, but he has, nonetheless, to account for the fact that this idea does somehow arise. No impression can produce it, constant conjunction is not sufficient, so he locates the idea in the observation of resemblance or constant conjunction, which is an operation of the mind. In other words, observed resemblance induces the mind to pass from one object to its usual accompaniment. Thus, observation of constant conjunction is what gives the mind a habit, but so far as our knowledge of the processes of nature is concerned, "anything may produce anything".

Given Hume's account of the origin of impressions, the build-up of

complex ideas, the contention that knowledge beyond what we c
obtain in present experience rests upon the principle of causation; a
given that causation cannot contain the idea of necessary connection, b
that causation must consist only of constant conjunction, the observati
of which forms a custom or habit of expecting the future to conform
the past—given these sparse preliminaries, Hume is concerned with t
question of how to construct the external world. In other words, h
far do the principles just developed suffice to justify our belief in t
continued existence of natural objects. Justification cannot be provid
by reason, nor by the senses which cannot reach beyond present
perience. Thus, if I glance at a picture, turn away my head, and th
look at it again, the connection between the two experiences, whi
leads me to speak of them as being of one picture, such a persiste
identity can be regarded only as the effect of repeated experiences. He
again, if we are attempting to extrapolate the notion of custom or hab
then it would be invalid to extend the notion of custom or habit
identify experiences that can never be either experienced together
experienced as one and the same. Hume is therefore confront
with the problem of identity, that is to say, of the persistence of a natu
object through time. Such identity cannot be located in objects in natu
behind our perceptions which they resemble, because, as Berkel
pointed out, there can be no possible test for this—ipso facto what
beyond experience cannot be compared with what is within experien
So here "experience is, and must be, entirely silent".

Hume has now reached the first of his sceptical conclusions, main
that there is no way of justifying the belief in the external world
no way of justifying the notion of identity as applied to natural objec

Hume now turns to the human mind, and subjects it to the sar
treatment that he has just meted out to natural objects. Hume consid
that there is no idea of the self, that no impression yields an idea of t
self, and therefore that no experience can yield the knowledge of t
mind any more than of natural objects behind impressions. This is tant
mout to saying that there is no mind in the ordinary sense. There
however, some notion, a very thin one, of what takes its place.

The mind is a kind of theatre where several perceptions successively make th
appearance; pass, repass, glide away, and mingle in an infinite variety of postures a
situations.

In other words, for Hume the mind is a congeries of impressions
perceptions.

This is the second great sceptical conclusion that Hume reaches.

It will hardly be surprising to find that there are other sceptical conclusions, that is to say, that no room is left for the existence of God or immortality of the soul. Freedom of the will, in any ordinary sense, also goes, because Hume was a determinist (though he had to maintain a form of determinism which excluded the notion of necessary connection). In fact, Hume takes freedom of the will to be acting in accordance with determinism, essentially Spinoza's view.

Can we now assess Hume's position? The application of his principle of empiricism leads him to formulate knowledge in terms of a principle of causation, and then, as Moore has pointed out most clearly, he dissected the notion of causation in such a way as to destroy the possibility of knowledge of processes in the natural world which could give coherence to our impressions and experience. Thus, Hume's principle of empiricism leads him inexorably towards total scepticism.

It is noteworthy that Hume ended up, in effect, as a subjective idealist which is the position that Berkeley ought to have reached if he had been more consistent, and which has been traditionally, though wrongly, ascribed to Berkeley.

Let us now try to sift out Hume's main questions.

The origin of our ideas or experience Hume attributed to impressions. Here he was giving vent to a basic empiricist principle that all knowledge must be rooted in experience, but this was a subsidiary issue. What it was subsidiary to was the question of causation, but for him even the principle of causation, while more important, comes in the category of a subordinate issue. And what it was subordinate to was the question of knowledge. Penultimate questions were concerned with the impossibility of knowledge of processes in the natural world or of the human mind. Hume's ultimate goal would seem to have been plainly scepticism about the existence of God or atheism.

In view of this conclusion and of the fact that Hume was a dedicated atheist, it is especially interesting to note the depressing effect that Hume found philosophy to have upon him. His way of shaking off his melancholy was by dining, playing a game of backgammon, conversing, and making merry with his friends.

It is well known that in the present century, which after all has reiterated Hume in a new form, the empirical approach to knowledge apparently makes it impossible to evade solipsism.

Could it be clearer that Hume was mesmerized by a philosophical principle of empiricism, which confirmed his deep sense of depression, his feeling completely alone in the world?

2 OF SCHOPENHAUER

I deliberately refrain from offering even a tentative account of Schopenhauer's aims until I have described his philosophy.

Die Welt als Wille und Vorstellung (1819) runs to fifteen hundred pages in the English translation; the material could probably be completely expressed in fifty pages; now the merest outline of his metaphysic and practical philosophy must suffice.

Schopenhauer's logical weapon is his Principle of Sufficient Reason, which has four derivative forms; its general purport is that there is a reason why a thing should be as it is rather than otherwise.

His metaphysic divides into four parts. First the world is considered as *percept,* exactly as with Berkeley: natural objects exist only when someone perceives them. Following Kant, he gives perception an a priori framework of space, time and causation. (I am using "percept" instead of the more customary word "idea" to translate "Vorstellung".) Like Berkeley, he cannot remain in this position, for, underyling fleeting percepts, there is something permanent or persisting to be taken account of. This he describes by means of Kant's *thing-in-itself,* though, unlike Kant, he holds that the thing-in-itself is knowable. This brings us to the second part, where the world is considered as *will.* A man knows his body as percept but his inner nature he knows as will. The percept is a manifestation of the will; a movement of the body is an act of will objectified, i.e. passed into perception; and this applies to all actions, voluntary or involuntary. Motives determine only the form an act of will may take; the will itself is beyond motivation, and it is therefore simply a blind striving. The manifestations of will must obey the natural laws of phenomena, as with Kant, but the will itself, again as with Kant, is independent of all restriction. In the third part of his metaphysic, this conception of will is extended to all parts of nature, on the basis of analogy. It is clearly at work with animals and the point is easily argued for plants; but he extends it to the inanimate because of intermediate phenomena, such as the behaviour of the magnet and the crystal. The argument is not clear; one is supposed to apprehend the result intuitively; then, one will understand the force through which crystals are formed, bodies gravitate, life lives, and the magnet attracts. Schopenhauer calls this general élan vital by the name "will" after its most important species; but, because it is far removed from what can be known to a man's inner consciousness, the designation *mechanical conatus* will be more appropriate. Thus far, then, the world is entirely percept, will, and mechanical conatus—the phenomenal world is the mirror of the will; and, because the will underlies phenomena and because it is knowable, it is identified with the thing-in-itself. The fourth part treats of the world as *archetype* (a more suitable translation of "Idee" than the word "Idea" spelt with a capital). There are various grades of objectification of the will, the lowest, for example, being the universal forces of nature, such as gravitation, while the highest include man. Corresponding to every objectification is a universal archetype, which is an Idea in Plato's sense; the archetypes multiply themselves throughout nature. Archetypes may conflict with one another : thus the pattern of behaviour of the magnet conflicts with and seeks to dominate that of gravitation. From the strife of the lower arise the higher—no victory without conflict; the more completely the lower form is overcome, the more the higher archetype is expressed. Now in the order of objectifications of the will—gravitation, man, and so on—the most adequate objectivity is the archetype. Since the archetype is the most complete objectification of the will, Schopenhauer regards the archetype and the will as complementary—they are not, of course, the same. The important question now arises how archetypes are known, for they lie outside the knowledge of particular things. The general way of attaining to knowledge of them is by self-transcendence, relinquishing one's knowledge of things through the senses, so that one can no longer distinguish between perceiver and perception : then arises a pure, will-less, timeless subject of knowledge; in this condition archetypes can be known. The media by which self-transcendence may be attained are philosophy and art, the adequate pursuit of both of which require genius; hence to reach the archetypes one has to be a genius.

This concludes Schopenhauer's *metaphysic* according to his conception : *The World as Percept, Will, Mechanical Conatus, and Archetype.* As a metaphysic it is not of the first rank. Its interests, however, lies in the practical philosophy and other ideas he based upon it. To these we now turn.

Schopenhauer's practical philosophy places an enormous stress on pessimism, the will to live, and the denial of the will to live. His pessimism is unlimited. Optimism he regarded as "a really *wicked* way of thinking, as a bitter mockery of the unspeakable suffering of humanity" (I, § 59, 420). In opposition to Leibniz, he held that this was the worst of all possible worlds. He gives a most graphic account of human striving, suffering, insatiable desire; every satisfied desire only gives rise to a new one (III, 383–5).

Whence did Dante take the materials for his hell but from this our actual world? And yet he made a very proper hell out of it. And when, on the other hand, he came to the task of describing heaven and its delights, he had an insurmountable difficulty before him, for our world affords no materials at all for this. (I § 69, 419).

None the less he finds ways of mastering such a lot : by repudiation the will and through the power of art and philosophy. These are co nected, for the pursuit of art and philosophy is simply a means of silen ing the will. This takes on additional significance from his belief th love and sexual pleasure were founded on a delusion :

> nature can only attain its ends by implanting a certain illusion in the individual on account of which that which is only a good for the species appears to him as good for himself.

Thus nature impels man towards propagation, but having attained its er it is indifferent to him and cares only for the preservation of the speci (I, § 60, 425). Chastity, therefore, provides another way of silencing tl will. The trouble is due, of course, to the inordinate assertion of the w to live; the will wills life and "the will" means "the will to live Schopenhauer believes in no ordinary kind of immortality. Individua may come and individuals may go, but the will persists and it alon His view may perhaps be described as *transmigration* of will. In co sequence we need have no fear for our existence, even in death, and li cannot be ended even by suicide (I, § 54, 354, 358–62); the will persist like gravity when a pendulum comes to rest (III, 259). In particul; the sexual passion leads beyond one's own existence and continues li indefinitely : parent and child are different as phenomena but identic as will and as archetype; generation is only the expression, the sympton of the begetter's assertion of the will to live; with this assertion, sufferin and death have been asserted anew (I, § 60, 423–4). How, then, is tl will to live to be denied? This is achieved by a strategy of indirect a proach, which depends upon the power of the intellect, for, apparentl upon gaining full self-knowledge, volition ends, i.e. upon gaining fu knowledge of the human archetype, one finds in it a quieter of the w (I, § 54, 367). The goal may be achieved also by voluntary renunciatic of the sexual impulse (I, § 62, 430).

Schopenhauer lays a good deal of stress on the unity of will throug out all mankind : the will of the agent and the sufferer is one and tl same; because of this identity, love and friendship for others help n only them but oneself, just as this identity is a reason for not takii revenge upon others (I, § 63–7 passim). This notion is strikingly simil to some Indian thought, in which Schopenhauer steeped himself : th it is said that a Hindu holy man, when bayoneted by a soldier, remark calmly, "And thou also art He" (Bouquet, 1941). It was a truth to l seen through the veil of Maya. He who has this insight must take (himself the suffering of the whole world. This is the reverse of the asse tion of life, from which the will now turns away. All this is closely bou up with the denial of sexuality, for, Schopenhauer remarks, the first step towards renunciation of the world is voluntary and complete chastity (I, § 68, 489–94). Regarding the idea that in hurting others, one hurts the will in oneself, it is interesting to find that he disapproved of vivisection (I, § 66, 481 n.).

It is noteworthy that suicide, so far from being a denial of the will to live, is a strong assertion of that will; for suicide is due to dissatisfaction, which implies desire, and it occurs because a man cannot endure the breaking of his will (I, § 69, 514–17).

Looking back over Schopenhauer's philosophy, we first have four conceptions: The mind-dependence of percepts; the thing-in-itself which gives identity and persistence to them, which is interpreted by Schopenhauer as the *will*; the extrapolation of this notion as a mechanical urge operating through all nature (thus, the will in a magnet is what attracts); and archetypes, which are the will in objectified form. It scarcely needs to be argued that everything is subsidiary to the question of the will as at least a penultimate goal, and we might reasonably take the ultimate goal to be a problem of obtaining knowledge of the archetype.

However, Schopenhauer's practical philosophy places an interesting slant on this. He graphically brings out the appalling nature of our lives under the domination of the will, and is confronted with the task of coming to terms with it and, if possible, silencing the will by a wholesale policy of renunciation, renouncing the will, the sexual impulse, and life itself. In short, the goal here is nirvana.

In the case of other philosophers, such a conclusion would have naturally been categorized as an extra-philosophical goal, but Schopenhauer is completely overt about it, explicitly makes it the be-all and end-all of his philosophy, and plainly conceives of philosophy as including what would otherwise be classified as extra-philosophical. Thus, for Schopenhauer, the goal of nirvana must be regarded as the ultimate goal.

Nonetheless, one is prompted to raise the question if there is, after all, another goal which is extra-philosophical. Was there something else sought after in depicting a philosophy with such an end, publishing it in order to reveal it to others and possibly persuade them of its validity?

The suspicion that Schopenhauer, too, was concerned with a problem of communication with others receives some light support from the way he develops his pessimism. First, there is the abnegation of will, which he closely connects with the abnegation of sex, almost certainly turns on his attitude to women. It was said two thousand years ago (by a Roman who was happily married even) that men could neither live with women nor do without them, which has been said many times since and doubtless was also said for centuries or millennia before him. Now,

Schopenhauer epitomizes this outlook, perhaps as strongly as can be found anywhere in literature. Thus there is an indication that his pessimism meant that he completely despaired of being able to form a relationship with a woman as a person.

3   OF BRADLEY

With Bradley, likewise, I shall not attempt to give an account of his goals until I have given some description of his philosophy. He is usually placed in the tradition of absolute idealism and thought of as a Hegelian. This must be taken with very strong reserve, but there is something in common between Bradley and Hegel. For Hegel, the ultimate was a pan-dialectical network called the Absolute, and the dialectical relationship was such that the Absolute both preserved and resolved all differences. Such was the nature of the universe.

With Bradley also, the Absolute was the ultimate, and the theme of his famous work, *Appearance and Reality,* is that all contradictions disappear in the Absolute. One may stretch out this one sentence to six hundred pages but not much more is added beyond a variety of illustrations. Bradley develops logic in his own fashion to provide a fundamental type of argument to this end. It centres on the doctrine known as internal relations, which means that a relation is part of the nature of the terms it relates, and also that the terms so related are in part determined by the relations that relate them. Thus, the earth would be inherently different if it had no moon. The kind of argument he uses to achieve this end runs somewhat like this: If a relation is external to the terms it relates, then there must be some further relation to relate that relation to the terms. Each new relation of this sort would require a further new relation to relate it to the terms, and so on indefinitely. Hence, the distinction between terms and external relations is impossible; that is to say, all relations are internal and this successfully obliterates the separateness of terms and relations. The distinction we make between terms and relations is, therefore, one of *mere appearance,* and it embodies a contradiction, but this contradiction disappears when we see terms and relations in the Whole. Extrapolating this notion, we see that everything has to be connected in the same way with everything else, and all contradictory mere appearances are seen to vanish in the Whole, which is the Absolute.

Bradley goes on to conduct the same sort of argument in innumerable contexts, for example, with the concepts of space, and time, and thought, truth, etc. The outcome is a conception of the Absolute that is an all-inclusive harmony, which, perhaps surprisingly, also includes sentient experience. We do have knowledge of the structure, that is, in the very thin sense that contradictions and appearances vanish within it. We have no knowledge of its content. Although Bradley is very dogmatic in his mode of procedure, he is modest about his end for he admits to a kind of scepticism in the sense that he admits that we end up in ignorance of the Absolute due to human limitation. His confidence is restricted to the belief that there *is* an Absolute because there *must* be one.

Bradley wrote sublimely and his work has enormous historical importance, for though it is in itself thin in comparison with the much richer Hegelian philosophy that preceded it, his philosophy was the immediate target of the realistic movement begun by Russell and Moore at the beginning of the twentieth century, which arose through opposition. But it is regrettable that his relationship to his predecessors should be widely misconstrued.

Conceived as an absolute idealist, he belongs with Hegel insofar as the Absolute was an ontological conception. But Bradley, unlike Hegel, conducted some of his central arguments in epistemological rather than ontological terms, which makes him rather like a subjective idealist, and he in part accepts the doctrine of *esse* is *percipi,* which lays him open to the traditional, if incorrect, interpretation of Berkeley.

Turning to his relationship to Hegelian philosophy : just as in Greek days Socrates was followed by the semi-Socratics, it would be reasonable to say that Hegel was followed by the semi-Hegelians, and Bradley was one kind of semi-Hegelian. That is to say, in a nutshell, he emphasized one aspect of Hegel to the detriment of another. Thus, Hegel's conceptualization becomes more and more concrete as he approaches the notion of truth, whereas Bradley's becomes more and more abstract. Hegel believed that the notion of contradiction was to be used for positive purposes. Whatever value-judgment we may choose to put upon this now, the point being made here is a purely historical one, that Bradley looked upon the matter differently. He viewed contradiction as something to be discarded. He had no use for the identity of opposites in Hegel's sense; for Bradley did, like Hegel, equate opposites, but he did not, as Hegel did, preserve the difference between the opposites thus merged. However difficult it may be to understand this, the two philosophers meant entirely different things. As a result, the Absolute, when attained, according to Bradley, was free of contradiction and characterized by some principle of self-consistency. For Hegel, the self-contradictions would be preserved but for Bradley they would be mere appearances arising from seeing the Absolute not as a whole but as a part. Self-contradictions in the Absolute would be apparent only, not

F

real. While Hegel made a bold bid to characterize the Absolute, Bradley'
defeat by this project amounted to an ad hoc claim that the Absolut
simply must exist to avoid self-contradiction.

If any comparison of this sort is valid, it would be more reasonabl
to liken Bradley's Absolute not to Hegel's but to Schelling's. It is, per
haps, curious that Bradley nowhere explained where he differed from
Hegel or followed him or where he thought that Hegel was wrong
Further, it is worth pointing out that there is a closer link betweer
Bradley and Kant than there is with Hegel, insofar as Bradley's entir
philosophy can be said to be a multiplication of antinomies; that is t
say, self-contradictions are paradoxes which he could not resolve, fo
which he postulated a unifying principle that somehow would resolv
them. This is extraordinarily like the positivism left by Kant in that h
sets forth a small number of antinomies, and explicitly contends tha
they cannot be resolved by the human understanding.

If we try to look at Bradley's goal in perspective, it seems plain tha
his quasi-dialectical procedure was subsidiary, that questions of trutl
were penultimate, and that the all-embracing harmonious Absolute wa
the ultimate goal.

It is hard to doubt Bradley's pessimism. The Absolute was unttainabl
(even though he held it must be in principle attainable). A note of caln
resignation seems to me to pervade his writing. But there is, in addition
an interesting clue.

Bradley discusses the problem of evil. The result is predictable. Evi
is evil only when seen as a partial view of the universe. Seen as fittin
into the Whole, it loses its character of being evil. This is not the sam
sort of view as Leibniz's for whom evil was a necessary evil, for it
absence would not be compossible with the rest of existence. Bradley':
view is virtually identical with Spinoza's, for whom evil does not hav
the character of being evil when seen to be a necessary determinatio
of God.

If we take Bradley's excursion into the problem of evil as reall
significant, the possibility opens out that what deeply concerned hin
was the evil of the world and that he was overwhelmed by it; and that
if this is so, the only way he could cope with it was by a tour de force
constructing a conception of the world in which evil vanished.

Thus one extra-philosophical goal for Bradley would have been th
liquidation of evil.

This may not be the end of the matter, however, because Bradley als
overtly discusses solipsism and held that there is a one-sided truth about
solipsism. Now this would seem to mean that while solipsism is not true
when seen in the Whole, it is the experience with which man is con-

fronted. So we seem to find the extra-philosophical goal turning up once again concerning isolation from one's fellows. The linkage presumably is that this isolation is the product of evil.

If we look back over the philosophies of our three Pessimists, we see that they all were depressed. Hume said he was. I have gone into Schopenhauer's philosophy closely and come to the conclusion that he suffered from one of the more deeply rooted forms of depression, and I think it is fairly plain that Bradley, too, was a depressive. In all cases, it seems fairly clear that what they were depressed about was the possibility of effecting communication with their fellows.

Our group of Optimists, on the other hand, seem to be beset by exactly the same problem of communication; but they found salvation, or at least escape, in philosophical devices that worked for them sufficiently well to hold depression at bay. It is true that Schopenhauer and Bradley also produced devices for coping with their depression, but they seem to have dimly realized that these devices would not work, and, hence, were more of a prey to their depression.

The review given in the last two chapters would indicate that a great number of the most renowned philosophers, even of opposite schools, were concerned fundamentally to cope with, to avoid, or to evade, a depression manifested philosophically in the problem of solipsism, but arising psychologically from personal isolation.

In linking solipsism or scepticism with failure of communication and depression, there is no intention to suggest that the philosophers in question were overtly suffering from depression. They might have been or might not have been, or might have at one time and not at another. What is meant is that they had a depressive constellation in their character (which therefore might have become overt). That is to say, where there is scepticism in this philosophical sense, there is a lack of communication (though not necessarily conversely for it may come out in some other form). This, moreover, is not intended to mean that such philosophers were overtly shy, for example, or had no friends; what is meant refers to a much deeper level of relationship, in which it may be said even of some friends that there is little real communication between them.

CHAPTER XVII

One Dogma of Apriorism and Empiricism

MY THEME IS what I would describe as a kind of anthropology. Anthropology as a social science studies customs and institutions, and things of that sort. But I do not see why an anthropologist should not study philosophy : that is to say, philosophy in its role as a social institution. For not only does it have an individual role in a person's life but perhaps also a social role. That is the background or framework for what follows.

Let us begin with a dominant facet of twentieth-century philosophy. It concerns the old tag, "Nihil in intellectu quod non prius in sensu". It is no doubt irrelevant to existentialism, but the influential empiricism of the century from the early days of Russell and Moore to, perhaps, the later Wittgenstein and so on was all dominated by it. The adage is older than medieval days,[1] it comes (in some sense) from Aristotle. It runs through most of the middle ages and then there is a lengthy history afterwards, which I want to go through very briefly; the barest allusion will do. Locke was largely imbued with it. Berkeley used it and Hume used it. It would, of course, be oversimplifying to say these philosophers never went against it; all I want to claim is that it was a dominant tendency in their thought, even if not the only one. Thus Berkeley had a doctrine of notions and a notion was something that was not rooted in the senses. And Locke, of course, had a doctrine of substance, which does not square with the principle (his doctrine of knowledge, by reflection, however, is, I think, an application of it). So these philosophers did not hold it unadulterated, animating *every* corner of their philosophies. But they probably would have liked their philosophy to have conformed to this principle if this could have been managed. But that was unworkable. In other words, it seems to me that the principle dominated their philosophy as far as it was able to but that they had to make concessions. Hume strove to adhere to it.[2]

To revert to the stages of twentieth century empiricism, first comes logical analysis, beginning, say, with Moore's "Refutation of Idealism" in 1903 and lasting to, say, 1925 when Moore wrote "A Defence of Commonsense". That was the period in which the outstanding characteristic was the priority of the senses, e.g. in discussions of perception and so forth. The characteristic concept of the period was sense-data. And phenomenalism was the sophisticated outcome of that period. It is in Russell, it is in Moore, and it is in the entire field, it was the dominant philosophy of the time. It lasted, of course, much longer than 1925 and quite a number of philosophers did not give it up till 1940 or so. That was the period when this sort of outlook was first created or flourished, when it was defended, and when it had its autumn (or, should I say, fall). The point that I am concerned with is that the period was very much empirical in the sense of reducing everything to the senses.

The second period centred on logical positivism, which ran from the early 20's to the second world war. And this was characterized by one central doctrine, though there were one or two other concepts that were closely connected with it. The central doctrine was the verifiability principle of meaning. The early formulations or the late ones, the sophisticated or simplified, all hold that the meaning of the statement has to do with the observations that bear on its truth or falsity. Thus there would be nothing in the intellect that would not be capable of being checked up on in his way. This sophisticated twentieth-century approach seems to me to be in this respect no different from the classical one.[3] It is true that the original form of the dictum referred to the impossibility of ideas arising in the mind without psychologically and indeed logically originating in the senses, while the positivistic form of it is that the former can have no meaning unless they are describable in terms of the latter; but this modification would seem to make no significant difference to the question at issue.

Further, the unity of science was hardly different from the language of physicalism.

There is a point here I think that is worth mentioning: that when twentieth-century philosophers were concerned to reduce everything to one language they never stopped to discuss why that language should be the physical language and not some other; it was just taken for granted that the only sensible thing to do would be to reduce things to the physicalistic language and not the other way round. Now that seems to me to be a bias of western Christendom which I find particularly fascinating (though when I say bias I do not mean that I am supporting the opposite view because I think they are both equally misguided). If there is a reason for a unity of language one ought to have an additional reason to say which way the unification should go. Again, in old-fashioned terms you have the question of whether we should talk of idealism or materialism, which, though less mentioned nowadays, is just as good a way of handling the matter—do we reduce everything idealistically

to mind stuff or materialistically to matter stuff? Why should we reduce
one thing to the other rather than the other way round? Positivists have
simply offered verifiability, which settles the direction of reduction, and
have left it at that. All philosophers of this persuasion pursue the same
path in this respect.

The third phase was linguistic philosophy, which began to flourish
after World War II (but which became attenuated in the sixties in a
noncommittal form of philosophical analysis). Linguistic philosophy was
devoted to the study of the *use* of linguistic expressions (in a philosophical way not articulated). It aims at being liberal and not proscriptive
like its positivistic parentage; but in tendency it exerts a pressure in the
same direction. So it seems reasonable to interpret linguistic philosophy
as being in line with the doctrine of the priority of the senses.

It is to my mind striking that twentieth-century philosophy is unique
in being the only period down the ages that was, broadly speaking,
governed solely by this doctrine. In the past, alongside this doctrine, we
can also find other doctrines that are also highly important, and that
sometimes had the ascendency contemporaneously. Thus the apriority of
ideas, concepts, or essences, which was widely and often held, was such
that they were not dependent on the senses. This idea is as old as philosophy and does not need remarking on. And it is also in some of the
same philosophers that I have mentioned as conforming to this doctrine.
Thus it is in Berkeley, for whom the concept of a notion of persons did
not originate in the senses. What I am trying to depict from earlier
centuries is a split between this doctrine of the "Nihil" and an apriority
doctrine about essences.

Now I am not giving any rounded account about what empiricism
consists of. You see the senses in which Russell would call himself an
empiricist, or a Wittgensteinian, or Locke, Moore, Ayer, Ryle, or Austin.
There are empiricists in different senses no doubt, but there is a family
resemblance between them all and you know more or less what is involved. Naturally, if we are going to compare empiricism with its opposite, we might have to do so with some precision, because the opposites
would be different in each case. But it is with a very broad distinction
that I am concerned. There is a very broad difference between rooting
things in the senses, either building things up from knowledge gained
from the senses or reducing things to the senses, and on the other hand
a priori notions like Plato's ideas or Kant's categories or Hegel's, and
so on, which makes a complete contrast. This apriorism dominates Plato,
Aristotle, the Cartesians, Kant, and Hegel, after which it drops out in
this century. Thus we had parallel streams, which to me raises a curious
problem: why have we got only one of the streams in this century?

What is there about western man or society that has given rise to these two streams of philosophy all down through millennia but that is missing now?

Closely connected with the doctrine of "Nihil trans sensum" (to which I shorten the aged form) are two other concepts that are relevant here. First is the conception of reductionism, which is seldom emphasized enough. The reductionist tendency that philosophers suffer from has a very respectable ancestry and has led to very remarkable and fine results. Thus it is a wide notion; "Nihil trans sensum" is a form of reductionism, not identical with it; there can be other forms of reductionism that are not the same as this; reductionism has been very widespread in various forms and at all times. But what makes it rather a dangerous kind of doctrine is its great successes. One is apt to forget that its great achievements have lain in mathematics and logic, and there the achievements have been genuine. For instance, the start-off of the trend in modern times came from Dedekind. This is a bit peripheral to the present theme; but briefly the point involved is that Dedekind reduced the irrational numbers to rational, thus solving Pythagoras' problem. He showed in what way irrationals are numbers because they could be defined completely in terms of these—by reduction. Such a procedure is common in mathematics and in logic. And there are other beautiful examples too. Whitehead reduced points to Chinese nests of boxes or concentric spheres. So far as I know this method works perfectly well. The point that I want to draw attention to here is that the reduction is animated by our adage, because Whitehead's goal was to get rid of such peculiar entities as Euclidean points and lines—contradictory entities—and replace them by perceptual objects. There is one more which perhaps may not be so familiar: Broad, in his examination of McTaggart's philosophy, treated the notion of "proposition" by such a method. This was related to the philosophy of the day, when propositions had a kind of Platonic subsistence which puzzled philosophers. Broad defined "proposition" in terms of co-referential judgments, a class of judgments that referred to the same objective (whether he quite brought it off or not is hardly the point). It was a very bold effort. The goal as before was to reduce propositions, which were limbo entities, to judgments, which are factual. The mechanism of reduction works nicely in the logical mathematical area. But when you try to go further, as in phenomenalism, you get into a morass; phenomenalism has gone out (not that this in itself disproves it); clever philosophers over many years were concerned with phenomenalism and they failed to work it out; and the situation has convinced most philosophers sufficiently that the programme could not be realized (no one has actually disproved phenomenalism but that is another matter). Thus it

would seem that when we go on from mathematics and logic to episte[m]-
ology, the reduction can no longer be carried out.[4]

Thus we have reductionism as a facet of our topic. Next I want [to]
add another "-ism" which is characteristic, and that is that the approac[h]
is *monistic*. And further, it is worth noting that almost the entire histo[ry]
of philosophy has been monistic, with only one or two exceptions, e.[g.]
Descartes and William James. This contention requires that we ta[ke]
another look at reductionism, i.e. at what happens when the reducti[on]
is in the opposite direction. Descartes seems to have had a shrewd[er]
grasp of philosophical problems than his successors, but he left an u[n-]
solved problem to do with three substances—God, matter, and min[d.]
Now substances in that period were things that were wholly independe[nt]
of each other, operating in accordance with their own principles, a[nd]
they were not reducible to anything else. Descartes' successors, t[he]
occasionalists, Spinoza, Leibniz, Wolff—all the Cartesians were co[n-]
cerned with the tremendous problem of relating substances, a task th[at]
in the terms in which the problem was presented could not be do[ne.]
However, the misguided effort to solve a problem in terms which pr[e-]
cluded its being solved is not what I am concerned with. My conce[rn]
is with the attempt to *reduce* substances. At its peak, in Spinoza or
Leibniz, the substances were supposedly reduced to one. Thus in th[e]
great rationalist period—and these were very fine intellects—the dri[ve]
was reductionistic, though it was reductionistic in the other direction [to]
the one considered above. In a recent paper by Gunderson, he was pu[t-]
ting in a plea for physicalism, trying to answer objections that have be[en]
brought against it, and put it back on the map. In this he made a ki[nd]
of confession that maybe the opposite was the same thing, i.e. that t[he]
idealistic philosophy was in effect the same as physicalism. This stran[ge]
comment carried all the aura of a real anxiety, a fear of having ma[de]
a real bungle, and a serious doubt about the matter. For if idealism [is]
essentially the same, this would undermine all that he had to say [in]
favour of physicalism, for his arguments could equally be used the oth[er]
way round. In my view, physicalism and idealism are identical in stru[c-]
ture—you put different fillings into the mould but the mould is t[he]
same. There are fundamental entities in physicalism; and there a[re]
sophisticated complexes of a larger sort which are all reducible to the[se,]
e.g. Locke's complex ideas which are reducible to simple ones, or t[he]
phenomenalist conception of a physical object. But the structure [is]
essentially monistic—basic ingredients plus non-basic ingredients th[at]
are reducible to them. The non-basic ingredients in nature may be co[m-]
plex molecules, or, in idealism they may be complex monads. In phy[si-]
calism, there are the more material ones and the less material ones, b[ut]

they are all different kinds of matter. In idealism there are the more mental ones and the less mental ones, but they are all different kinds of mind-stuff. Thus there is no difference between physicalism and idealism, except to say that ingredients are different—the structure is the same. In other words, the reductionist tendency is just the same only in the opposite direction with the rationalists or apriorists.

Thus monism is characteristic equally of this apriorist tradition as well as the empiricist.

With this canvas in front of me, I now wish to ask three questions. (1) Why the tendency towards apriorism (or might we call it "psychism")? (2) Why the tendency towards physicalism? (3) And then more generally, why monism?

These tendencies are shot through 2,500 years of philosophy. I want to put forward certain conjectures which are in the area of—perhaps we could call it—anthropological philosophy, because it is an anthropological way of looking at philosophy.

What was it that upset the Cartesians, for example? Let us grant that it was incommensurability—that is, the incommensurability of substances. Incommensurability is what I call the principle that "like could only interact with like". If you had unlikes there could be no interaction, no concourse at all, no relationships at all. This is a very old tradition which is hard to pinpoint in the literature. Certainly there were natural scientists who were imbued with it for a long time: they held there could be no interaction between magnetism and electricity, because of unlikeness. In philosophy you find it in Spinoza and in Gassendi, for example. What, then, was the fuss about? The immediate demand was for an essentialistic reduction: they wanted to be able to reduce substances (or even essences[5]) to one another. Why? The conjecture that I have put forward is that they sought one main thing: a communion of souls, including other people's souls and God. Collateral with that conjecture would be a fear of isolation; being cut off either from one another or from God would have been the ultimate disaster, implied by the incommensurability of substances in the intellectualist philosophy.

To turn to the empiricists. What upset them? This is difficult to answer, but it seems to me that the empiricists were worried by superstition. Thus Bacon reacted against the middle ages by trying to abolish superstition; that is clear. Further, one gets the impression from nearly all empiricists down the line that they were fighting against being fettered by certain kinds of moral and religious beliefs. (An exception was Berkeley, who is normally regarded as one of the great orthodox empiricists; he was of course trying to depict a God-centred universe; in any case I have reclassified him with the apriorists.) But the general tendency was the other way. So I am suggesting that the empiricists were engaged upon a search for freedom of a certain sort, because of feeling *fettered* by ideas. So much is this so that one often gets the impression that empiricists are afraid of ideas of every sort. If you let in ideas of one kind maybe there is a danger that the dark, superstitious, ideas, liquidated over the centuries at much cost and suffering, might get in at the side door. To ward off this danger may have been what made them tick, explaining what they were trying to assert and what they were trying to deny.

Now in suggesting that they sought freedom in the sense of being unfettered by ideas of a certain kind, I want to draw attention to a price they had to pay. All empiricists who are rigid enough to construct knowledge on or reduce it to immediate experience have to pay the price of solipsism. This was a bugbear to Hume, and in our own day to Russell and Ayer—the latter was still writing about it only a few years ago. Empiricism has always ended up in solipsism, and there is nothing anyone has been able to do about it. Of course, the quests of some of the later Wittgensteinians display an attempt to get around the difficulty; but they do so, as it were, by jumping outside immediate experience (denying the possibility of a private language), and it is hard to see how this squares with the "Nihil" which seems to be implicitly retained. No one would deny that solipsism is a major difficulty for an empiricist.

Let us now consider both the notion of solipsism and that of communion of souls. I have suggested that both parties of monists were faced by the same problem underneath all this—they both faced the problem of isolation. But if this was their fear, they faced it in different ways. What I am suggesting is that the apriorists faced the problem of solipsism but not openly. They never devoted themselves to discussion of solipsism, for example; it was never very close to their consciousness. They were almost overtly concerned with monism in a way the empiricists were not; but they did not go closer to the question of isolation. In other words they feared it but did not face it. However, the empiricists on the other hand have faced it, insofar as they have overtly and explicitly written about it. And their general attitude at the end is quite different. They face it, they accept it reluctantly, they dislike it, but they lump it.

Although the attitudes towards it are different, there is possibly a common problem at the root of the matter. Supposing you invent a problem like one that has been put on the stage. Supposing you are in hell, as a Sartre's play called "In Camera" or "No Exit". Now suppose you have two choices. You could live with some nasty sadistic devils; in other words, following Sartre's sophisticated view, hell equals other people; or less sophisticated, hell is persecuting devils. But hell could also be isolation. Hell might consist of being put in solitary confinement. (These would seem to be the tortures underlying the notion of too much central heating.) Which would you opt for? Could it be that, if you hold that hell is other people, you would opt for isolation and go the route of the empiricists? Whereas if you think that isolation is the ultimate misery and think it better to have the company of torturers than none at all, then perhaps you would go the route of the apriorist?

What is at stake here is whether there is not a central problem that was getting under the skin of these two very opposite kinds of people. They both do seem to have the same basic similarity of structure, to do with reductionism and monism, though they differ in the way they cope with it.

And lastly there is the question of why the difference. This requires a comment on monism. Why does all this make sense only in terms of monism? That again is a bit difficult to answer. But it seems to me to be connected with monotheism. Until, one might say, 1918, or 1914 to 1918, God was in his heaven and all was right with the world. Everybody knew his place and his role in the world. Since then "God is dead". This refers to a kind of social reality, with the dynamism gone out of religion. Lots of people still believe in God but the dynamism is gone. It does not enter into their lives, it does not enter into their decisions when wondering what they ought to do either with themselves, their families, or anything else. This is a change such as I think has never taken place before. The monotheistic phase of mankind which has lasted to 1914 or 1918 has had a pretty long innings, from about the time of Amenophis IV or Moses. Before that in the face of polytheism it might have been perfectly possible to have had a pluralistic philosophy. But monotheism was shot through people's thinking, even if there were sceptics like Hume or the deists in England in the 18th century, and would thus be in the culture of the period. They could philosophize only in a monotheistic setting—even when attacking it. So whichever side you were on you were psychologically almost forced into consequences of the monotheistic outlook. And monotheism almost inevitably carried with it reductionism and monism. For monotheism implies one overriding principle; an independent source of power or an independent principle would be incompatible with it; therefore other strong influences must be derivable and reducible—and hence monism.

Thus for apriorists you do not have isolations constituting a problem. With the empiricists it is more difficult to see why monism is needed. But if an empiricist seeks freedom from fettering ideas and he has to kill off ideas, he has to live in a world dominated by sensory, non-ideational experience. And that is monistic. If their monistic doctrine of the "Nihil" is disrupted, then the door would be open to something else, and that would be non-physicalistic, and could admit ideas, and once more the fetters of superstition.

That is the broad conjecture I want to put forward. I have been trying to explore the possibility of understanding philosophy as having a specific role in our intellectual culture—to keep us together as a society of selves secure from isolation.

FOOTNOTES

[1] It is an interesting question how the medieval theologians squared it with their theology.

[2] For Hume, however, and also in later times for the logical positivists, logic and mathematics were admitted to be unempircal. But these subjects constituted one kind of knowledge which gives the impression of being simply an excrescence. For mathematical and logical knowledge, though mentioned, seemed pushed to one side the whole interest and verve of the philosophy centres on empirical criteria for intelligibility and meaningfulness.

[3] I am not trying, by the way, to disparage this philosophy by reducing it to a middle-ages doctrine; indeed, I think it is a compliment to some of the twentieth-century philosophers to put them in the same breath as some of the ancient. I am, on the contrary, more interested in the fact that there is something quite the same in mankind's thinking down the ages. But mainly I am trying to track down basic principles.

[4] It is interesting in connection with this that in all these areas you can strictly refer to definitions. Definitions play little part in human knowledge, but it is interesting to note where they do and where they do not. They appear in logic, they appear in mathematics, but they do not appear anywhere else, e.g. in science (except for units like the volt), and they likewise seem to have no role in the theory of perception and so forth. There is such a process as trying to specify roughly what you refer to when there is a vagueness about the scope of what you want to refer to. But specific kinds of definition that philosophers looked for from Aristotle to Moore seem to be irrelevant. It is curious to my mind that definition should be appropriate to those fields in which reductionism applies and that neither reductionism nor definition works outside them. It may be that there is a link between definition and reductionism, because definition suggests a reductionist approach.

[5] It is less clear that philosophies of essence are monistic, for a salient feature of an essence is to be utterly distinct from another essence; hence reduction would seem to be ruled out. Yet there seems to be a hierarchical idea involved, such that essences are seen in the light of a monistic principle.

CHAPTER XVIII

Social Motives

By SOCIAL motives is simply meant motives underlying a philosophy which are shared by a sufficient number of philosophers to suggest the possibility that a motive was absorbed in part from their society or civilization.

While it would be a mistake, obviously, to try to make all philosophers fit into a Procrustean mould, there seem to be evidence that quite a number shared a deep-seated motive. We may acknowledge that the phenomenon of evil touched Spinoza, Leibniz, and Bradley much more nearly than it did Descartes or Berkeley. We may acknowledge that in seeking for communication with their fellows, some of these philosophers needed the community of spirits emphatically to include God, while others would seem to have placed the emphasis on communication between human beings, while a few wanted to include human beings only and definitely to exclude God. A further difference may show up in that Schopenhauer was the only one to put any emphasis on women, in that he revealed a need to have communication with them, but, as his relations with men were bad too, it is unlikely that the only form of communication with other persons he required was with women and not with men. With the other philosophers considered, one gets the impression of a need for communication with others, without specific regard to sex differentiation; and therefore what was implied was a community of men, at least at the level so far entered upon.

With all these differences taken into account, it seems clear, nonetheless, that the philosophers discussed all shared a need for fellowship (this being for the most part an extra-philosophical goal, though in one or two cases it was articulated overtly and included within the published philosophy and therefore constitutes an ultimate goal rather than one that is extra-philosophical). When we went on to consider schools of philosophy, dividing them into the apriorists and the empiricists (this being slightly wider than the traditional classification into rationalists or intellectualists and empiricists), the general positions of these schools seemed to yield the same results, though by a different route. Empiricism, though, reaches out from experience in the present, i.e. tries to justify knowledge about what is *not* present on the basis of knowledge of what *is* present, notoriously ending up in solipsism; and this implies that there can be no knowledge of natural objects outside one's experience, and, what is from the present point of view more to the point, no knowledge of other persons. But this result is explicit in the case of empiricism. We found that it was not so clearly in evidence in apriorism. Here we notice the enormous stress on the need to reduce substances from many to one, or at least to ensure inter-relationship between substances, which was a fundamental apriorist difficulty. The construction I have put upon the commensurability of substances in general, and of the mind-body problem in particular, was that unless it could be solved, human beings would be isolated logically from one another. Thus, it seems that apriorism faced the same problem as the empiricists, though they did not make this overt.

Now, if we begin to look at this situation from a social point of view and raise the question what underlay this common problem, or in a more abstract form, what underlay the drive towards monism, which was common to both parties, it seems possible that we might be able to initiate historical enquiries that would be relevant to consequences of this position. Although I have suggested that underlying monism lay monotheism, another kind of presupposition is possible, and if correct might explain both the need for communication and also the underlay consisting of monism and monotheism.

Let us revert to the mind-body problem which I have urged is ultimate, and let us consider the possibility that in the culture shared by the philosophers concerned, there was a sharp divergence between sensuality and personal attachment. First let us amplify what it involves. It would mean, for example, that a man might have a close relationship with a wife who did not attract him sexually and, on the other hand, that where he was attracted sexually no feeling of personal involvement arose. The extreme form of this phenomenon is well known to characterize men who frequent prostitutes, but, while the extreme form may not be very common, some degree or other of it might be more widespred. It is also well known that romantic love in the middle ages was taken for granted to lie outside marriage and never inside marriage, and also that it involved an unattainable goal. This phenomenon appears to have been built into the social structure. It is worth noting that it is the opposite phenomenon to the pathological one concerning prostitution. All I am concerned to point out here is that there are different ways in which sentiment and sex may become split off from one another.

Now let us recapitulate the predicament of communication.

In order that mind₁ should be able to communicate with mind₂, mind₁ has to be able to affect $body_1$. $Body_1$ can certainly touch $body_2$, but $body_2$ has the same sort of task as $mind_1$ had, for it has to be able to affect $mind_2$. Given the incommensurability of substances, however, it is clear that $mind_1$ cannot affect $body_1$, and $body_2$ cannot affect $mind_2$, and consequently that only the two bodies can meet. If, now, we take this into the realm of personal sexual relations, we can see at once that if incommensurability holds, then the possible relationship is bodily contact, that is to say, sensuality, for a personal relationship is ruled out by the incommensurability of substances.

It is therefore possible to specify further the conjecture that behind the mind-body problem lay an unsolved problem of personal communication, and the further specification would be that personal communication could not be satisfied through the sexual channel. Now, it seems just possible that a hypothesis of this sort might be testable historically, that is to say, one could attempt to investigate the intellectual and social history of the times to see whether there was an unusually strong strain of bifurcation between sensuality and personal relationship.

To turn to a different aspect of the theme, we have noted that Koyré and others have depicted the change from the middle ages to Renaissance man as involving an overwhelming loss in his basic world outlook, for with the Copernican revolution man lost his place in the universe as being at the centre. With his amour propre undermined, one would expect a depressive reaction and this would, in its turn, lead Renaissance man to seek some new form of self-value to make good the loss. The triumphant march of progess in science and the arts would have mitigated this (perhaps even had its roots in it) and given to man a new sense of dignity. It would help to restore his feeling of being his own master, or perhaps even add to that, because supernaturalism after the Copernican revolution inevitably became more and more replaced by naturalism, which would strengthen his sense of mastery of the physical world.

This further pursuit of the matter enables us to see within the mind-body problem a depressive root, which answers to the depressive constellation noticed above in the philosophers of optimism as well as in the philosophers of pessimism, and also in the mostly extra-philosophical goal that underlay the apriorists and empiricists alike.

CHAPTER XIX

Rationalist Tendencies in Twentieth-Century Thought

THIS HAS been a remarkable century for the development of theoretical knowledge. It has only two equals in recorded history, one being the flowering of the Renaissance period and the other being the peak of Greek thought (even with its powerful intellectual achievements, the last century can hardly stand comparison). But what is, perhaps, most remarkable about the present century is the split between rationalist and antirationalist tendencies. Anti-rationalist tendencies come readily to mind, so that one might be forgiven for thinking that this was a century of anti-rationalism, but some of the most important developments of all have been rationalist. I propose to examine these briefly, largely with the aim of making it easier to understand the other tendency.

While it is not necessary to begin with any detailed account of the notion of rationality, a brief indication of what is to be included and what is to be excluded will be in order. The broad dichotomy that underlies what follows is between objectivism, however this may be sustained, whether by logic or what may be upheld by evidence, as contrasted with an opposite that takes various forms, namely subjectivism, relativism, or intuitionism. It will not be relevant here to dwell on the distinction between deism/atheism on the one hand and supernaturalism on the other, nor between knowledge and faith. A complication that does come in, however, concerns a very real phenomenon in which aims and means are rational, while the implementation in fact leads to an anti-rationalist position. Let us now turn to the rationalist endeavours.

Where would you look if you were looking for a rationalist tendency? I would say that you would find this in, of all areas, the theory of relativity. We must first note that the general theory of relativity is the most absolute theory of physics ever founded, more absolute than Newton's despite its curious name. It should never have been misnamed relativity because of its various absolute features—it even utilizes a new form of algebra known as the absolute calculus. The central idea in it has to do with invariants—invariants of metric and of the form of a law of nature. For a relativity law has to be expressed in such a way that it retains the same form, no matter what frame of reference is used. It is a theory which is testable and does not depend upon the point of view of any observer (though often spoken of as if it did). The reason the word "relativity"[1] came in is because motion and length as ordinarily conceived turn out to be relative to a frame of reference—thought as conceived in relativity they are absolute.

A totally different reason for saying that there is a rationalistic trend concerns the new turn philosophy took at the beginning of the century, which I put at 1903 when Russell published his *Principles of Mathematics* and followed up with later work designed to provide mathematics with rational foundations, and Moore published his "Refutation of Idealism", substituting an absolute realism for the Anglo-Hegelian idealism with its overtones of subjectivism. Russell and Moore were both concerned to find something they could really assert with complete certainty. Russell was looking for "hard data"; in fact, he introduced the term "sense-data" in 1911 (following, of course, a very old tradition in British empiricism). Moore also believed that some perceptual judgments are certain. (He probably believed there was a limit to the possibility of being taken in by conjuring tricks or illusions of the senses.) It was a favourite device of his to argue that the existence of his hand was more certain than any philosophical argument that you could bring against it. Moore's and Russell's search for certainty was a notable feature of philosophy at the beginning of the century, and it went on for perhaps the first quarter of the new century. Whatever the turn philosophy took thereafter, this movement of logical analysis began and ended as a rational enterprise.

We may now turn to Tarski, most famous perhaps for his theory of truth, which came towards the end of the twenties. It does not make truth relative in any way; it does not make it subjective in any way. We need not go into the nature of his theory beyond noting that it is a version in modern dress of the correspondence theory of truth. The main point is that it constituted an objective rationalistic approach. Tarski also provided a solution for a two-thousand-year-old problem which had defeated Aristotle. Although Aristotle was familiar with all the ingredients required for providing a solution, he failed to put them together to form a definition or theory of valid inference; Tarski did this and it was a rational endeavour of the first order. In general, the developments of meta-mathematics come under the same heading.

Turning from physics and logic to philosophy of science, Popper, in 1934, introduced a new theory of the nature of science; it is the theory that science is empirically refutable, or testable by intersubjective means.

And his theory is objective—and has since been claimed, not without good reason, to provide a foundation for rationality.

Arising out of Popper's work, in opposition to the various theological figures of the present century who have flirted with relativism, Tillich, Barth, and so on, who use certain anti-rationalist arguments, there has appeared the work by a former student of Popper's, W. W. Bartley III: in his *Retreat to Commitment* he has tried to counter the anti-rationalistic arguments of these theologians, and show that rationalism does not hinge on an anti-rationalist commitment to rationality.

Freud's attempt to make of psychoanalysis a natural science was rationalistically inspired.

From these manifestations of rationalism, I want to turn to two cases which are ambiguous in the sense that they might belong to either camp or might, for some reason, have a foot in both camps.

One of these concerns behaviourism, at least as put forward by its originator, Watson. Reacting against the introspectionism that characterized some of the psychology of the time, Watson may well have introduced a breath of fresh air into the subject. In trying to reduce all psychology to observation he was unquestionably trying to render psychology scientific. That was an avowed aim. And so far as this was his aim, psychology would have been objective and rational. Whether psychology developed further in a rational way is another matter. Here it suffices to note that it had rational beginnings.

The other feature of twentieth-century thought, which has an ambiguous status, is the movement of logical positivism. This succeeded the rationalism of the logical analysis of Russell and Moore and, like behaviourism, it began with a rational objective. If the behaviourists objected to obscurantism in introspecionist psychology, the logical positivists objected to the obscurantism of metaphysics, and the aim was undoubtedly to transform philosophy into something definitely meaningful in the first place and to provide a definite method of checking up on its meaningfulness, and of its truth or falsity, in the second place. Logical positivism petered out because it could not implement its programme, and the question will be raised below whether it ended up in an irrational position. However that may be, as with behaviourism, it began by having thoroughly rational aims.

One has to try to distinguish between the intention of its proponents and the message that actually comes over, should the two things not synchronize. The logical positivists, who constituted the Vienna Circle in the 1920's, wanted to get away from all sorts of vague, nebulous, meaningless philosophy; and to attack metaphysical doctrines by a method that might be regarded as satisfactory from a rational point of view because established by means of the principle of verifiability; and they wanted to replace metaphysics by certain other doctrines like the unity of language in which all scientific statements, and hence all truths, could be made, and so forth. Whether or not anyone agrees with this, it seems to me to have been a programme in which positivists were trying to establish knowledge on a rational basis with a rational method which would stand up to any rational criticism.

It may be added, however, that the list does not presuppose a judgment of success. Some of the foregoing movements have been either a failure or of a success that is questioned by many, while others have been a success. Success and failure are not relevant, however, to the rationality of an enterprise.

This concludes the present review of rationalistic tendencies in the twentieth century.

THE NOTION OF RATIONALITY

We may now return to the concept of rationality itself. It will be discerned that the notion of truth, where given some relative interpretation, renders knowledge also relative. And this was taken to mean that objective knowledge was impossible, and the tendency was taken to be anti-rationalistic. Now, it might be suggested that after all the impossibility of objective knowledge might happen to be a fact about the universe, that all it was possible to know in some areas was relative to some particular framework. And if this were so, would it not be irrational to demand an objective knowledge going beyond this, and would it not therefore be fully rational to make the assertion of this relativistic knowledge?

To answer this would seem to require a new characterization of rationality. The tradition has been that beliefs, theories, attitudes, expectations, approaches, and so forth, are rational—and nothing else. These things do indeed constitute the stuff of rationality, but it may be questioned whether there is also not something else. We may notice that these ingredients are all *assertions,* but no reference is made to *questions.* On the face of it, it looks as if there is no essential difference between assertions and questions, for to every question there is an assertion providing an answer, and every assertion is an answer to some question. But a little reflection will enable us to challenge this view. A feature that is very prominent in twentieth-century thought, and in logical positivism in particular, is the introduction of assertions that *forbid* certain questions.

To illustrate. Behaviourists treat only of disenminded bodies. That is, they study human beings as if they were rats, and rats are studied as if they have responses, but hardly minds. If you leave out minds, and persons, which we think we have to do with from day to day, and deal only with bodies behaving (that is, moving), then this seems to me to leave out the essentially interesting feature of the whole subject and to be a case of problem-avoidance, or desiccation, for it dries up the whole affair. It seems to me unsatisfactory to rule out a question.

Let me put it this way more neutrally. I think one should try to begin by saying that there is a question to be raised, e.g. whether there are such things as imagery in people's minds or whether there are such things as feelings, although we cannot observe anything of such a kind. I would put it that we first of all allow the formulation of the question and then try to find reasons why those assertions are false—that is, to allow the question to be raised. But if you adopt a philosophical approach that does not allow the question to be raised, this seems to me to be prejudging the issue. It is rational to find a view false and then to throw it out, but it is anti-rationalist not to allow a question to be raised.

In short, the anti-rationalist characteristic, I am suggesting, consists of problem-avoidance, which leads to the desiccation of a subject. Conversely, rationalism requires the addition of a new characteristic of questioning—that is, questioning with no holds barred. Then, and only then, would there be a question corresponding to every assertion.

Let us consider further examples. We have already noted that behaviourism precludes the most significant questions being asked about minds and persons. It hardly needs to be reiterated now that logical positivism precluded discussion of many great questions, and linguistic philosophy does the same. To mention one brief example, if Being is the ultimate question in metaphysics—that is, how does anything come to be at all—we have an extreme example of a question which could not have appeared on any philosophical platform in the Anglo-American type of philosophy that has swept over Scandinavia, Austria, Australia, for over three-quarters of a century. It may not be possible to say much about such a question, but the correct attitude to it, I submit, is that the question should first be put. Then any philosopher is entitled to say, "I do not propose to work in that field". What is anti-rational is to preclude the question by a ready-made philosophy.

Some of the other examples of anti-rational tendencies need only a brief remark. Theology based on a commitment precludes a question. All the philosophies of science mentioned, which turn theories into manipulations of observations, preclude this question: what knowledge does science give us about the world? Marxist epiphenomenalism, whatever the merits of its powerful sociological theory, precludes our raising the question: in what way and how far can individual people effect marked changes in society? Psychiatry, in its worthy endeavour to come to grips with personal relations in the psychiatric area, distorts existentialism into a subjectivist relationship between people, and a subjectivist interpretation precludes the basic questions concerning the truth of psychodynamic theories. The cultural relativism that has arisen from social anthropology has sprung from a worthy endeavour not to talk down to "savages". It is also true that one should not talk to children as "mere children". But this does not mean accepting an irrational confusion between treating other peoples and children as human and maintaining that our knowledge is no better than theirs. If two cultures have two diametrically opposed beliefs, relativism precludes our asking the question: which is correct? (It probably implies, moreover, that the two beliefs do not really contradict one another because their meanings are incommensurable, so that there can be no communication between the two cultures at all.)

This chapter may fittingly be closed with a contemporary observation. New questions have been raised for the first time by mankind, including the young, which would seem to have been precluded by the social structure of the past. At the same time, some of those very people who raise these questions, and should be raising them, are introducing their own restrictive framework, e.g. the generation gap, the belief that knowledge emerges from involving one another in groups, and discarding all objectivist procedures. This seems to me to illustrate very well the fusion between rationalist and anti-rationalist tendencies in the present period.

In amplification of this characteristic, whenever a new theory, scientific or otherwise, is put forward, even with the best of rationalist intentions, the maxim might be observed of asking: may the theory inhibit knowledge? Or more specifically, the question would be: what questions does a great new development forbid? (We could even institutionalize the procedure of having a committee to investigate, in connection with any new corroborated scientific theory, what questions it rules out.) Looked at another way, many rational endeavours are limited as regards rationality by pursuing rationality up to the hilt but not including the hilt. So what is being suggested here is to substitute for constrained rationalism unconstrained questions. Otherwise expressed, this amounts to challengeability unlimited, perhaps involving the notion of levels of challengeability. Alternatively the point of view might, perhaps, be summarized as trans-pragmatic, that is to say, a theory is anti-rational if it forbids questions and a theory is rational if it is comprehensively challengeable.

FOOTNOTES

[1] I have suggested names which would seem to be more appropriate for Einstein's investigations. It seems that he introduced a totally new method of enquiry in constantly looking for invariant forms for metrics of space-time (which is a generalized form of the notion of length). The special theory of relativity (1905) might be called "the theory of flat symmetric invariant metrics". The general theory of relativity (1915) might be called "the theory of curved symmetric invariant metrics", and the bold, if unsuccessful, attempt to unify gravitation and electrodynamics (1950) might be called "the theory of skew symmetric invariant metrics".

CHAPTER XX

Anti-Rationalist Tendencies in Twentieth-Century Thought

ANTI-RATIONALIST tendencies would seem to be more numerous and perhaps spread over a wider area of human knowledge.

When Bartley put forward his theory of rationality as not involving any rational commitment to rationalism, he was opposing a fairly substantial group of modern theologians characterized by a certain liberal tendency, not in what is usually accepted as the good sense of the term, but in a sense allowing that any position is justifiable, depending on what initial commitment one has made. Whether or not this accusation is or is not true of all the theologians Bartley discusses, it would seem that a considerable number of influential thinkers in this area do hinge their views on a commitment that lies beyond the possibility of rational support.

Since there is, perhaps, something pragmatic in flavour about the foregoing theological position, it is worth pointing out that the spirit of pragmatism pervades the twentieth century, both as a general standpoint and in particular manifestations. The notion that a doctrine is true if it works must imply that the truth of a theory is independent of inter-subjectively acceptable evidence. The short way of saying this is that pragmatism is subjectivist.

One of the most striking manifestations of pragmatism lies in some of the current interpretations of the nature of science, that is to say philosophies of science, put forward by the most eminent practitioners of physics. Three interpretations—instrumentalism, conventionalism, and operationalism—have been widespread for many years. The slight differences that characterize them need not concern us here. The common element is what matters, and it consists of two special features. One is the ultimacy of observation, and the other is that there can be no objective truth, not just as a matter of difficulty of obtaining it, but in principle; for the acceptability or so-called truth of a theory consists solely in the power it confers of manipulating observations, that is, passing from observations in the past to observations in the future. But this is simply a power to manipulate; it provides no information about the nature of the world. In the sense relating to objective information, truth does not exist in these philosophies of science. Hence, so far as truth is an ingredient of rationality, these approaches must be reckoned as anti-rationalist.

It is worth pointing out an interesting way in which an anti-rationalist tendency has been manifested about quantum mechanics. As is well known, according to quantum mechanics it is not possible to state the exact position and the exact momentum of a particle simultaneously. The more exact one can be known, the less exact is our knowledge of the other. More specifically, the error in estimating the one multiplied by the error in estimating the other must always be less than a certain cele-brated quantity $h/2\pi$. This relation has as a corollary that neither of the two errors can be zero, far less both of them. Now, this perfectly correct consequence of quantum mechanics has often been referred to, both by physicists and by philosophers, in the form that it is meaning-less to speak of the exact position and the exact momentum. This way of putting the matter is strangely erroneous. What should be asserted is not that it is meaningless but simply false to speak of their being exact simultaneously. Let us begin with a slightly simpler example such as that in non-Euclidian geometry, which is required by modern physics, say, the three angles of a triangle do not add up to 180 degrees. To assert that the angles add up to 180 degrees is not meaningless in the non-Euclidian system; it is false. For it is well known, and indeed a cardinal principle of those who have spoken of meaninglessness, that if a proposition is meaningless, then so also is its contradictory. So if the assertion in non-Euclidian geometry that the angles of a triangle add up to 180 degrees is meaningless, then so also is the assertion that the angles do not add up to 180 degrees. Likewise, if we consider the assertion "the error of position multiplied by the error of momentum is equal to zero", it is not meaningless, for if it were, then so also would be the assertion "the error of position multiplied by the error of momentum is never less than $h/2\pi$". Now, this latter assertion is required as a theorem in quantum mechanics and cannot be discarded as meaningless. Hence, the assertions from classical physics should not be described as meaningless in the framework of modern physics, but as false. The mistake so commonly made about this point might be written off as being simply the result of a lax way of speaking on the part of those whose main job lies elsewhere. But when philosophers of great ability like the late Waismann make the mistake, it can hardly be written off in this way, and I would suggest that it is a manifestation of a tendency, not to criticize, but to write off—that is to say, of an irrationalist tendency.

To this positivist way of thinking, there came as its successor linguistic philosophy. Now, this movement has introduced a questionable kind of liberalism rather like that characterizing twentieth-century theologians in that it is so permissive a philosophy that "anything goes". It is almost, even though not quite, a philosophy in which nothing is claimed or asserted and nothing is denied. The first part of this assessment is correct without qualification. No claim is made; in fact, all claims are admissible provided you make sure you imply nothing misleading in asserting them. On the other hand, it is not quite true that nothing is denied. Anything that results from categorial confusion is ruled out and there is a tendency in line with this throughout the philosophy to abort any philosophical claim, or even abort a discussion of any point that would spark off in the minds of linguistic philosophers the suspicion of a categorial confusion. Since linguistic philosophy, or its still more attenuated successor, philosophical analysis, operates by assuming the virtues of the discarded logical positivism, preserving these in disguise, it is operating either on the basis of something it has overtly discarded, and contains inconsistent attitudes, or else operates on the basis of a confusion. Thus it cannot be accounted rational on the grounds of content. At most, it is rational on the grounds of method. But if the method centres either on a contradiction or on a confusion, it cannot be credited with being rational.

Let us turn next to Marxism. Marx's own economic theory of society is a highly rational endeavour and would have been included as such, had we been dealing with the last century as well. That is to say, it was rational so far as it aimed at providing a general dynamic theory about social change. It had a consequence, however, which has become prominent in the present century. For one part of the broad doctrine is that man's ideas are, if you like, epiphenomena of economic forces. Man's social behaviour, and perhaps individual behaviour, is determined (as one might say nowadays) not by his genes or by his own conscience, or by his mother or by his education or what-not, but by economic forces. The point about this is that man's individual activities have virtually no power to influence the course of events. Marx did admit that by taking certain actions you could act as a midwife to accelerate slightly the inevitable course of history or that you could, if you were a wicked capitalist, hold things up a little bit if you work against the course of history; but you could not do much—there is only slight play in the steering wheel. You could not do much more than accelerate or hold up the inevitable tendency that would unfold. In other words, the broad picture is that man's activities, including his intellectual pursuits, would be powerless to exercise any influence in their own right. That is to say, they would have no independent role, they would be shadows cast by the real nature of things, namely the economic reality, or, if you like, they would be epiphenomena. Now, this seems to me to be susceptible of being put under the heading of a kind of relativism. For a person's views or society's views will reflect the economic forces of the period in which he lives. In short, it amounts to economic relativism. (There is also, perhaps an element of irrationality or at least of paradox in propounding a theory of action when action is not of our choosing.)

Now, take something closely similar in structure, though vastly different in content—a modern psychiatric intuitive approach. Although Freud's aim was objective, numbers of psychiatrists hold that what they know in clinical contact with the patient is intuitively grasped, and, though they do not discuss the matter, they seem to think that intuition is essentially valid, i.e. that well-sharpened, well-trained intuition is self-guaranteeing. Now, on this basis, a psychiatric assessment would be a subjective psychiatric intuitive judgement. (Not that there is anything against intuitive insights; they are the only thing anybody ever has to work on; they are more often right than wrong, or we would not survive, and without them we should get nowhere; but one has to check up on them.) Moreover, an anti-rationalist tendency is manifest in the use of the notion of rationalizations of unconscious motivations; for this is felt to suggest that the conscious reason for an action is never the "real" reason, which is attributed to the unconscious. Here we have a psychological relativism. There is a certain parallelism to Marx's epiphenomenalism here. In both cases we have corollaries that can, and I think very often do in practice, lead to a subjectivism or relativism. This would, in fact, be historically unfair to Freud, who was very careful about rationality, and probably also to Marx, but I am not so much concerned with the historical intentions in these cases as with the effects and the way the message has been subsequently read.

Here is another example, which I think is quite powerful. Social anthropologists have sometimes subscribed to what is called cultural relativism, and some of the above views could be put very nicely under this heading. By this is meant simply that value-judgements, or other assertions made by people in a society, have been interpreted as true, relative to the social structure or functioning, or the culture, and do not hold true of all cultures or all people of all kinds. Of course, a great many things are of this sort. A great many things naturally do hold only of certain periods in history and certain peoples and so forth; but the cultural relativist claims that every assertion that can be made about society is relative to a culture precludes objectivism. For example, one thing to be ruled out would be any cross-discussion of a question of right or wrong. Thus an ethical moral judgment would be right in one culture and wrong in another. Take the case where in medieval or in post-Renaissance England monarchs were constantly chopping off heads. Today we find this totally unacceptable. This may have been part of the socio-political structure of the time making it "understandable", whereas it would not fit into our society. But if we adopt cultural relativism, we cannot raise any objective question of right or wrong.

Now comes one other -ism of the present day, and that is the sociology of knowledge. It suggests that the structure of knowledge itself is relative to the period or an outlook or a country or what-not. Without discussing this in general, one point may be mentioned. In Kuhn's fine work on the theory of scientific revolutions, which contains magnificent features, he holds, for example, that two scientists belonging to two culturally different epochs, so far as science is concerned, cannot communicate with one another. Thus a Newtonian and an Einsteinian physicist cannot understand one another. They both talk about mass, space, time, force, and length—all the fundamental terms that are used for building up physics they both need; but they mean different things by every single one of them—not just that the concepts are differently applied and that the theories are different, but the meanings of the concepts themselves are different. But why there should be no communication between the two parties remains obscure. For one thing, Einstein surely knew Newtonian theory very well before he began his work, and he did not lose contact with that understanding after he developed his new theory. And for another, Einstein took particular pains to deduce the Newtonian theory: you make deductions from it, you make the necessary approximations, you make the radius of curvature of the universe equal to infinity, and deduce a result which is the Newtonian theory. This on Einstein's new theory and for the new physicist will be meaningful. For the sociologist of knowledge, on the other hand, it will be not understandable. But how are you going to make a deduction, with or without approximations, if you have the premiss meaningful, the conclusion meaningful (but in another framework), and no meaningful connection between them? To hold water, this requires very tortuous interpretation. In fact, of course, there are many people nowadays who understand both theories perfectly well and can work with both. Now there is something odd in holding that people with different theories cannot communicate when we all know well that in practice they can. True, there are large numbers of cases where people with different views get hot under the collar and cannot communicate; but Kuhn is not concerned with that; he is concerned with something much more fundamental, that in some logical sense there can be no communication. As developed further in Feyerabend, the sociology of knowledge interprets the natural sciences in a way akin to cultural relativism as understood by some social anthropologists, because scientific truth is taken to be relative to a paradigm, the dominant theory of a period, and "anything goes". The fundamental point, however, is that this approach leads to solipsism, just as in a different way Hume's empiricism led to it.

It probably should not be thought that the exponents of these points of view, some of whom were most distinguished and highly rational, were aiming at something anti-rational. On the contrary, in several instances they were baffled by difficult problems and used deep-seated rational considerations in arriving at these results. Nonetheless, what comes out is that they were in one way or another relativistic and, therefore, anti-rational.

From these overtly relativistic approaches, we turn to the two that appear to have a footing in both camps.

Watson's behaviourism started out with the avowed aim of being objectivist. And carrying out his programme required reduction of all psychology to observation. Now, this referred to two distinct features of his method. On the one hand, Watson thought that the subject matter of science had to be observable, so that psychologists could not discuss *thinking* scientifically, they could only discuss subvocal *talking*. Thinking was thus equated with oscillations of the larynx. The second feature was that only observable entities could enter into scientific explanations (later behaviourists introduced intervening variables which went beyond observation, but these were not admitted by Watson). This was observationalism gone to extremes.

The criticism cannot be diluted that Watson, who wished to render psychology scientific, had, in certain fundamental respects, no understanding of natural science. It should have been apparent to him that physics had long studied entities like atoms, which are not observable. It is true that many scientists have had reserves about this sort of procedure, but many have not, and in any case physics has progressed not only very effectively in this way but also characteristically. For the atom is not an exception as an unobservable, and, on the whole, it would seem to be that most philosophers of science now recognize that such entities are the norm in physics. Returning to Watson, whatever the author's intentions, if what he was doing was based on a mistake, his work can hardly be counted as rational. Watson's approach, moreover, was a prominent feature of the twentieth-century thought, for his influence has lasted for more than half a century. Subsequent behaviourism, insofar as it attempted to introduce unobservables, was approaching more closely the procedure of the natural sciences. But there are different kinds of unobservables; and intervening variables are not the fundamental kind with which physics deals. Therefore, they represent only entities inside a black box which would be observable if only you could open the box, whereas the basic unobservables of physics are in principle unobservable. Moreover, subsequent behaviourism continues to proceed on the principle that psychology cannot study hidden mental processes without replacing these by observational equivalents (known as operational definitions). Thus, this whole movement in psychology continues to be rooted in two myths. The strength of this tendency must be accounted one of the major anti-rationalist features of the age.

The other movement which had a foot in both camps was logical positivism, which overtly aimed at rendering philosophy as objective as science, and brought a great rational apparatus to bear on this task.

The fact that it did not work out suitably can hardly be held against positivist intentions. The fact that an attempt is a failure does not necessarily put it in the anti-rationalist camp. But we have to take a second look at the central doctrine of logical positivism, the principle of verifiability: according to this, the only realities are sensory observations. There is great difficulty in finding out what these are because they turn out in the end to be atomic facts or what is given by protocol statements, that is, hard data, of which there are no specimens. Hence, logical positivism, although fundamentally an epistemology with the aim of destroying all metaphysics, and therefore out to destroy all ontology, had to allow that there are some things in the world, for it did allow that the world has some ultimate furniture, consisting roughly of sense-data. So positivism had an ontology of sorts. The main substance is that you have the grin of the Cheshire cat but not the Cheshire cat itself. In other words, what positivists were portraying was a universe with pure observational components but no underlying reality.

The epilogue to the story of logical positivism is an epitaph. It could not in principle deliver the goods. It died of inanition around the end of World War II, when it was realized that the principle of verifiability could not be constituted in such a way as to do its work. For it either excluded the higher levels of explanatory physics and science generally, or else it readmitted into the corpus of meaningful statements the metaphysics it was designed to eliminate. However, let it be stressed, mere failure does not constitute anti-rationalism. But the nature of the failure indicates that the seeds of failure should perhaps have been detected at an early stage and, indeed, could have been, had the Vienna Circle of logical positivists not been so imbued with fervour that they failed altogether to take note of criticism existing even at or near the beginning. For Popper, quite early on, was making fundamental criticisms about all central aspects of positivism. Indeed, when Kraft, after World War II, wrote his short history of logical positivism, it came over very clearly that positivism had accepted Popper's criticisms one after another.[1]

This refusal to heed, or attempt to cope with, criticism is an indication of an anti-rationalist tendency in a case where the criticism was carefully worked out and of a rational kind. Far from being merely incoherent opposition, the positivists' path, which swept over the philosophical world and dominated it for about a quarter of a century, and even spread its influence over natural science and psychology, reflects something charactistic of twentieth-century thought.

It would seem that all these anti-rational tendencies of the period centre on two themes—observationalism and values. A philosophy of observationalism underlay the attempt to reach objectivity, but conceivably also what prevented its attainment. Values are equally significant. They enter the scene because of the failure of philosophy to establish objective values and because of the growth of humanism. These two facts add up to a cultural relativism.

In distinguishing, apparently sharply, between rational tendencies and anti-rational tendencies, it should not be overlooked that the two are often fused, and if the preceding separation has been over-sharp for purposes of exposition, it is now necessary to enter a caveat. Thus, the observationalism of Russell and Moore, which displayed a rational tendency at the beginning of the century, assumed an irrational form later. But it is, after all, not so surprising if both rational and anti-rational tendencies are to be found both in the same movement, and even in the same man.

FOOTNOTES

[1] The structure of Kraft's work is odd in certain respects. He calls Popper a logical positivist, but quotes him at length always against the tenets of logical positivism. He never says that positivism gave way under the criticism by Popper, and this may be in part, or even in large part, true, because a movement will often not give way until its own members discover the flaws for themselves.

CHAPTER XXI

The Twentieth-Century Sophists

The subject matter of what follows is linguistic philosophy, considered as a social phenomenon. Before formulating the problem involved, it is worthwhile trying to place its main features in perspective. However vacuous we have found its content, it has a Weltanschauung—never to my knowledge articulated—that would be regarded as admirable, at least in some respects, even by those who do not agree with them. Let me attempt to outline its character.

i) Linguistic philosophy is, broadly speaking, a philosophy of contextualism, that is to say, there is no meaning in words or language apart from a conceptual context in which they occur. This is a noteworthy advance on the early work of logical analysis by Moore, for example, who treated the meanings of words and of statements independently of their context. And meaning for him gives the impression, at times, of being a platonic idea. Contextualism is not, perhaps, so new as might be claimed because it is characteristic of absolute idealism, for example— a bedfellow that linguistic philosophy would abhor.

ii) Linguistic philosophy, at the "liberal" end of its spectrum, allows for the possible existence of unobservables. This is a noteworthy advance on the restrictions from the period of logical analysis, and also from the period of logical positivism. Linguistic analysis, unfortunately, makes no use of this liberality because it is too thin in ideas.

iii) Linguistic philosophy is anti-essentialist. Thus instead of seeking an essence of reality or an essence of thinking, what is mapped is a spectrum of real things or of kinds of thinking, which may shade into one another.

iv) Linguistic philosophy aims at being anti-obscurantist. Although it ends as being obscurantist itself in high degree, it should not be overlooked that this was not the desire. Thus, consider a celebrated contribution from language analysis by Austin: one of his "insights" was that the verb "to know" is distinguished from the verb "to believe" by being a "commitment" word. That is to say, if a person believes it is

177

going to be fine, and it pours, he is not in any way to blame for your leaving your umbrella behind, and cannot be held responsible for any ill consequence. On the other hand, if a person claims to "know" that it is going to be fine, he is, according to Austin, making a commitment; and if he is wrong, he owes a forfeit. If on the basis of his "knowledge" you leave your umbrella behind and get soaking wet, then it is up to him to have your suit pressed. Now, this may be a remarkable insight about the difference in the way the verbs "know" and "believe" function, but it has nothing whatever to do with the main epistemological problems of knowledge. Thus the enterprise is obscurantist, although Austin wished to attack obscurantist ideas such as the essence of knowledge.

v) At least at one end of the spectrum, even if this looms very small, linguistic philosophy is concerned with the traditional question of the limitations of human knowledge. For as a kind of English neo-Kantianism, however watered down, it imposes a synthetic a priori categorial restriction upon what can be known.

vi) Contrasted with this atypical feature is the well-nigh universal one, which may be described as linguistic relativism, and which is in line with, though not a necessary consequence of, contextualism.[1] That is to say, since the meanings of words and statements are relative to a context, then, assuming that they cannot have a universal context or universal language, whatever is asserted must be relative to the particular language in which it is couched.

It is interesting to observe how many of these features would be shared by philosophers of very different schools, which whom linguistic philosophers would not like to share anything. Thus, categorial restriction is shared with Kant and Bradley, contextualism is shared with the absolute idealists, though the relativism is not. Contextualism is also shared with Popper, who holds that in the realm of science all scientific theories belong to a context and cannot be treated "in themselves" (we must, however, be cautious about the comparison, for some contextualists assume it implies an out-and-out relativism).

Linguistic philosophy also shares with Popper a feature that is often overlooked about his philosophy of science, that one can work with unobservables. It shares his anti-essentialism and his dislike of obscurantism.

Probably what matters most to practitioners is anti-obscurantism, in that they really think that they undermine it by tracking it down to linguistic misuse and that in so doing they are carrying out a large, difficult, and worthy task, and help to turn the world into a civilization of reasonable men, free of Baconian-type Idols.

A curious feature of the movement is the absence of a standard name. We find linguistic philosophy, language philosophy, and most recently, philosophical analysis, which seems to be an admission that it contains no ideas. But let us turn from the Weltanschauung to the question of content.

1) As the heir to logical positivism, it seems at times to have been handled as if it were logical positivism in a new form, that is, in linguistic form. Procedures of verifiability yielded place to procedures involving the examination of the use of expressions. There is clearly no difference in the following respect: If a statement is verifiable, then the statement has a linguistic use. Doubt arises over the converse equation: If a statement has a use, it is, or is it not, then verifiable? If the first line is taken, as it seems to have been done by some philosophers, then there is a complete identity between linguistic philosophy and logical positivism. Then, linguistic philosophy would imply meta-ontological negativism exactly as did logical positivism. It would be a dogmatism and would fail in its objective, exactly as did the principle of verifiability.

2) If the other line is taken, so that a statement can have a use without being verifiable, then linguistic philosophy is not identical with logical positivism. This is superficially the more usual line, and it has been developed in such a way that any assertion can be made with sense, provided great care is taken not to allow the misleading implications of old-time philosophy, which the analytical ventures of the twentieth century have liquidated at such an enormous expenditure of effort. On this line, linguistic philosophy is wholly devoid of content; it makes no assertions; it makes no denials;[2] as Gellner (1958) has put it, it makes "good sense of everything".

3) The actual practice of linguistic philosophy[3] probably constitutes a spectrum between these two poles, with most exponents sliding uneasily from one to the other. The overt intention is the "liberal" second line of allowing anything to be asserted. But taking linguistic philosophy in the "liberal" sense, you will be hard put to it (apart from clearing up confusions, methodological prescriptions, and elaborating small technicalities) to find a work containing a contribution of any breadth. The first line, inherited from positivism, shows itself very quickly if one attempts to raise the classical questions from philosophy in substantive form. Linguistic philosophers are then very quick on the draw to show that this is logically misguided—though the word "meaningless" is never actually used. Thus, linguistic analysis has all the appearance of being liberal, while preserving an apartheid programme, which can be operated when required. There seems to be a somewhat arbitrary application of this,

G

since the tendency is to rule out some philosophical questions of the old-fashioned kind by permitting others without specific justification or attempting to show why any line may be drawn.

The image linguistic philosophy presents is such that one might be accused of supposing that we are in one of the great ages of the decadence of philosophical thought, of which there have been others. But this might be an exaggeration. The Sophists of old are distinguished by historians into, in effect, "good guys" and "bad guys", although the popular meaning of sophist and sophistry is pejorative. Likewise, among the twentieth-century sophists, we can find examples of philosophers who have worthy aims and interesting ideas (though very, very few). A striking example with a thesis is Ryle's work in the concept of mind. This is very far from a "liberal" work, in which "anything goes", for Ryle introduced the very restrictive postulate of "category-mistake", as a result of which he introduced a new theory of the mind, which I have called "adverbial". And he could also be regarded as showing that mental processes are on a different level from bodily processes (though this way of putting the matter would not square with his attack on dualism, but to aim only at showing there is no problem.) Ryle's other work in philosophical analysis, however, would seem to lack such characteristics.

The great bulk of linguistic philosophy, on the other hand, seems like a self-perpetuating computer, programming itself to re-programme its programmes, all content for the programming to programme having been omitted by an undersight. If one end of the spectrum is regarded as a philosophy of the categorial strait-jacket, the other end of the spectrum might be regarded as paraphilosophy.

There is a strange incongruity between the vacuousness (or worse) and the general approach of this movement. How can we square such a reasonable, or at least partly tenable, and apparently dignified general approach, with the dross that appears under its banner? Perhaps we may get a lead on this by looking at the manner in which a great deal of argumentation is carried out.

There is often a quality manifest that the philosopher was a reincarnation of Alciphron, the minute philosopher as portrayed by Berkeley. It is not that language analysts spend their time trying to score points. This is most atypical, that is to say, they do not do this in general by overt means, but it does seem to be the strategy of indirect approach. In other words, one gets a picture of an attempt to destroy, in a certain way, though usually clothed in a very sophisticated and suave form. One does not see the smart boy in his teens attempting to humiliate by unfair means to render others helpless (by offering a match from a box with sham matches or by making an apple-pie bed). For the means used are much more subtle. It is to provide a framework with a degaussing gear built into it, preventing an opponent from entering into a discussion.

There is a strange example from an extreme end of the spectrum. Austin, at philosophical meetings, is reputed to have reduced his colleagues to philosophical impotence by his technique of humiliation, when he turned his microscope on the fine structure of the differences between the various words they used. He could, and apparently did, make able men look like dunces. An interesting example appears in print where Austin brings his battery of small arms to bear on Ayer and makes it look as if Ayer has committed the most elementary and stupid logical mistakes.

Now the reality factor in this is important. If these philosophers have made mistakes, it is correct to point them out. But when clever men of known ability are made to look like dunces, one begins to suspect that something has gone wrong. Whether or not Ayer himself introduced any new philosophical ideas is beside the point (I do not seek to defend his philosophy, for I do not think he developed a philosophy to defend; I seek only to defend his intellectual ability against Austin's subversive attack). For even his most extreme opponents would probably agree that Ayer is one of the most acute practitioners in the field of logical discrimination that have existed for a very long time. Indeed, he stands comparison, for sheer intellectual quality, with Abélard; and of how many during the last few hundred years could the same be said? (Ayer was more fortunate in his destiny than Abélard in that Austin was only a philosophical Canon Fulbert.)

Such an enterprise seems to rest on a total unwillingness to see what the other philosopher wished to say. Ayer is well known to be extremely lucid, and if we bear in mind that absolute lucidity is a myth, obscurities will always be obtainable when subsequent discriminations are made. But this does not show that the writer was stupid. It is surely very odd that Austin failed to recognize that Ayer was not stupid in the way portrayed.

Now the smart-boy tactic seems to depend largely on taking the letter and not the intention. So what I am suggesting is that a large part of linguistic philosophy is a sophisticated form of smart-boy stuff.

We can begin to see some sort of fit between the approach to the subject and the practice of the art. While contextualism, anti-essentialism, anti-obscurantism, and categorial restriction, not to mention the use of unobservables, can all be used constructively, one group being used for instance by Popper, another group being used at times by Ryle, they can very readily play into the hands of the smart-boy philosophy and almost inevitably do so when supported with linguistic relativism. Thus, what might have been constructive in the general approach of linguistic philosophy has tended on the whole to be used mainly for the purpose of harrying other philosophers. The linguistic philosopher, on the whole, so far from trying to understand a philosopher of another mode of thought, is more like a barrister conducting a hostile cross-examination. (It is perhaps not without relevance that in this circle the one outstanding mark of a philosopher is originality of argument—surely an important one among several but even then hardly the top of the list.)

If this is the scene, how do we account for it? Smart boys have no doubt existed all down the ages in philosophy,[4] but they failed to get away with it. In the twentieth century, however, it has become the establishment procedure and carries great status. If we look at the matter evolutionwise as the survival of a strain, the smart boy did not survive or make his mark in most periods. And if he has succeeded in doing so in the present century, this surely means that the environment was propitious. What we are up against, therefore is a problem of the soil.[5] What is there about the soil of twentieth-century outlook that facilitated, encouraged, or possibly brought to fruition the seed of the smart-boy philosopher? Once it arose at all, it would be increased by positive feedback. Professor Alciphron,[6] once he has obtained a chair of significance, would modify the soil in his own favour. So the question is: how did the inital change in the soil first come about?

First of all, there is the obvious factor of disillusionment because of the poor-grade quality of Anglo-Hegelian philosophy during the latter part of the previous century, which was, on the whole, poorly practised. But disillusionment has arisen before and would not alone be sufficient to account for the change. The new factor, which, though it has had parallels in the past, has had very few of them, was the social sense that metaphysics was dead. There seem to me to be two social reasons why this was so, but here I shall confine myself to one of them. The overwhelming influence that penetrated right through the population was the consequence of the Darwinian revolution, showing that man was an animal. But what has this to do with philosophy? I would suggest that it has everything to do with philosophy, for the consequence was that the notion of distinct species was socially finished, and, hence, metaphysics was at an end, that is, in the blood and thunder sense understood by philosophers. Philosophy could no longer create. All it could do was use the one tool of philosophy that had taken on a new lease on life, namely, logic, and use it in the final destruction of metaphysics.

But the decadence did not set in all at once. The philosophy of realism, i.e. the period of logical analysis, given an established position by Russell and Moore, had some epistemological content even though this was somewhat thin, and in logic was immensely rich. There was still an earnest drive towards solving problems about the world. After the first quarter or third of the century when logical positivism took hold, decay began to set in. For, although it aimed at disinfecting knowledge and at giving scientific knowledge a secure foundation, it contained the seeds of an all-pervasive negativism. Even then there was no intellectual obfuscation. It was only in the third period after World War II that intellectual integrity became questionable, displayed in the tendency to slide between a principle of meaninglessness and a "liberal" principle of "use" in which "anything goes".

This last attempt to have it both ways is equivalent to an anti-essentialist standpoint coupled with allowance of essentialism, manifest for example in the thesis of the "paradigm case", suggestive of a nostalgia.

The smart-boy philosophy resulting, and there was plenty of overt facetiousness in the twentieth-century presentation of it, amounts to pulling faces at dethroned elders, for whom no understanding or wish to understand was left.

The half-concealed bitterness of linguistic philosophy's handling of metaphysical ideas, the content, the facetiousness, the spoliation (apparent also in the period of logical positivism and discernible even in the initial phase of logical analysis), could hardly have been pursued on a national scale if there was no deep-seated disappointment or sense of deprivation by the older philosophers who had failed to deliver the goods. And even this attack would not make much sense unless the attackers really wanted to make just these demands on themselves, but knew they could not fulfil them. I am suggesting, therefore, a fundamental identification between the hopeless hopes of the twentieth-century analysts and the Anglo-Hegelians who promised much but proved effete (the latest ones being disillusioned with the efforts of their predecessors to set this right). The overall attitude might otherwise be expressed in terms of the notion of envy, the envy by philosophical analysts of their predecessors, who, however disappointing the outcome, would seem to have had a richer philosophical experience. Envy may be regarded as the spoliation in phantasy of others not seen to be a reflection of oneself. In this we may see, also, not only the lack of creativeness with the depression that this covers over, but also the denial of that lack, for we can understand the denial of the lack of creativeness as a hypomanic enthusiasm of twentieth-century analytic empiricists.

It is possible, moreover, that the smart-boy philosophy with underlying envy is but part of a larger social attitude that forms part of the reaction to Victorianism.[7] The overall change is, of course, emancipation; but while emancipation may consist of a positive breakaway leading to a burst of creativeness, it may also contain an element of rebellion for its own sake, of just being the opposite of what it displaces. The latter kind of development would seem to be rooted in envy of what has gone before, because of being unable to make a genuine break with it. Thus the greatness of the early part of the twentieth century would seem to carry in its bloodstream the seeds of decadence.

FOOTNOTES

[1]Gellner (1958) has brought out very sharply that Wittgenstein's later philosophy is functionalism (in the anthropological sense), with all the difficulties this encounters when taken to be central and universal.

[2]The question should be considered whether Austin (and ?Wittgenstein) might have broken new ground, instituted a new form of philosophy. For though Austin seems to be solely (a) attacking others by his linguistic analysis, and (b) claiming to solve old problems thus, e.g. epistemology by his theory of the use of "know", he *might* nonetheless, though these attempts were fallacious, be developing a new idea (from which the above targets and fallacies distracted attention): namely an anthropology of language in the sense of studying the social role of key words, e.g. finding that the social role of "know" is "commitment". Where such a study might lead I do not know, or whether it would lead anywhere. But I do not know (!) it would lead nowhere. So, if we are not to put a priori confines on new conceptions of philosophy, we should leave it open as a possible new one for those it interests. Criticism should be, not that it is not philosophy, but that it has nothing to do with philosophy in existing forms (at most it would amount to a new style of presenting an argument against essentialism).

With regard to Wittgenstein, who is widely regarded as conducting a defence against being mislead by the grammar of our language, a positive aim is ascribed to him by Cavell (1966), namely the pursuit of self-knowledge by studying its boundaries due to this grammar.

[3]This has been exhaustively gone into by Gellner (1959).

[4]And probably almost every tyro in logic, and even intellectual learning to use his intellect, will possess a streak of showing others up.

[5]Gellner (1959) was the first philosopher in contemporary times to point to the strategy and tactics of linguistic philosophy from a sociological angle. This is taken up here at a somewhat different level.

[6]In tilting against Alciphron, I am not supporting the somewhat self-righteous Euphranor.

[7]Neither the assessment of language analysis nor the reaction to Victorianism are relevant to European existentialism, which is taken in positivistic and linguistic circles to be a decadence because of its woolliness and lack of argumentation or not really philosophy at all because of its alogical subject-matter (could this turn out to be the grand error of the century?).

REFERENCES

Cavell, Stanley (1966), "The Availability of Wittgenstein's Later Philosophy", *Wittgenstein: the Philosophical Investigations*, Ed. Pitcher.

Gellner, Ernest (1958), "Time and Theory in Social Anthropology", *Mind*, **67**, 183–4.

CHAPTER XXII

The Place of Goals and Motives in Philosophy

The various modes described are ways of handling different types of questions. It is easy to understand the raison d'être of metascience and the ontology of science, and easy, at least up to a point, to understand epistemology, perhaps including the epistemological form assumed by logical positivism. And in a different way it is easy to make sense of the question of the way of life. What gives rise to difficulty is cosmological ontology (including parascientific ontology), because of the elusive nature of the questions involved in that there is no way of answering them nor yet a means of disposing of them.

By bringing to light the possibility of extra-philosophical goals, we have before us a new raison d'être for the questions of cosmological ontology, i.e. for the most central kind of metaphysics. Thus a philosopher, and even a school, may be struggling with a personal problem such as a barrier of communication with fellow men. It was not suggested that philosophers have been conscious of such goals; on the contrary it was suggested that they generally are not. In rare cases, however, they seem to have been conscious of them. Goals, or their cognate, motives, that are not usually conscious but may sometimes be conscious or may become conscious are not what Freud regarded as unconscious. He introduced the notion of the preconscious for this level. The unconscious proper, however, is regarded as a deeper level and a different kind of level, for it concerns phantasies that have at no time been conscious and that cannot become conscious unmodified. We thus have the notion of unconscious goal or of unconscious motive.

We have now examined and illustrated or noted the following types of goals/motives :

> Subsidiary goals
> Subordinate goals
> Penultimate goals
> Ultimate goals
> Extra-philosophical goals/motives
> Unconscious motives/goals

The first four are not too difficult to sort out approximately. They form a perspective of *philosophical* goals. And they concern *goals* because they concern *problems* to which a *solution* is sought or offered, or because they concern *principles* or *methods* for which *validity* or *applicability* is sought or offered. There is a rationale which lies in a problem (or question) or a heuristic challenge; and this is to be located in the *intellectual situation*.

An intellectual challenge can lie objectively in the intellectual situation; for the overall situation to which a certain problem points, whether of explanation or of discovery, is to be found, even if not always fully articulated, in books and journals, set against the warp and weft of relevant existing knowledge *and* the gaps in it. This is so even though the human race has disappeared, provided libraries survive (Popper, 1972).

The articulation of a problem or the way the problem is seen depends upon the existence of a human being. This is so whether the problem is one of physics or of philosophy.

Not every specialist in some area of a broad field will recognize the problem fully or be particularly interested in a particular problem. There is something individual about the person who takes it up. There is something individual about the way he transforms it. There is something individual about the novelties he brings to bear on it. There is something individual about the respects in which his solutions fall short (given that they are objectively in the situation as he transforms it, i.e. "within his grasp").

Thus a scientist or a philosopher tackles a problem as a result of his character (or preconscious nature), his way of seeing things (or preconscious disposition), and his originality (or preconscious type of creativeness), and his defects (or preconscious guilt, anxiety, inhibitions, or water-tight compartments).

I have exhibited a number of philosophers as tackling a problem in a way that betrays a barrier of communication between them and their fellows. Their philosophies both manifest this deficiency in their lives and also constitute a fantasy world in which the lack is made good, i.e. in which there is an attempted wish-fulfilment of the wish for fellowship. In this they were also reflecting a generalized, characteristic, social need extending over centuries and dominating the lives of most philosophers.

This finding sets us a further question: why this phenomenon? In answering this, we are inevitably led into investigating other individual features of each philosopher; and we are forced to go below the preconscious to unconscious factors. We could, of course, go directly to these without the intervening step of explicating the preconscious goals. But to leave out this intermediate investigation can make a man's philosophy look deprived of all rationality, and this is misleading and unnecessary. The unconscious level provides us with an explanation of the choice of problem, or goal, and of the philosopher's need to tackle it, in terms of his unconscious "problem" or inner world.

What reason can be offered for supposing that unconscious motives are relevant to the raison d'être of philosophy? A problem opens up, either directly because we want to explain the extra-philosophical goal and therefore seek the explanation in the unconscious of the philosopher, or less straightforwardly because, if, for example, a cosmological ontology seems wholly unrealistic, we are at a loss to understand how it came to be. In either case the philosophy would seem to be an unconscious autobiography.

Lest anyone should suppose that such an approach should be inherited from the mystics, it is worth drawing attention to a sober ancestor.

Several moralists have recommended it as an excellent method of becoming acquainted with our own hearts, and knowing our progress in virtue, to recollect our dreams in a morning, and examine them with the same rigour, that we would our most serious and deliberate actions. Our character is the same throughout, say they, and appears best where artifice, fear, and policy have no place, and men can neither be hypocrites with themselves nor others. The generosity, or baseness of our temper, our meekness or cruelty, our courage or pusillanimity, influence the fictions of the imagination with the most unbounded liberty, and discover themselves in the most glaring colours. In like manner, I am persuaded, there might be several useful discoveries made from a criticism of the fictions of the ancient philosophy, concerning substances, and substantial forms, and accidents, and occult qualities; which, however unreasonable and capricious, have a very intimate connexion with the principles of human nature.

And this remarkable passage comes from Hume, in his most important philosophical work, and must therefore have been read by innumerable philosophers.[1] I have given several examples of investigations of unconscious motives elsewhere. (Wisdom, 1945; 1947; 1947a; 1953.)

Let us come closer to what problems the unconscious origin is relevant. It begins by being invoked to explain mistakes, gaps, incompleteness—in a word shortcomings, though shortcomings not as measured by ideals but in terms of what might reasonably have been achieved by the potential of the author with the facilities available and the knowledge of his time. An additional form of incompleteness could arise if an author failed to utilize ideas available in his circle. The unconscious origin continues by being invoked to explain why a certain problem (or, more weakly, topic, area, theme) was selected for study. The first hints at psychopathology; the second need not. Is there more to be asked of the unconscious origin? Specifically, can it be invoked to explain in a certain way an author's interest in a theory and, as developed by him, the theory itself? What light can it throw either on a theory or on an author when he deals realistically with a real problem?

One point, though not fundamental, is yet important. The unconsious origin in such a situation would have to be such that the author can draw only on the reservoir of unconscious factors available to him from his own unconscious. Given that he selects well, i.e. is able to handle his objective problem, it might seem that this selection can throw no light on his own mental make-up. This is to exaggerate. It tells us something about his mental make-up; but in view of the constraint to use the factor effectively in connection with an objective problem, it may not tell us the most significant things about him; and in particular it may not reflect the more pathological aspects of his nature. Thus, the more realistic is the use made of his mental potentialities, the less sure can we be of what it signifies about his nature, from the point of view of gaining a *balanced* perspective.

Now this is not the most fundamental issue, for it *presupposes* that an unconscious origin can be sought in an author dealing with an objective problem and even lacking a pathology. Is this possible? Apart from the interest of following the unconscious psychical processes involved, it would be conceptually very awkward if this were not possible. For, before we could legitimately start to investigate the unconscious origin of a theory, we should have to determine what parts of the theory were realistic and what parts had shortcomings (and the unconscious factors relevant to the shortcomings would be barred by an iron curtain from being applied to the healthy parts). Such an outcome does not disprove the restriction, but it makes the restriction unplausible.

We now reach the largest claim: that the unconscious origin can explain the details of the concepts of a theory and their interrelationships. Let us look at this from the perspective of objections. It might seem as though theory can have no explanation other than the function it is designed to fulfil. But it seems natural enough that a person might use for making a realistic and highly functional theory the ideas he was most fond of; and this would be a psychological process.

But then we need to understand the connection between the functional explanation of a theory, which consists in its being designed to solve an objective problem, and the psychical explanation of its make-up. An analogue would be that certain properties of a phenotype are explained both by interaction with the environment and also by genetic coding. Thus there would seem to be no incompatibility in having an unconscious explanation of a theory that has a rational role in solving an objective problem.

Now, in advance of making any investigation at all into the unconscious origin or explanation of a philosophy, we know that for any human product there must be a psychical explanation (unless we are epiphenomenalists), but we might expect to find only a concatenation of instincts, drives, impressions, images, associations, just put together in an odd way. What is unique about a psychodynamic investigation is the psychical *meaning* of the underlying factors and the extraordinary parallelism to be found between a man's philosophy and his dreams or unconscious inner world, which has led me to call philosophy an unconscious autobiography (Wisdom, 1947).

An unsolved problem arises here, to explain why the unconscious conflict should seek out a philosophical expression rather than some other (which is a particular case of the unsolved problem of the "choice of neurosis").

The next question that arises is whether these preconscious and unconscious constructions throw any light on the philosophies manifesting them. This question may be broken down into questions to do with the truth or falsity of a philosophy, its meaning, and its being undecidable by rational enquiry.

As regards the question of truth and falsity, the "genetic fallacy" is well understood: that tracing a view to its origin does nothing to invalidate it. And this is important. But some qualification is needed.

When I first began to enquire into the unconscious origin of philosophy, the problem that puzzled me was this. Logical positivism (which was in its hey-day) said that metaphysics was meaningless; I could not understand how so many great intellects had managed to understand so much that was meaningless, discuss it rationally with their colleagues, and make modifications that commanded rational assent (or dissent). I came to realize that the positivist contention was, however, a tautology: metaphysics is indeed meaningless in the positivistic sense of "meaningless", i.e. having no bearing on perceptual experience; also that this should have been obvious, because metaphysicians never would have defiled their metaphysics by allowing that it could have a bearing on perceptual experience, for they would have insisted on a "transcendental" meaning. Positivists had at least, however inadvertently, drawn attention to the difficulty of grasping or articulating transcendental meaning. And I came to the conclusion that it might refer to a transcendental world in the sense of a world picture as a projection of a philosopher's own unconscious structure.

Now it was clear that this did not *disprove* a philosophy; it explained the need to have a philosophy that otherwise claimed or seemed to claim to say nothing about the world.

Despite this, however, the unconscious investigation did seem to have an *undermining effect:* if you show that a philosopher was pre-occupied with an anxiety about potency or castration, one wonders about the stability and reliability of the views that stem from such a pathology. No disproof; but confidence is shaken. Consider a colleague on a committee whom you suspect of having an ulterior motive in making a certain proposal; you are somewhat dubious for *this* reason about the merits of the proposal. You do not throw it out, because it could be a very good one even though put forward for an ulterior motive; but you check up on it more carefully than you otherwise might. Again, you distrust an idea put forward by someone known to be rather incompetent or lacking in relevant knowledge; his idea may be sound but you are right to be additionally careful. What the matter comes down to in the present context is whether a man's unconscious conflicts do or do not swamp his attempt to deal with a real problem. In the case of philosophy, there is no standard method for checking up; so the unconscious investigation serves to confirm the impression that the philosophy has no objective content or meaning, says nothing about the world, is neither true nor false, simply by finding an alternative raison d'être for it. The reservation remains that such a conclusion would have to be altered if someone were to find a way in which philosophy informs us about the world; in other words, the undermining effect of the unconscious investigation depends upon the (presumed) absence of any way of deciding upon the objective validity of a philosophy.

It must be possible for a "realistic" venture like a physical theory to have an unconscious origin, just as with a philosophy. The point is that the unconscious origin does not disprove the theory.

What light may be thrown upon a philosophy by investigating its unconscious origin?

The first obvious claim is biographical. We should learn something about the philosopher which we could not learn in any other way. Thus we may find convincing grounds for thinking that Descartes was not guilty of hypocrisy in religion; or that there was a split between his sentiment towards women and his sexuality. Then we may be induced to seek tests: we may look again or further in the philosopher's life for evidence bearing on this. Thus an understanding of the man is more within our grasp.

Does this heighten an understanding of his philosophy? The well-known musicologist, Ernest Newman, maintained that some music could not be adequately understood without coming to grips with extra-musical factors about the composer. Is this kind of claim—in the philosophical field—at all true?

It is easy to see that a more balanced perspective can be obtained.

Thus, if in the classroom we teach Leibniz as the inventor of the monad who tried to solve the mind-body problem by a principle of pre-established harmony, and the problem of evil by the contention that this is the best of all possible worlds, we shall lose sight of his picture of the City of God, and get his philosophy out of focus. Moreover, we shall understand his philosophy not merely as an intellectual venture but as the outcome of the evils which he felt to be overwhelming. Popper is fond of pointing out that Kant was not concerned with an artificial exercise in epistemology but that he faced the devastatingly difficult problem of understanding how Newtonian science was possible, and that we fail to understand Kant's philosophy if we divorce it from its setting in philosophy of science. True. Likewise I think we fail to grasp the fulness of Leibniz's philosophy if we do not understand it as the philosophy of a man dismayed by vanities and evils, and constantly haunted by certain horrors. Leibniz—and also Spinoza—was saying that the universe is "all of a piece", and that we are all, as elements reflecting or in causal connection with the rest, equally responsible for what goes on in it, and that we have to accept our position in it. This is in Leibniz's philosophy, but is not easily discernible without the unconscious' being investigated; and I think it considerably alters our understanding even of the content of the philosophy.

Thus the investigation of goals and motives adds to our biographical understanding of men, correcting misassessments or resolving questions of assessment, enables us to see a philosophy in better perspective, even to seeing the problem of that philosophy differently (and more adequately).

All this places the focus on *understanding,* rather than on the question of truth and falsity. But it bears on this question also. Despite the necessity to acknowledge the genetic fallacy—and I have continued to regard it as decisive—too much *awe* of it can lead us to overlook something so that the respect for the genetic fallacy can lead to a one-sided assessment. For a knowledge of preconscious and unconscious motives can legitimately *undermine* a philosophy in the sense of leading us to suspect it, to suspect it of saying nothing about the world, a suspicion we may then look into further to see whether it is objectively undecidable—although, and here we again pay heed to the genetic fallacy, the *undermining fails* if we find an objective function in the philosophy. And investigations into unconscious structures can point to whether the structure is inherently pathological or oriented maturely towards a real conflict in real life.

APPENDIX

LAZEROWITZ'S INTERPRETATION OF METAPHYSICS

Professor Morris Lazerowitz is practically the only philosopher I know of who has given an interpretation of metaphysics with a strong family resemblance to the one I have put forward, though it could be said that many years ago Carnap threw out a hint of something similar. Despite the family resemblance, however, there is also a considerable difference, at least about one fundamental particular, and as Lazerowitz has given a very full and closely reasoned, not to mention finely written argument, I wish to present his view, bring out the difference, and give the reasons for my different assessment. Lazerowitz names and discusses at length five interpretations which he discerns throughout history in the literature on the nature of metaphysics, all of which with cogent argument he rejects. (i) The first deals with metaphysics as empirical. The upshot is that no observation is allowed by metaphysicians to count against a metaphysical proposition, hence no such proposition is empirical. (ii) The next concerns metaphysics as a priori. He holds "there cannot be a priori descriptions of natural phenomena" because these make no difference to our knowledge of any fact about the world. (It deserves more than a passing mention that this part of his discussion takes no account of synthetic a priori propositions.) (iii) He regards as inadequate a conventional current view according to which metaphysics is verbal. One reason he gives is that if this were true it should be a straightforward matter to resolve philosophical disputes. (iv) This concerns the former positivistic view that metaphysics is nonsense, because it condemns a metaphysical statement for referring to realities beyond our experience instead of conforming to the positivistic requirement of relating to our sense-experience; the positivistic requirement he regards as arbitrary.

We come to Lazerowitz's own sixth interpretation, according to which metaphysics is rooted in linguistic innovations.

He points out very clearly that in metaphysics certain key terms are not used in their ordinary sense; they are therefore innovative. I take this for granted without the need for further argument. His interpretation then involves three parts. (1) Metaphysics purports to state a view of reality produced by altering the use of words, i.e. produced by linguistic innovations. (2) These innovations are concealed—not only from the reader but from their author. (3) Metaphysics is empirical in another way, by being an empirical description of an *unconscious* view of reality.

As regards the first of these as mentioned above, I think metaphysics not merely purports to but actually does state a view. Lazerowitz has expressed the third one very happily; the content of it he partly attributes to interpretations of particular pieces of metaphysics, which I have put forward on various occasions, and partly to his own investigation of the psychology of change, which he deals with at length, eliciting many interesting and pertinent factors.

I would, however, add a qualification about the first component of his interpretation. If it is true that metaphysics hinges in some way on linguistic innovation, it does not follow that metaphysics is even in part brought about by linguistic innovation. Nothing said so far precludes the following alternative: a commonplace point of view cannot be expressed otherwise than in some language; neither can metaphysics; innovative language may very well be no more than a vehicle for a theory. Certainly in a roundabout way language influences our thinking and attitudes, points of view, and so forth, as all institutions do; but this is not to say that metaphysical linguistic innovations constitute a creative force in producing metaphysical ideas, for the vital factor may lie simply in the attitude built up.

Much as I agree with a good deal of what Lazerowitz has contended for, the respect in which I differ from him concerns the second component of his view. It is clear that language that is both innovative and a disguise constitutes for Lazerowitz confusion. (So his interpretation of metaphysics could be expressed as linguistic confusion, together with unconscious motivation). It is this that I would cast doubt upon. One could justly claim that advances in natural science are impossible without linguistic innovation. Indeed those who have not gone carefully into matters of science can scarcely be aware of the enormous extent of linguistic innovation involved. But an inspection of a few examples will probably be enough to convince most readers that this has had nothing to do with the generation of theories. One example would be the term straight line in non-euclidean geometry and relativity physics. Here, however, the innovation might not have been concealed, so let us look to one of the oldest and time-honoured examples, namely the Newtonian conception of force in celestial mechanics; but I very much doubt if anyone realized until modern times that there was an innovation, and a very great one, in the use of the term.

The difference between Lazerowitz's view and mine might be expressed in a broader way. Lazerowitz seems to retain a general principle from logical analysis, logical positivism, language analysis: that the confusion, or alternatively lack of reference of a term, can be elicited by a philosophical examination of the use of the terms. To my mind, however, innovation, concealment, possible confusion are wholly irrelevant; and the question of reference is to be determined in a wholly different way, namely, by testing consequences (or, in other cases, by enquiring whether they are consequences of testable theories, for it has been my contention that some metaphysical views are refutable in the latter way). These metaphysical views are thus not confusions but simply false. This way of handling the matter would also cover the one interpretation of metaphysics that Lazerowitz missed out, namely, that it consists of synthetic a priori propositions. I have, I hope, shown that some such cases, when we are particularly fortunate, can be refuted by a testable and corroborated scientific theory, so that they are not innovative or confusions but simply false.

In short, my view is that the metaphysician is constructing a fantasy about the world, and to do this he has to do several things, one being to make linguistic innovations in order to express what he has in mind.

REFERENCES

[1]But it may have been missed. It was kindly pointed out to me by H. H. Price. Another interesting passage comes from Plato's *Republic* (Bk. 9, 571), where he remarks that in our dreams one can see or commit the most horrible deeds, such as intercourse with one's mother, or man, god, or brute. How many of the thousands if not millions of those who have read the *Republic* have somehow missed this passage? I am indebted for it to Sir Karl Popper.

BIBLIOGRAPHY

Lazerowitz, Morris (1955), *The Nature of Metaphysics*, London.
Popper, K. R. (1972), *Objectve Knowledge: an evolutionary approach*, "Epistemology without a Knowing Subject", Oxford University Press, London, 106–52, esp. 108.
Wisdom, J. O. (1945), "The Unconscious Origin of Schopenhauer's Philosophy", *International Journal of Psycho-Analysis*, 26.
———————— (1947), "Three Dreams of Descartes", *International Journal of Psycho-Analysis*, 28, reprinted in *The Yearbook of Psycho-Analysis*, New York, 1948, Vol. 4.
———————— (1947a), *The Metamorphosis of Philosophy*, Cairo.
———————— (1953), *The Unconscious Origin of Berkeley's Philosophy*, Hogarth Press & Institute of Psycho-Analysis, London.

Part IV

PHILOSOPHY AS A SOCIAL AND PERSONAL
WELTANSCHAUUNG

CHAPTER XXIII

The Idea of Culture and the Role of Philosophy

CERTAIN PHYSICAL things like the climate or indigenous types of food help to shape the nature of man. The interaction is two-way. The orang-outang, for example, alters his environment when he eats a nut and throws away the husk, or a herd when it eats away the grasses, or uses a river as a bathroom. These activities are, of course, deliberate but the aim has nothing to do with the environment but only with the animal himself. That is to say, the activities are not deliberate attempts to alter the environment. Thus, a significant early phase of culture arose when man began to reconstruct his environment for his own ends, not instinctively as in nest-building, but with deliberate intent. Discovery of fire was no doubt accidental but the attempt to imitate outbreaks of fire by making them was not accidental. Let us imagine a man first trying to make fire. Other men had not thought of doing so. But they saw him do it. Whatever meaning fire had for them when it occurred by accident naturally would be there also when seen to be made by one of them. Whether it was magical or useful, they would then try to make fire, too. Tasks like this would tend to promote identification. The group would feel as one, at least as regards the fire-making. Now this development could not have taken place if only one man had the conception of making fire, and if the others watching were unable to have the conception even after being shown it. Another way of saying this is that the members of the group would have to have the conception, at least potentially, if fire-making was to be institutionalized. Otherwise, one man might make fire and when he died, fire-making would no longer occur. Thus, fire-making presupposes a certain level of conceptualization among members of a group and cannot be explained as a purely individual activity.

But this is not the beginning of culture. What we have at this stage is a group of men, having some primitive potentiality for conceptualization. Now before making fire or the like, men made tools of a more primitive kind. Fire is no doubt a tool which can be used to cook meat. But more primitive tools did exist in the form of clubs with which to attack other men. There would have been a phase in which a club was in some degree fashioned, maybe a branch of a tree would have been rubbed against a rock so as to alter its shape and made it more effective. And this again would have been a basis for identification among members of the group—making in a highly significant sense for club-membership. But even club-membership presupposes some primitive degree of conceptualization. Prior to that would have come the first phase of clubbery, consisting simply in picking up a stone or a branch of a tree and belabouring someone with it. In such circumstances, the environment would not be deliberately remodelled. Some degree of conceptualization is present even here, however, and even if it is the most primitive possible, it is still remarkable. It involves the notion, however intuitive, that a piece of wood or stone can be used as an extension of one's arm for additional strength, for use near at hand and even at a distance if thrown. This is no mean imaginative achievement, and it involves the idea of something which is not present.

There does not seem to be much place for identification between members of a group in such circumstances. The actual use of the club would arise perhaps in response to an urge of hunger or sex. One man might want to take away another man's dinner or his female. We can hardly find in this sufficient ground for identification. Here I think we can no longer seek identification in pursuit of a common task; for roots we must go back on something of a different kind, namely to those factors of identity and difference that cement groups of similar animals together into one herd.

In the phase discussed above, however, the focus is not on herd animal-identity, but on a cultural identity, springing in the first place from a common task.

Given a group, then, cemented culturally in some such way as this, what are the main factors that affect the lives of its members? As before, we have the environmental factors such as climate and type of food available. But our interest focusses on the cultural influences, all the more as the cultural influences enable man to control to some extent the environmental influences. For instance, if the climate is bad, he can build a roof over his head. Before leaving this, however, we should take note of a highly significant environmental factor which is not amenable to control for a very long time, namely disease. For it is an enemy that is concealed and mysterious, not open to the view like another man with a club.

What, then, are the chief types of factors that influence the cultural behaviour of man? Here is a list: hunger, sex, self-defence, power, possession, fear, unseen powers, law, custom, hope, self-respect, position, achievement, need for fun, companionship, concern for others, need for children, exercise of skills, appropriate degree of social, political, and individual freedom, appropriate degree of tradition, knowing where one stands with respect to each of the above, role and goal of man.

These may be conveniently classified as follows : environmental, bodily needs, political, religious, legal, social, human relations, gamboling, ideals, identity, knowing the system.

What influences dominate?

There have been several notable instances of pre-eminent thinkers supporting one factor to the exclusion of others. Thus, some have held that everything is accountable in terms of organic processes, rooted in instinct. In other words, all human behaviour is explainable in terms of neuro-physiology. Again, Marx held that all human behaviour was determined by economic causes. Adler held that power, in the sense of the wish to dominate others, was the decisive factor. Freud located it in sex and defence. Hobbes attributed it to a need to obviate a war of all against all. Strangely enough, one of the most important, strongest, and most decisive factors of all in governing the behaviour of groups and societies has, from the beginning, till say 1945, been religion, and it is a question of some interest why this should be underplayed now. Once the point has been made, it seems so evident as not to be worth spelling out at length.

What does need spelling out is the relationship between religious inferences and other factors, if, as I assume, no one of these factors is the only significant one, not even religion, if indeed it is the most important. The enormous role of economic factors, likewise, seems hardly worth emphasizing. The influence is visible all around us. And I suppose it is more or less understandable that people should think it is, at bottom, the decisive influence. But this is clearly false because it is possible to adduce counter-examples in which economic sacrifices are made for other ends. It is noteworthy, for example, that economic sanctions have proved ineffective in international relations. One knows of a non-economic motive that dominated the economic sanctions between the United Kingdom and Ireland in which, as was easily predictable by anyone who knew the country, Ireland refused to give way under economic pressure. The United Kingdom itself was prepared to make stupendous economic sacrifices rather than give way to Hitler, and history is full of such examples. Apart from counter-examples of this kind, there is the general fact that economic gain is, after all, for some non-economic purpose, which may be enjoyment, prestige, development of culture, etc. And in addition there is the very general kind of counter-example consisting in the fact that people as individuals and to a very small extent in history, people as groups, will make economic sacrifices for others. In other words, altruism both as an individual and a social phenomenon is incompatible with, and a counter-example to, the theory of economic determinism. Despite these three reasons, however, while economic determinism is not the sole factor, it does remain an outstandingly important one. In a somewhat similar way, it is fairly easy to see that the other factors considered play an important role but not an over-riding one.

Now, religion does seem to be somewhat different in that it has dominated virtually all peoples, and the direct influence of it upon their lives, customs, economics even, and so on, is very easy to see. Yet it is clear that even religion is not the sole decisive factor. What it constitutes is a control, meting out sanctions both positively and negatively, that is to say, it affords permission for some activities and prohibition for others. Its role is no doubt extremely complex, but one obvious feature of its role is that it reflects mankind's helplessness before the task of controlling, broadly speaking, his sexuality and aggressiveness. The outcome is that no one of this mixed bag of factors is over-riding. It is, perhaps, worth mentioning that sociology is sometimes thought of as providing the basic answer. This, of course, is not true, if sociology is understood as the collection of all these components nor is it true if sociology is understood in a specific sense as the study of the relations between institutions or their historical origin. There may or may not be a fundamental societal explanation embracing some or all of these as individual components, but if there is, it has not so far been discovered.

Given, then, that culture is made up in some such way as that described, whether or not there is a fundamental societal theory to explain it, the present focus is on the relationship of philosophy to these various components. It clearly underpins some of them. Indeed, a carefully worked-out case might well be developed to show that it underpins all of them, but it will suffice for present purposes to show that it is deeply engaged in one or two of them.

Thus, consider organicism or physiologism. This amounts to the a priori policy that no theory endowing mentality or society with autonomous power to operate is conceivable, and that such entities merely reflect the real causal efficacy lying in the organic world. This is a philosophy rather than an empirical theory in the sense that it does not consist of empirical content, empirically testable, or empirically refutable by observation. (The doctrine is indeed extraordinarily unrealistic and dull to anyone who is concerned with significant problems about human beings and society, and it is a social question of some interest to find out why so many able intellects have been indoctrinated by it, just as it is an interesting question why many of the high-level physicists and philosophers of Galileo's time refused to listen to the evidence he wished to put before them.)

Perhaps the most obvious case of underpinning the approach to knowledge concerns religion or theology through hundreds or thousands of years. Till recent times this underpinning was obvious, but it has dropped out of notice since the end of World War II, and this may indeed provide two reasons why subsequent philosophy has become so thin and uninteresting. For religion itself has ceased to have a hold in a way unprecedented in previous history and therefore philosophy has lost one of the most important of the subjects it used to underpin. Secondly, philosophy has shown little desire to underpin something else instead.

On the other hand, there have been indications of underpinning in the field of social theory. Thus, the Nazis went to some trouble to have an official philosophy for their social theory of Aryanism. Also Communists continue with the philosophy of dialectical materialism. At the other end of the scale, Popper's work, *The Open Society and its Enemies*, may be regarded as a philosophical underpinning of liberalism or, as he has called it, the "philosophy of muddling through". This tendency, of course, is not entirely new. Hegel's philosophy was also interpreted politically, and clearly Plato's philosophy in the *Republic* and the *Laws* was a philosophy of what constituted the good society. The history of philosophy, however, has never been written from this angle, as though philosophy was not an underpinning of social theory; and in a certain important sense this is correct—it never was, for the chief field it underpinned was probably religion. Now, religion, in its turn, provided the structure justifiying the nature of society as it existed, so only at a second remove was philosophy such an underpinning. But with the great social changes, which have gathered momentum in the second half of the twentieth century, although they really started with the end of World War I, it is possible that philosophy might now take its place as a direct underpinning of the theory of society, and this is perhaps borne out by the growing use of phenomenology among sociologists.

Such a role for philosophy ascribes to it a position of great influence, namely that it shapes the kind of theories that shall occupy the attention of the learned, and in the end, of the unlearned.

But there is a two-way traffic. There is a feedback between philosophy and culture. Changes in culture can also lead to changes in philosophy.

Let us consider some examples. The development of cybernetics, centring on feedback mechanisms, has given an immense boost to neurophysiology and therefore encouraged an organicist theory of mind. On the other hand, the growth of psychosomatic medicine has worked precisely the other way round. Thus, the age-old philosophical problem of mind and body is in a state of flux. Again, it is quite possible that the uncertainty relations of quantum mechanics, the phenomenon of Brownian movement, and so forth, have shaken the attitude that determinism is the only thinkable outlook, and perhaps helped to reconcile philosophers to taking seriously the possibility that, in some significant sense or other, a man does have free choice, even if only on a modest scale. Decay of the influence of religion is probably responsible for banishing the problem of substance from the philosophical scene, where it occupied such an important place for several centuries. Quite probably, the great number of developments that favour relativism in one form or another—the misunderstood theory of relativity, the kind of equalitarianism that allows the central views of a primitive society to be just as valid as ours, the apparent impossibility of resolving questions of aesthetics or taste, or of finding any firm criteria for judging in these areas, discoveries that human action is either economically determined or determined by unconscious forces beyond our reach, and further such highly specific discoveries that even mathematical truth is not beyond the possibility of challenge—all these conclusions undermine the world of intellectual standards, leaving us without criteria of intellectual, moral, aesthetic, political or social judgement. So in a very real sense no one knows where he stands. Philosophy faithfully reflects this position not by producing great numbers of prophets, all with different and incompatible messages but simply by floundering and having nothing to offer at all.

Thus, the transactional relationship between philosophy and culture is to be seen not only in historical periods of social and intellectual stability but also in the twentieth-century social and intellectual flux and uncertainty.

CHAPTER XXIV

Philosophy as a World-Outlook
(Weltanschauung)

LET US cast our minds back to the seven modes of philosophizing. It is noteworthy that all of them have to do with enquiry. They may be right-headed or wrong-headed, but this was their activity. Natural science and epistemology have to do with the nature of knowledge in one way or another. The ontology of science, parascientific ontology, and cosmological ontology are all enquiries into the nature of the universe. Logical positivism or, as I have called it, meta-ontological negativism, is a negative ontology, based on a sceptical epistemology. Thus, it is concerned with the limits of what is knowable. The remaining mode—philosophy as a way of life—centres on the human predicament, but despite its dislike of norms does lay down a norm of free disingenuous living. I have set these modes out because they all seem to have been a genuine part of philosophical activity from the dawn or recorded philosophical history. That is to say, they were the deliberate enterprises of philosophers. In setting them out, I did not wish to suggest that philosophy had no other function. In fact, the whole tenor of the subsequent discussion seemed to unfold several other functions, which, however, had not been pursued by philosophers overtly.

In this way, philosophy has been revealed as subservient to individual goals, as autobiographical, as a powerful subterranean—powerful because subterranean—influence shaping individual and social attitudes concerning vital cultural factors, and as reflective of social outlook, even being expressly influenced by social attitudes and outlook.

Thus, in addition to philosophy as enquiry (assertions about the universe, claiming knowledge of it, and laying down how one shall act or live), I have also interpreted philosophy as reflective of the nature of man, philosophy as a king-pin of human and social goals, as a determinant of man's culture, and philosophy as reflective of the nature of society and moulded by it.

The two that reflect the nature of man and the nature of society constitute what I would call philosophy as a Weltanschauung. This does not include unconscious autobiography. It does embrace individual pre-conscious goals, and also social attitudes towards cultural factors. And about these, it covers both the general outlook that influences cultural factors and the general outlook that is the result of cultural factors. Thus, when Spinoza saw all the world as God-centred, with all mankind in communication, even communion with him, or when Leibniz saw the City of God in the same terms, these were individual instances of a Weltanschauung, i.e. the way these philosophers saw the world. It so happens, also, that this Weltanschauung was common to the period, was a social Weltanschauung. On the other hand, when the Copernican revolution was under way, this changed the Weltanschauung of the times from seeing God as the sole active cause of the fall of every leaf or every sparrow, and replaced it with a Weltanschauung in which God continued to be present, still in a significant way, either in the form of the one who started the celestial spheres rolling, or as one who, from time to time, intervened to obviate an untoward concatenation of circumstances, but apart from this, allowed the world a great measure of dominion status, responsible for its own physical affairs. Another example of a great change of Weltanschauung came about with seepage of Darwinism, which produced a Weltanschauung in which man no longer possessed a divine identity. A further great change of Weltanschauung is upon us now.

Although metaphysics in the sense of cosmological ontology, investigating for example such questions as the number of independent substances that compose the world, expresses a Weltanschauung, I do not think the philosophers engaged in these activities intended to portray their Weltanschauung, or the Weltanschauung of their times, or to create one. Their Weltanschauung emerges as a by-product of their more deliberate activities. The case may be somewhat different, however, with the philosophy of the way of life. This mode of philosophizing virtually presents a close connection between a way of life and a Weltanschauung; for to advocate a certain way of life is also to reveal how one sees the world, and conversely if one spells out how one sees the world, one implies a way of life. So the existentialists of the twentieth century have come nearest to being overtly connected with a Weltanschauung. And indeed there is no reason why a philosopher should not deliberately engage in the activity of depicting the Weltanschauung of the times as he interprets them (indeed, this book, among other things, is doing that), but he might even go on to advocate a certain Weltanschauung, urging in effect "this is how we ought to look upon the world". I do not say he would have any method or proof available to him for justifying his portrait, but that is no reason to prevent him putting his portrait before us for our consideration.

Such portrayals have, in fact, occurred, though in the eyes of many people in very disreputable circumstances and far removed from philosophy. Nonetheless, we should not overlook them. When Hitler put forward his programme for generating an Aryan race which would last for a thousand years, he had a vision. This is how he saw the world (and he was unfortunately within striking distance of bringing it off). Because a vision is bad, at least one that many of us would disapprove of, this does not mean that the vision does not exist or that it is not a Weltanschauung. Another example would be the Weltanschauung put forward by Marx. It was nearer to philosophy, for it was related to the political philosophy of Hegel and to the Hegelian metaphysic. This was the vision that the world would consist of a dictatorship by the proletariat. It would probably be unworkable in practice and even in principle, but that does not prevent its being a vision. Presumably King Charles I's claims in his *Eicon Basilike* amount to a Weltanschauung. The Middle Ages had a Weltanschauung with a very rigid social structure, centred on what was virtually a religious caste system. Perhaps it should be conceded that Plato's aim in his philosophy was to advocate a Weltanschauung of a patrician society ruled by philosopher kings (it is not clear to me why Plato was so keen on this for, although he never met the modern Alciphron, he certainly introduced a rather irresponsible cabinet minister into his *Republic* in the character of Thrasymachus), with a second level of power consisting of the Pentagon, General Motors, and influential families, all served by the third level provided by the child labour of the Lancashire cotton mills.

I would suggest that a fruitful way of trying to understand twentieth-century society as it has developed in the second half of the century would be to try to articulate its Weltanschauung.

Philosophy in this sense might be described as meta-culture.

CHAPTER XXV

The Downfall of Values
(Die Götterdämmerung)

PRESENT-DAY man has clearly lost his former Weltanschauung and is groping after a new one. Existentialism has filled this void to some extent, and even to some extent successfully. We are faced with the question why our Weltanschauung has tottered and how such a new growth as existentialism has come about. It seems to me that the pieces in this puzzle are few in number but that a historical cum social psychological theory is needed in order to put them together.

The historical component is this : from the dawn of recorded history, until comparatively recent times, man has always operated under the aegis of divinities, while now, for the first time for many thousands of years, this is in large measure no longer the case. We must now explore this phenomenon and draw out its implications.

In the western world of Judaism and Christianity—though also much more widely—it is particularly striking that man has endowed himself with a special status in the universe, privileged by divinities or a divinity or at least able to sway the divinities or divinity in his favour and, although a lesser breed than the divinities, regarded himself as to some extent partaking of the divine. Thus, he saw himself as part of a structure headed by a Great King, under whom came man's King, under whom in turn each man regarded himself as a little king, because, however humble his station, he regarded himself as lord over the beasts. No other creature in existence was accorded the status of being a king, however minor.

The divine hierarchical structure implied an essential difference between man and all other creatures; they possessed different essences.

The pride of place that this gave to man enabled him to put up with his lot, to put up with an unbelievable amount of slings and arrows of outrageous fortune. Whatever hovel he lived in, however low in the scale of respect from his fellows, he had the satisfaction of knowing that he was superior to the beasts in the eternal scale of being and also he "knew his place" in it. Therefore, whether he was low down or high up in the chain, he regarded it as part of the natural order of things that the lowly should render service to the lord of the manor. This needed no proof and any other idea would have been unthinkable, laughable, or heretical.

The hierarchical structure may even be spelled out more fully. Under the Great King, and then the King, come all the little kings, themselves with numerous gradations. First would come the nobility and gentry and closely allied with them would be the upper reaches of the priesthood and the armed forces, then would come the professional classes, merchants, business executives, white-collar workers, tradesmen, farmers, yeomen, and peasants. With a social structure divinely prescribed and universally intuitively understood, each would render to the other his due. Envy might be present but would not normally be manifest. Social manners would reflect these relationships and would be formed in such a way as to avoid introducing tensions. Indeed, the need to avoid tensions between social groups had operated to strengthen codes of manners and hence perpetuate the social structure.

A further consequence would be that each group would find itself with its own occupations and interests, that is, those that it was possible to pursue within the structure, and a group could develop its own scale of values within these activities. This could even lead to a value concerning the clothes that were worn. Thus, it would be wrong for one group to wear clothing that was appropriate to another group, either because it would be pretentious or because it would be demeaning. Each group would develop a pride associated with its own group based on superiority to the group below, but also, and very far from lacking in significance, from participation in or, if you like, identification with the group above. While this would have produced numbers of social requirements of a more or less moral flavour, e.g. a man might touch his forelock to the squire, there would also be various forms of what in other groups would be called moral laxity. Thus, petty pilfering from the squire would not raise an eyebrow among the group practising it (only it was desirable not to be caught).

Within a group it would be proper for each man to do the best he could for himself, but woe betide him if he tried to change groups or at least some groups. The reason for the lack of "social mobility" between groups is fairly obviously that it would have transgressed the notion of the fundamental structure and therefore been a threat to the entire system.

This is in keeping with another feature of enormous importance. It is, I think, a direct consequence of the social structure depicted that the social and economic doctrine of laissez-faire inevitably held sway. Whatever *is* forms part of the structure arising from divine ordinance, and to interfere with it is to interfere with the divinely prescribed order of nature and might even incur the wrath of the divinities or divinity.

It is even a natural consequence of the structure that scientific doctrines less closely related to society than that of laissez-faire might have restrictions put upon them. Thus, it would be more open to a group or an individual to study something harmless like mathematics or physics or astronomy, but only so long as it remained harmless, that is, that nothing came out of it that would conflict with the fundamental structure. Thus, it is clear that within such a social structure the natural sciences could flourish up to a point, but the social sciences would be likely to be stunted.

Thus, the divine hierarchial structure would have prescribed social stratification, fairly general rules of obligation between one group and another, the level responsible for government, the role of the clergy, and would even have led to codes for inter-group relations and for intra-group relations, and, of course, some form of "natural" law embodying these. Perhaps the most striking thing of all about divine hierarchical structure is the huge number of things that all men may take for granted within it, in a totally unquestioning way. You know what you wear, you know whom you salute, you know what you have to do on Sunday mornings, you know what you must do on weekdays, you know what obligations you must render by certain dates during the year to the lord of the manor, you know what rights you may exact from your tenants. You know more or less how far you can go; in short, you know where you stand, and within the divinely constructed hierarchical society, you have a clear-cut identity which is a particular form of your essence, man.

Let us turn now to the period of change. Structure began to crumble a little bit just before World War I and would probably have crumbled slowly and steadily had World War I not broken out, but the four years from 1914 to 1918 wrought havoc on this structure. The structure was not demolished, and what was left after 1918 continued for another quarter of a century with considerable, but not overwhelming, modification. World War II completed the disintegration——in the large that is, for there are many small pockets of the old structure that remain. Thus, manners are gone, inter-group relationships are gone, social structure has tremendous mobility, laissez-faire is gone, and most strikingly of all, the dynamism of religion has gone. Let us dwell on this last.

In bygone days, religion entered into the daily lives of people first in the sense that they considered, for example, what God would wish when they were about to take some important decision. It was not only that they considered religion in the case of an action which would have moral overtones, such as whether it would be right in the eyes of God to give a slave his freedom, but also actions lacking moral overtones, such as the choice of a career. Even in late Victorian days, many men and women would have asked themselves, about something they were contemplating, whether this was what God would approve of. After 1918 the situation was completely altered. A small proportion continued to go to the church services of their respective denominations and a slightly larger proportion would have retained some belief of a religious kind, perhaps rather abstract or attenuated. But the dynamism was gone. People's attitude toward religion was no longer one of *gut belief,* and so, while it is still part of the social system in some attenuated way, it is far from entering into the daily lives of people in the majority of western countries.

This historical assessment has no relation to the objective truth or any theological claims, nor in itself does it make any attempt to make a value judgement. Some would be nostalgic for the religion of the past, some would celebrate their release from it, some would hold, calmly or vehemently, that certain theological beliefs were true and others would hold, calmly or vehemently, that certain theological beliefs were false, but all these attitudes are irrelevant to the present point, which concerns only the sociological effects and nature of the change that has taken place, whether or not we like it. One practical matter should however be alluded to : though we may repine, it is in general impossible to put the clock back. So I make this historical assessment in the setting of the assumption that the areligious society has come to stay, at least for the foreseeable future of the short and middle term.

It remains to consider the causes of this sweeping change and its social consequences.

There were obviously many contributory causes. Some would point to the writings of Marx as being basic; others would point to Freud; some would mention Ibsen and Bernard Shaw; some would emphasize the disillusionment resulting from World War I; others might think the great advances of natural science centring on Einstein at the turn of the century were relevant. No doubt, all these influences played their part, and indeed I would think that Marx and Freud added very greatly to a change that was coming about; nonetheless I would consider that it was set in motion by a different influence altogether. The king-pin of the change, to my mind, lies in the Darwinian revolution.

If we go back to 1543 when Copernicus started the great revolution of physics and astronomy, what he did was to replace a Weltanschauung in which God and man were at the centre of the universe, not to mention the earth itself, by a new Weltanschauung in which the sun

H

was at the centre, and natural causes were supposed to operate without perpetual divine intervention. At least this was the development that took place at the hands of Galileo. It has often been remarked by historians, notably by Koyré, that the appalling impact of this revolution was to deprive man of his sense of dignity and importance in that he was no longer at the centre of the universe.

This revolution lasted well over a hundred years, but its aftermath persisted for 300 years. Then arose the Darwinian revolution. Whether it was right or wrong, the Weltanschauung of the Darwinian revolution consisted of the consanguinity of man and the animal kingdom, that is to say, man was not a distinct species from other animals, in the sense of being an essentially distinct species or a distinct essence, for, according to the theory, man evolved by degrees from some primate. This consequence would be devastating in a certain respects. While the Copernican revolution would make a dent in man's dignity, man would still remain some sort of a little king under God, but as a result of the Darwinian revolution he would cease to be God's lieutenant and instead find himself no more than the first of the beasts. It is easy to see that the ideas of Marx and Freud would find a ready soil here for further undermining man's belief in himself.

This dethroning of man in the sense that he became part of the "extended family" of the primates and no longer participated in the divine nature was bound to percolate down through all segments or layers of society. The message of that dreadful man Darwin, that we were descended from the apes, could hardly have escaped universal notice, and was bound to torpedo the social structure. Man no longer participated in the divine, so the divine could not save him from his fall; this would induce a loss of reliance on the divine, and gradually undermine the upper reaches of the hierarchical structure from the top downwards. It is, perhaps, no accident that constitutional monarchy was becoming a reality only about the same time as Nietzsche's message that "God is dead" began to be a social reality. Since then, there has been a steady erosion of the influence of the aristocracy and gentry; democratization of a social kind has taken place in a massive way. No doubt, in principle it should be possible for democracy, whether political or social, to exist with a structure in which people of different levels related to one another with mutual respect. The recent growth of social democracy does not seem to have conformed to this pattern. It seems to have depended on the undermining of the relationships of the different social groups. With this has come about the spread of mass education that is also an evidence of a decay, whether to be hailed or bemoaned, of the standard values of the preceding age. At least, there is a widespread *questioning* of former values and there is, indeed, a questioning of anything and everything. With this has come, and this is also a significant accompaniment, the end of laissez-faire, that is, social and economic. Time was when it would have been considered wrong to interfere with the natural order of things, even to save people. The Pharisaic Weltanschauung, for example, was clearly in evidence after the Irish famine when food was made available and imported into Ireland and obtainable through the usual merchant channels, but the afflicted starving and dying could not afford to buy it and, of course, the government could not interfere with nature by doing relief work. It is, perhaps, no coincidence that the economics of laissez-faire was swept away by Keynes shortly after the creation of the change being considered here.

But apart from all these consequences, there is one that is outstanding. Since the divine hierarchical structure has tottered, man cannot identify or participate in the social group above him, nor can he allocate to himself the status of being a little king above the group below him, and consequently he has lost his identity. Herein lies the twentieth-century identity crisis. All existing philosophies have sprung from a setting rooted in the divine hierarchical structure, and it is no coincidence that the downfall of this structure, the disintegration of its values, should be accompanied by two philosophies: one, existentialism, a desperate attempt to find a new way of life, the other the vacuous philosophical analysis, heir to the moribund philosophical tradition. A revolution in this area is slow in making a start—and it is slow also in the social sciences (except for psychoanalysis and economics). It would be hardly surprising if contemporary man were in search of a new Weltanschauung.

Die Götterdämmerung means the passing away of social structures of the following kind :—

DIVINELY ORDAINED SOCIAL STRUCTURE FOR COPERNICUS TO 1914

God as Super-king

Monarch as Great-king

Man as Little-king

Nobility and Gentry

Merchants

Yeomen

Peasants

Beasts

With consequential inter-group roles and observances regarded as axiomatic

CHAPTER XXVI

Ultimate Social Values: Current Options

IF THERE are now no *standard* values forming a more or less universally held Weltanschauung, this is not to say there are *no* values. Each person has his own; and so does each group. But confidence is lacking when they are group-relations: an individual does not know how far, how widely, they hold—which arouses a doubt about their validity. It may prove worthwhile to inquire what some of the more prominent sets of values in fact are, where "values" includes norms present or to be attained.

One set would seem to comprise the following:

PRAGMATIC SOCIAL STRUCTURE FROM 1918

A home

Sex

Large and increasing income

Fun

More gadgets

Being a good neighbour

Status symbols

Status in the eyes of neighbours

Status in the eyes of other groups significant to oneself

Prospects of increasing status

Individual power

Defence of one's group and individual rights against encroachment by others who have less

The right to hamper the development of rival groups

The norm that one would never do anything really shady

The norm that one's efforts are of value to the country

The norm that one's country is (making due allowances) one with high ideals

Another set would be :

INTERPERSONAL, IDENTIFICATION, SOCIAL STRUCTURE EMERGING FROM 1945

Sex

The materially good things of life

"Enough" is not enough

Instant results

High ideals of aid to mankind

Abolishing hypocrisy

Abolishing the power of the establishment

The need for guidance

No one shall tell one what to do

Resolving difficulties (individual, group, etc.) by honesty, confrontation, sensitivity interactions

Man (unmolested by authorities) is basically good, generous, harmless, helpful, willing to share

Irrelevance of parental attitudes

Modified loyalty to country (country not regarded as an ideal entity)

The norm that life must have a meaning

Intimate personal relations

There is a fundamental clash between pragmatic values and non-pragmatic ideals. The scientific revolution, from Copernicus in 1543 to 1914, with its social finale after the World War I, 1918 to 1939, with part II of the finale, presto vivace, 1945 onwards, has meant the gradual ascendency of pragmatism over God. Pragmatism proves empty on its own, when lacking idealistic supports. The search for an ideal is felt to be desperate when God is no longer accepted as a value. It becomes easy to oscillate between striving for an ideal and, feeling this to be futile, to slump back into a despondent pragmatism.

To preserve perspective, it must be recalled that pragmatism has been one of the most powerful instruments of freedom and of good that has ever been tried. Born in America, as a result of the frontiership that helped to consolidate the nation, it resulted in the outlook of the 'good neighbour', dropped many (though not enough) persecutions because these did not pay, and was a philosophy that valued change (America being the only country that actually likes change). An element of pragmatism is still and probably always will be needed. But it has to some extent outlived its usefulness (and therefore Hegelianwise ought to acquiesce in its own demise)—that is to say, as an overriding Weltanschauung. It has filled the belly in North America and also in Western Europe where it has spread[1] (even the "poor" are not poor as this has been experienced from the beginnings of man). But the owner of a full belly very, very, soon forgets what it is like to be hungry, comes to feel he has got nothing really. In fact, he feels empty! And he is right. Now that he no longer has to go out with his bow and arrow to do his shopping or else he will have no lunch, he has time enough to realise (assisted by relinquishing his hunting interests) that life has no meaning. "You never had it so good" quoth the Welfare State. True. But consider the two top cases. One is a small country which has given the impression of deep unhappiness and the other is a larger small country which for many years gave the impression of having lost all initiative. This is not to say that the ideal of a welfare state is a mistake. It is to say that without the welfare state, a country is not in a position to face its real misery and advance to a new stage by coping with it. Pragmatism removes a few real aches and pains, only to reveal that, important though they are, they are of minor significance. The success of the policy of pragmatism, which at the same time renders it no longer necessary, it to uncover the deeper aches and pains.

Pragmatism is also responsible for the disastrous split that pertains in the social sciences. A policy is often adopted because it is economically profitable, because however unfortunate in itself, it is a "political necessity" to ensure an important end (such as the selection of an American Vice-president or the burning of Joan of Arc), or even because it is a social sop springing from generosity, without enough regard to its appropriateness. This kind of sectarian use of technological applications of the sciences must flourish so long as we are not clear, and to a fairly large extent united, about our values.

The first set of values listed centred on : pleasure, possessions, status, power, maintenance of status quo, and a shadowy retention of ideals. It is pragmatism and rejects the ancient Weltanschauung of the divinely ordained social structure. The second set of values listed centred on :

fun, instant satisfaction of wants, abolition of mentors (hypocrisy, establishment, laws, parents, etc.) and antonomy of the self, care for the deprived, and finding the focus of life in human relationships (achieved by "honest expression of feeling" in group relationships). The second set, then, wants to be irresponsible, and also to be responsible in a new way, the way of human "involvement".

Let no one merely criticize this for being contradictory—the first set would reveal contradiction if looked at closely, for the fact that it is not blatant does not mean it is not present. To *study* the contradiction, however, is most relevant. It is a pointer to a split attitude about aims. And the split is a sign of the straits people are in. The story of mankind is a story of conflicting aims, but not always in so stark a form as now.

There exists, therefore, a stark clash of value-systems, which may be crudely expressed as pragmatism versus ideals and involvement. This is not basically a clash between thirty-five year olds and twenty year olds (though it occurs there); for it is internal to the twenty year olds. Thus there are plenty of these who align themselves with the older pragmatists they hope to become. But the clash is even more internal, in that it exists within the new idealists themselves. If Cromwell advised his troops to put their trust in God but keep their powder dry, the new idealist with his eye on a vision, distant or instant, also looks over his shoulder at what he might regard as traditional pragmatic temptations.

Clearly the new idealism has a huge momentum and clearly the pragmatic undertow is deeply entrenched. Clearly there is no simple resolution and clearly the clash will be with us for a long time to come. What will emerge may be unpredictable; but on the way we may expect a see-saw effect with each philosophy temporarily in the ascendency.

What is the role of rationality? It is easy to suppose that where ideologies are concerned, rationality must be wholly impotent. And this may even be made part of a Weltanschauung, in the form that it dehydrates involvement. The issue assumes a different hue if we follow the suggestion that rationality has to do not so much with the logical deployment of supports for a position as with raising significant questions. The same? To every answer there is a question, but it is not necessarily the case that to every question there is an answer. And, more important, finding a significant question, answerable or not, may alter a situation.

We are surrounded by great numbers of clever people who can argue well and raise good questions about the working parts of some system under discussion, and this is of enormous value for the development of the system. It is more rare to get questions—at least from professionals, and others are not taken seriously—that are raised about a framework, about the warp and weft of a system, about its Weltanschauung. I suggest that a basic characteristic of rationality is the raising of questions about the Weltanschauung. There are strong reasons why this is seldom done and strong reasons for doing it.

To entertain a question about a Weltanschauung is often a shattering experience, because for what was apparently axiomatic one finds oneself without a rationale helplessly gesticulating.

It is also alarming because it is felt to be a threat to one's way of life. And indeed it may be undermining, but this may be illusory in that the supposed threat may be faced and met.

One reason for taking the risk of questioning a Weltanschauung is that it is to face the unknown, and thereby to become less a prey to alarm at the very thought of it.

Another is that one may emerge with a better founded strength.

Another is that the very act of doing so establishes a relationship with opponents for it almost inevitably involves understanding the opposing Weltanschauung. Though for many this would be something to shun, many espouse it on pragmatic grounds. The relationship may be crudely ambivalent: to understand your opponent in order the better to do him down. Less coldly calculating, to understand an opponent, particularly his Weltanschauung, may enable you to satisfy it wholly or in part at little or no great cost; it can open the door to satisfactory compromise.

Differences in Weltanschauung may be resolved or they may not. When not, in extreme cases the resulting social phenomenon is not one social world but two (or more), with an ideological curtain segregating them. In certain conditions, not fully clear, peaceful co-existence would seem to be possible; in certain conditions, not fully clear, this is not possible and the result is violence. If we divide the two segregates into the materially secure and idealist revolutionaries, for example, the materially secure will not resort to violence unless they feel highly insecure in some respect, not material, but threatened in Weltanschauung. Idealist revolutionaries on the other hand have no motive for being reluctant to put their possessions at risk and thus restrain the trigger finger; and they sense, in part correctly though sometimes exaggeratedly, that the Weltanschauung of the secure will be impervious to "reasonable" demands. Hence the materially secure, who have not yet been shaken in their Weltanschauung, will want to avoid violence, and will negotiate or make concessions, whether satisfactory or totally inadequate. The usual situation is of course "too little, too late". On the other hand, those who want instant world justice will often be impatient, but, however understandably, often take coercive measures which defeat their own object, i.e. block the attainment of goals that would have accrued readily in response to moderation. Thus "to little, too late" is met by "too coercive, too soon".

From all this it would seem that there are reasons for the secure to study their own Weltanschauung and that of their opponents; and, if they consider that there is or should be but one social world, make negotiated concessions with greater speed. Those desirous of instant redress could have the following reason for examining their own Weltanschauung : to enquire whether their opposition to existing power and privilege and the intention to wrest it from its possessors carries with it the ideal not only of taking their place but also of subjugating them. The point is that establishments fear the emancipation of ghettos for fear of being relegated to a ghetto for the former well-to-do. And it is not always clear that revolutionary idealists who want human beings to be treated as human and to have human needs met are willing to extend this impartially to former first-class citizens. It sometimes works out. Thus the Roman Catholic society of Southern Ireland, which became an establishment in 1922, treated the Protestants, who had been the Ascendancy, pretty well. But it is not usually so—and this was not expected. If second-class citizens, whether blacks, students, Jews, foreigners, or women, depending on time and place, in fact intend to accord equal treatment to those they wish to draw level with or supersede, they could attain part of their objective by making this overt and if possible providing a guarantee for it.

The general point I wish to draw from all this is that there are both pragmatic reasons and idealistic reasons for both groups though they are of different levels of power, possessions, and ideals, to consider looking to their own and their opponents Weltanschauugen; where the "idealistic" reasons involve the idea of people of every kind of Weltanschauung belonging to one social world.

I am suggesting it would help to clarify the morass of group-values for groups to consider their attitude to our having one social world. And I am suggesting that the notion of one social world if adopted as a norm would resolve some basic problems, not only of violence and of wealth, but of meaningfulness in human living. I do not think it is a provable proposition. But it could perhaps be given the form of a hypothetical imperative : "*If* you want to be at all fully a person, you will respect the Weltanschauungen of groups other than your own; and you *will* want to be such a person, *if* you want (but there is no reason why you should) a meaningful life."

CHAPTER XXVII

Pragmatism and the American Mom*

PRAGMATISM HAS articulated doctrines and, I think, unarticulated doctrines. The articulated ones are very well known. First there is the theory of truth. I think that comes first because the other doctrines are consequences of it. The theory of truth is a very simple one : broadly speaking, a theory is true if the theory makes some difference however slight to our experience. There are differences between the three main pragmatists, but this view would be accepted by all. With James it is specific : a theory is true only if it is useful. So the theory has to be not only an instrument, but it has to be a good instrument. It may be noted that this part of pragmatism has found its way into the main stream of scientific thought; practically every philosophy of science contains a component of pragmatism though, of course, most of them contain non-pragmatic ingredients; and it is rare to find one, such as instrumentalism, that is wholly pragmatic. This influence indicates its pervasiveness in the intellectual field. What it amounts to is that the value of a theory lies in its being earthbound, and this requirement applies to every interpretation of science except intuitionist ones—which, of course, are not really viable alternatives though they do exist especially in the field of psychiatry and phenomenology.

The next component of pragmatism is the rejection of metaphysics. The raison d'être of pragmatism was to get rid of unanswerable questions in metaphysics which, it was maintained, really made no difference to anybody's experience. This repudiation is important for understanding the movement.

These are the two main components. A number of fundamental objections have been raised by eminent philosophers including Russell and Moore to the pragmatic doctrine of truth. I do not propose to dwell on these because the doctrine is of merely scholastic interest, a doctrine that is of little value, the least easy to sustain, and one of the few philosopical doctrines that is very easy to knock over.[1]

Now we come to the unarticulated part of pragmatism, that is to say, the message it carries for ethics, politics, and society—what may be summed up as societal pragmatism.

Since pragmatism is a denial of metaphysics, it is in effect a denial of principle in the sense of high principle, unless that principle is realizable in practice and unless it is advantageous; for any principle that is so realisable cannot be metaphysical in any traditional sense. The societal doctrine means, I think, three basic things. One is material progress, implied by the denial of high principle of a metaphysical kind. The second feature is one I would call "good neighbourdom" as contrasted with personal friendship; that is to say, neighbours are persons with whom to have superficial cooperation; but you do not have them too close for comfort. In other words, there is a certain restriction on good neighbourdom, which means that a certain social distance is maintained. Now this restriction is due to the third feature, which is a correlative of it, namely individualism. An action done for pragmatic reasons is cooperative because the agent needs the fruits of co-operation, not because of his concern with the other party as such; for attaining solely one's own ends, even though by co-operative means, implies that the individual himself comes first. And he has the near ultimate right to act in his own interests alone. However, other people (for co-operative reasons) have a right to individual freedom; but strong as this right is, it is not quite unlimited, for it is restricted by good neighbourdom. These two principles, good neighbourdom and individualism, are correlatives, because you cannot fully formulate one without the restriction imposed by the other. They belong together in an integrated whole. Moreover, the good neighbourdom and individualism belong in a setting of material progress.

These three basic ingredients that make up the societal message of pragmatism[2] have a number of significant consequences: (i) There is a practical emphasis on material success. (ii) Change is a high value. Very few societies in thousands of years have liked change, most have disliked change and a few have tolerated it at best, but only the pragmatic society has actually valued change as a positive thing.[3] That means in broad (pragmatic) terms that you up-date machinery as soon as what you have gets a bit out of date; you do not wait to get the last ounce of use out of it, you scrap it, pull it down, and replace it by a new, a more efficient kind. (iii) No social change can be tolerated under the pragmatic aegis if the social change is going to conflict with the three basic components: that is to say, if it conflicts with material progress, good neighbourdom, or individualism, then the social change is ruled out. Which virtually means that there is very little social change possible though there may be some; or that it is difficult to get change at all other than technological change. (iv) By the same token, one can explain social conformity. (v) Social democracy comes under the heading of individualism and good neighbourdom. And (vi) naturally enough there is an ideal (not so guaranteed) of legislative democracy as well. Lastly, (vii) a pragmatic country will place great faith in the use of economic power to influence other countries.

To intervene with a comment or two, these characteristics are virtually world-wide though they do not dominate outside America. They are world-wide in the sense that, while there is a considerable infusion of pragmatism in this sense even, I think, in Asia, certainly in western Europe, other basics tend to dominate and pragmatism gains the ascendent only occasionally. But in its home, though not always dominant, it usually is. Incidentally, this may account for America's enormous difficulty in foreign politics; because it is a major task of re-orientation for a pragmatist to understand other countries which are not predominantly pragmatic. An example of a lesser degree of this difficulty would come from another country. Great Britain is not fundamentally pragmatist but it has quite a sizable infusion in pragmatism in the brew; and this, I would suppose is part of what leads to Great Britain's enormous difficulty in handling Ireland, which is grossly under-pragmatic for either co-operation, progress, or living in a communal world at all. So you can get pragmatism in full degree, very high degree, moderate degree, or practically non-existent. In high degree it is obviously characteristic of America. We should, however, associate it mainly with the upper portion of American society, the leaders rather than the led (though it may also dominate the led in some form).

In discussing pragmatism, I am speaking largely about America because it happens to be the example par excellence of a pragmatic society although it does have a non-pragmatic ingredient. The non-pragmatic characteristics of America are interesting and important; they show that though America is deeply pragmatic, it is, so to speak, not more than 80% or 90% pragmatic.

First, there are characteristics that seem to be only loosely connected with pragmatism. (a) There arises in America an administrative autocracy through distrust of decentralizing authority. (b) Legislative democracy can be, and is partially, undermined.

These consequences are a little different from the others because they are possible but not necessary, unlike the earlier ones which are more or less necessary; but these may be seen to be likely enough. (c) However, in America there is another feature which is not fundamentally pragmatic at all. Let us take this first.

As regards distrust and autocracy in America, there is, I think, a deep sense of hostile environment both overseas and at home. This is a feature that can be explained by the same historical origins as pragmatism itself. There is a stress on defensive power both individual and national, that is to say the nation is always watchful, even suspicious, and individuals own their own guns.

To come to the American characteristic which is peculiar in being almost totally unrelated to all the rest, America has provided an example of quite unparalleled generosity to underprivileged weaker nations. (There is only one other case in history known to me, and it is much weaker, where a dominant power behaved generously to a defeated opponent.) The degree to which America has rendered material aid internationally from the 1940's onwards calls for special comment. Now, I know some Americans to whom I have mentioned this do not agree with me that this is a bona fide feature, because they regard it as being dictated by such motives as maintaining trade overseas or gaining political control abroad. It is an economic truth that there are huge benefits accruing as a consequence from this huge generosity, but I think there is a complete answer to this showing that it is not the whole truth or even a large part of the truth of the matter; for although hard-headed people in Washington may have realized the economic consequence of benefit from being generous—or may have regarded it as a protection against communism—I do not know—they could not have got the measure through Congress or got it accepted throughout the country without colossal protest and great political risk, if the mass of people had not supported the policy out of generosity, and felt it was really called for; the American people must have felt a wave of sympathy for countries that had suffered unendurably from the Hitler onslaught (and tyranny is something Americans can understand from the way their nation was founded).

Let us glance briefly at the question of values. Pragmatism, like so many bases of ethics, whether individual or political, can be put to good use or bad use. For instance, the noble use of pragmatism was to get away from persecution, to respect the rights of the individual as an individual and to respect human freedom. These are the sort of things that most of us would regard as admirable. They are not of course peculiar to pragmatism for they are in other forms of ethics too; but at least pragmatism can boast of having these values in it (even if they are not rooted in basic personal respect). On the other hand, you can equally well put pragmatism to other kinds of ends altogether because it is very easy to turn it into a case of the end justifying the means. Here again pragmatism is not unique. Most systems of ethics can be twisted in this way also. Nonetheless, if the criticism can be made, even if it can be made against other forms of ethics also, it should be made. For instance, any means would be justifiable to defend the three basic principles that I have mentioned, that is to say, material success, good-neighbourdom, and individualism. So long as anything there is threatened, I think you will find it is natural for a pragmatist either individual or national, to regard any means as justifiable for defending those three basics. And this would give a rationale for scandals both domestically and abroad. So we find respect for individuals together with the possibility of committing scandals in the name of some sort of principle. It might be mentioned that respect for the individual and respect for cooperation is the sort of thing that was denied to a very large extent by the aristocratic type of society which the pragmatists were originally inveighing against. Thus we have a rather pliable doctrine, which can move from the kingdom of ends in Kantian terms to a doctrine of "might is right" as Thrasymachus put it. In other words you could say that the pragmatic principle would be "might is right"—subject to certain limitations implying not an absolute "might is right" but subject to individualism and good-neighbourdom. One might expect these two attitudes constituting a social democracy to have ensured the maintenance of democratic processes throughout. Certainly they led the founding fathers to pour colossal effort into framing a democratic constitution with all sorts of safeguards. How did it come about then that legislative democracy could become partially undermined and administrative democracy become strangled?

To answer, let us recall the sense of hostile environment, which reflected the realities of the English establishment, the frontier enemies, and construe it that America developed a habitual disposition of sentinelship. Although sentinelship in the first case was directed outwards, it was thus directed by equals. As soon as the country began to be "organized", with law, order, and a central government, it became—what is a truism—politically layered. The layers would easily unite under good-neighbourdom against a threat from without, but in the absence of such a threat, it would find an outlet only between layers. Hence a political pecking-order, distrust of decentralizing authority, and holding a tight-rein on subordinates—producing the paradoxical result that a country founded on democracy—of one sort—produced an autocracy as well. For the American Government can and does, subject to parts of the constitution that work effectively, take autocratic decisions that are reminiscent of the great dictatorships. This may make itself noticed but little to most Americans, but to conduct administration routinely in a characteristically autocratic way is highly paradoxical in a country that worships the concept of democracy; and it is maintained by non-recognition and by the huge scale of the phenomenon, for Americans seem to regard administrative autocracy as part of the natural order of things, accepting autocratic decisions (not with grace but putting up with them) that would be unthinkable and evoke immediate revolt, say, in a constitutional monarchy. While these two undemocratic characteristics perhaps need not absolutely occur under pragmatism, I think they are overwhelmingly likely. First, pragmatism could hardly develop without sentinelship. Second, pragmatism implies the absence of any deeper principle than good-neighbourdom to soften an extreme individualism. If we apply these to the administrative situation of superior and subordinate, the doctrine of individualism will not be generalized to those below, because good-neighbourdom fails to be applicable beyond equals; thus the field is ripe for "might is right" rather than fellowship; with sentinelship there is distrust; and the combination equals autocracy towards subordinates.

The obverse is displayed in generosity, so large as to remind one of the widow's cruse. It is true that this could embody a trace of what in psycho-analysis is called "manic-defence"—designed to compensate for guilt—but the circumstances of its use indicate a huge sympathy with the recipient's social situation. Thus this character of America does not stem from pragmatism (though it may share with pragmatism a common root).

We turn now to the social situation giving birth to pragmatism. I think individualism arose historically from the situation leading to the Mayflower enterprise, that is to say, from the situation that made America what it was—protest against the Anglican Church in order to preserve individual freedom, freedom for people to conduct their own religious observances, and also the individual right to other kinds of freedom to certain posts or positions that were denied to non-conformists—for if you did not conform to the Anglican Church of the day, a number of roads were blocked to you. So it was a protest of principle against the religion they did not want, and the social and (national?) consequences of that. This carries a parallel defiance of the social establishment—also a significant feature of the situation. These factors amount to individualism and to the denial of establishment principles which would foster a soil suitable for pragmatism; and the religious situation in England was reinforced by the religious situation in New England, which fostered individualism and a pragmatic attitude. To these factors we have to add frontiership. When these immigrants founded the colonies and reached out further west, the frontier dominated, wild and lawless: it was very much a question of the individual and every man for himself, but the individual was forced by the sheer need for self-defence into good-neighbourdom—rendering mutual aid. But this was mutual aid on a certain level, which excluded the deeper level of personal relationships. It quite easily led into material pragmatic aid because men were up against the raw difficulties of their physical environment and of warding off marauders. Their situation played into the hands of making a fetish of technology, which placed emphasis on materiality rather than the personal, and forming a society in which others around would develop a sense of equality with those similarly placed, while others who might be dangerous would become second-class citizens. So from the religious persecution in England came mutual aid and good neighbourdom, and this explains the outlook of pragmatism and how it assumed a purely material form. The outlook was not articulated at the time, but could constitute a powerful social dynamic[5] without ever being articulated.

The outstanding characteristics to be dwelt on are individualism and good-neighbourdom. The restricted defensive nature of social distance that belongs to good-neighbourdom precluded all but a minimum of personal relations; it fathered material success. The individualism was so marked as to approximate to the clinical conception of the sense of omnipotence in the individual. It would be reasonable to add the influence of a further consequence—the mobility of American society from its foundation to the present day; for this would militate against the formation of deep lasting friendships and play into the hands of consolidating social distance.

The most significant factor for what follows is social distance; for it produced tenuous personal relations, reinforcing individualism; it is to be expected that man will not house close relations of identity with other men. Male relations to other persons would have been predominantly concerned with other males, while women were treated rather as they are in many oriental countries, endowed with a place in the nursery and kitchen, with the image of what I call the womb-breast-hand axis, excluded from things of intellect politics, and even those forms of relatively sophisticated culture allowed to their European counterparts. This would have been facilitated by a relevant division of labour; but is this all there is to the matter?

Consider the revolt against the established Church; this was male; women would have acquiesced in their men's attitudes but not rebelled. It would—superficially speaking—have been possible to treat women on equal terms, even with some division of labour—but only subject to the conditions of individualism, good-neighbourdom, and particularly social distance. And this would be impossible; for men would have known that women could not so easily give up the deeper elements of the personal required by social distance. Thus the phenomenon of social distance required by the situation vis-a-vis the male was also required vis-a-vis the female. Such a restriction on the role accorded to the female, conforming to the womb-breast-hand axis, i.e. the body, must ward off the personality. This was both a necessary presupposition and consequence of the birth of pragmatism: frontier-man could not adopt a pragmatic attitude without having put a distance between himself and women; and its adoption ensured that this distance would become embedded in social structure. Pragmatism would be at risk if the female were allowed too close. Thus the possibility of equality of women would have been a constant threat.

Therefore, I now put forward the hypothesis that social distance fostered the growth in the American male of a dread of the female, of having women on more or less equal terms, arousing whatever inherent dread of this sort there may have been; and that from these beginnings there grew the phenomenon of the American Mom.

Let us look into the notion of the American Mom. The characteristics of the American Mom—as some American psycho-analysts will substantiate—amount to the wife-mother-cook instrument enshrined in a halo of selfless motherhood and with a taboo on the non-pragmatic aspect of personality and culture.

The hypothesis I put forward is (a) that the children of the pragmatic society are relatively fatherless in the decisive baby/toddler years, and (b) that man's life is extra-familial. Later boyhood relations with the father, though of some importance, especially in learning pragmatic pursuits, would not compensate for the lack of such relationships in the most formative years. Now these abstractions are the extreme end of the scale and we might say that they are limiting cases or approximations. The reality without approximation is, in other words, that the amount and intensity of paternal inference in the life of the small child was, though present, very meagre.[6] The influence of the other roles is much less than in other societies. In primitive societies and perhaps in rural communities in the west, later boyhood relations with the father might well be fairly close, both in pragmatic pursuits and in personal matters; but hardly in the west, particularly in urban areas.

Continuing from the interpretation that Homo-Americanus has a deadly fear of women, this is not a straightforward castration-anxiety of the kind familiar in classical psycho-analysis, but rather a fear of involvement with the female personality. Can we find any clue to its nature? Let us dwell on the nature of the fatherless son—not one whose father is dead but one who plays little of a father's role. The boy has (a) only the mom to identify with and (b) has only the mom as an object—a love-object. So both the object of identification and the object towards which he could direct his feelings is one and the same person, in contrast with the normal situation in which the object of identity is the father and the object-relation is to the mother (if we distinguish sharply between identification and object). And here the picture is one in which both are with the mom. That is to say, the son is more or less forced into a family set-up in which he has to adapt to a feminine attitude towards his mother instead of a masculine one; and that he then spends his life denying this and withdrawing from it. Thus the male social structure is a "substitute formation"[7] based on an attempt to break free from this basic relation with the mom.[8] If not perhaps the only way, the most easily available way of doing it, in the absence of a father's being around in a really influential way, is to make an impersonal adjustment. This is the most basic point of all that I am trying to make, that if one is trying to free oneself from the shackles of an identification and an object which are unwelcome and there is no other personal object around to substitute, then whatever serves as a replacement pretty well has to be material or physical rather than personal.

It is a simple enough conclusion that this female attitude towards the mom, forced on the child, whether boy or girl, will promote or perpetuate pragmatism. I have been concerned basically with pragmatism and not with America as a whole, and therefore have not dwelt on America's sense of generosity, which does not spring from pragmatism (though it may be linked with pragmatism). Mr. Russell McRae pointed out to me that the male identification with the mom can induce a mood of huge optimism and give vent to an image of an unlimited good breast, able to feed the world, and from his extensive knowledge of American literature he drew attention to Scott Fitzgerald's image of the American "green breast". Thus he showed that the underlay of pragmatism (though this does not mean pragmatism itself), namely the feminine attitude endowing the American male, would explain the phenomenon of generosity. (We might still have a further problem of explaining how this assumed a national rather than an individual form.) Mr. McRae also mentioned how strikingly the hypothesis reflects Henry James' own life; it would, however, take us too far afield to discuss the relevance of this significant point.

If femininity fosters pragmatism, the converse question is equally interesting: whether pragatism can produce this feminine attitude, and I think that the answer is that it can. If it is correct that the distance between men arose because of individualism, which arose from the persecution in England, and was exported to the frontier society, promoting good neighbourdom with social distance, then this kind of social distance between men means in effect a rather tenuous male identification as opposed to what one might regard as a more normal close identification; hence it would hardly foster the male-female personal relationship. So the conclusion I am reaching here is that the boy withdraws in virtue of his relation to the mom from the personal to the impersonal, a process that is rooted in the fact that there is only a tenuous male identification that he can fall back on—that is the thesis. Moreover, the daughter is brought up in the same situation and therefore, with a strong tendency[9] to have a female as an object; hence she needs a feminine attitude in her future husband. This situation amounts to a collusion-effect between husband and wife. Thus pragmatism and the feminine attitude in the male mutually foster each other.

To summarize. The original development of pragmatism was brought about by the English persecution, emigration, and frontiership, that is to say specifically the good neighbourdom, the individualism, and the social distance, and the consequential principles like expediency, success, conformity, and so forth. Further, the sense of social distance is important because of bringing about the tenuous identification with the male, which in turn brought about a withdrawal from the personal, because the only personality to fall back on for identification is the female which the male inherently objects to; and withdrawing from that, there is no other possibility but to place the emphasis on the material.

APPENDIX

THE INTERPLAY BETWEEN INFANCY UNCONSCIOUS FACTORS AND LATER SOCIAL INFLUENCES

Professor Otto Friedman pointed out to me that it would be a mistake to suppose that the mom produces a little pragmatist by five years old, and that, on my hypothesis, what she does is to develop him with a blueprint for it; for the explicit development of the pragmatic attitude would depend on a variety of social factors, notably in adolescence, ranging from the (belated) influence of the father, peer-group, the media, etc. Moreover, he added, these would have additional force in America where there are so many first and second generation young whose nuclear families would lack grandparents.

I agree that these superstructural factors are important. They would not, of course, operate without the mom-based underlying structure, and that was my main focus. I might remark that I do not subscribe to the doctrine that used to be attributed to Freud, though nowhere put forward by him, that the child's experience in the first five years of life determine, exclusively, his subsequent development. What I do think is that the early years dominate, i.e. play a larger role than later factors in shaping personality—the senior partner but not endowed with exclusive power. Thus I assume that later male identification plays a notable part in the development of the personality, and notably that it influences choice of career and social attitudes, but that they would not often appreciably counterbalance the lack of appropriate identifications that should normally take place during infancy.

The later factors raise many sociological questions. One would concern variations in the pragmatic attitude. Another would concern sub-cultures that do not share it. Thus Jewish Americans, with a long tradition that was anti-pragmatic, though with a pragmatic component, would not fit the image I have presented.

But my concern here is not to deny these other factors, and the need to investigate these other problems, though I would say they are subsidiary in that they arise out of my hypothesis; but rather my aim is to deal with what seems to be a more fundamental level.

FOOTNOTES

*Given to the Toronto Imago Group, 16 January 1972. I am grateful for helpful comments and criticisms to Professor Otto Friedman, Mr. Russell McRae, Dr. J. N. Hattiangadi, Mr. Alan Cobb and Mrs. Katherine Cobb, and Clara Wisdom.

[1]There are, naturally, differences between the exponents of pragmatism—the main ones were Pierce, James and Mead—but I am concerned with its general form in which it reflects social outlook, and I think this is undoubtedly closest to James's version, even though, as Perry has put it, "the philosophical movement known as Pragmatism is largely the result of James's misunderstanding of Pierce" (quoted by W. B. Gallie, *Pierce and Pragmatism*, London, 1952, 30). It is worth noting Gallie's (op. cit., 29) view of James as an individualist:

James . . . was an individualist, interested in the experiences, perplexities, and satisfactions of individual souls, and anything claiming to be more-than-individual he distrusted from the depths of his own Protestant and American soul.

Equally striking is in James's own stock view of truth: "The true is only the expedient in our way of thinking, just as the right is only the expedient in our way of behaving." (William James, *The Meaning of Truth*, New York, 1909, vii). Without going into the cogent philsophical criticisms that were levelled against this view, we may note certain serious difficulties: if 'being true' is equated with 'what is useful', we want to know not just that something is useful but that it is true; and we might consider that, however useful pragmatism itself may be, it may well be untrue.

[2]It is possible for some people to emphasize one component rather than another, and it is even possible for a clash to occur between them, but there is nothing really strange in having a general outlook that sometimes gives rise to internal problems.

[3]Only America and the U.S.S.R. have put a positive value on change. The relation between pragmatism and the doctrine of praxis is of great interest but would require separate examination.

[4]No doubt former German Realpolitik had a strain of pragmatism, and the same is sometimes felt about the U.S.S.R. While this may be true of their foreign policies, it is not characteristic of the ethos of the internal relations within these countries.

[5]I assume a framework according to which ideas can create or change a social structure.

[6]It is true that in almost all societies fathers spend less time with their babies/toddlers than do their mothers. This does not necessarily mean less influence. Mrs. Johnston-Abercrombie has estimated contact between mother and child by the amount of time she has picked him up and held him. A mother busy cleaning out the wigwam or buying the food in a supermarket (?while the baby cries in the pram) may have less Johnston-Abercrombie relation to the child than the father has, even though the amount in clock-time is greater.

[7]I do not go into the question why the male reacts against the feminine position.

[8]Clara Wisdom pointed out that it may be of interest to compare Philip Wiley's contention in *A Generation of Vipers* that the American mom produces a nation of vipers. On my thesis, the male and female have interacting roles in producing pragmatists (who are only sometimes vipers).

[9]I do not go into the question why she does not rebel against this upbringing.

REFERENCES

Gallie, W. B. (1952), *Pierce and Pragmation*, London, 30.
James, William (1909), *The Meaning of Truth*, New York, vii.

CHAPTER XXVIII

Existentialism as a Way of Life

EXISTENTIALISM constitutes a great new Weltanschauung. My aim here is to give an understandable account of it.

Existentialism is concerned with the question of decision, in the broad sense of human responsibility in the light of the nature of man.

Taking off from here, existentialists have brought to light all sorts of interesting matters, often of a very surprising kind. To explain the thesis requires that a number of topics should be discussed, notably the relation to logic, the relation to Platonic philosophy, the relation to morals, values, and standards, the background of phenomenology, the relation to empiricism, the form of freedom, and the question of objectivity. It shares some common ground with empiricism and logical positivism, with psycho-analysis and certain ideas of social structure, and partakes of the Weltanschauung of the twentieth century. Limitations in the light of psycho-analysis and the notion of social structure need to be dwelt upon.

LOGIC

When he first introduced his work on existentialism, Sartre developed the position by means of a lengthy excursion into logic. This was a misfortune because the logic was barbarous and also irrelevant. It was exploded in two articles by Ayer who carried out a highly efficient job of demolishing the logic, but he failed to point out that the existentialist thesis had nothing to do with the logic and might therefore be a serious position in its own right. Sartre's disregard of the need for competence in handling logic may have done the subject of existentialism harm in Great Britain where logic, at least of a sort, is highly prized. This is not certain, however, because the existentialist thesis, in any case, would have little appeal to the more typical kinds of British temperament, and elsewhere existentialism caught on, especially in countries like France and Germany, where logic is of less interest. To these comments on logic should be added a footnote on jargon. It takes sweat of the brow to penetrate the jargon that existentialists use, and this is a pity because most of it, and perhaps all of it, is totally unnecessary. If British empiricism, or language analysis, or philosophical analysis are in a high degree logical although they have nothing to say, contrariwise existentialism is usually inarticulate and totally undisciplined in the matter of expression, but at least it has something to say.

RELATION TO PLATO AND PHENOMENOLOGY

It is not standard to mention Plato in connection with existentialism. I do so because the notion of an essence which has dominated philosophy for two thousand years effectively saw the light of day in Plato, and again in Aristotle. It can, of course, be discerned in the pre-Socratics, notably Parmenides, but in Plato it is fully explicit. Sartre launched a great attack on essentialism. This was not, nor has it been claimed to be, original with him. Essentialism was attacked in modern times, first by Berkeley and then by Hume, but Sartre's attack on essentialism has more in common with Bergson, who inveighed against the intellectual carving up of experience into frozen segments, destroying the flux or process of living. For Sartre, I think, an essence was in effect the result of petrifying a slice of lived life. Reality was the fulness of experience at any moment of existence. Thus, if a man wonders what he ought to do, he petrifies his lived response by determining his action in accordance with precepts which he considers he ought to follow. This leads us to the next topic.

MORALITY, VALUES, AND STANDARDS

Sartre inveighs against standards or codes, at least in the sense of being a standard code presented to be obeyed.

What he condemns, for example, is acting in accordance with a moral code which you have learned at your mother's knee, from your school teacher, from your clergyman, from your professor, in fact from anywhere. To act in accordance with such is to act in accordance with a foreign body and not out of yourself. To be an existentialist is to act out of the depth of oneself. Qualification is, of course, required here for Sartre realizes and explicitly holds that a person may very well go into the matter of alternative codes, values, standards, etc., and adopt one of them as his own. In that case, if he acts in accordance with it, he will be acting from himself and not just because it is one that has been given to him. The difference therefore lies between acting in accordance with a code that is another's and a code that is one's own. Only the latter counts as a case of free action—similarly for free decision.

It is in this connection that we meet with certain interesting adjuncts. Thus, the man who gets up routinely at 7:00 and catches the 8:21 to town typically leads a vegetable existence and is not acting existentially from himself. The contrasting point to emphasize is the notion of *self*-responsibility for one's decisions and action. However, to act otherwise, that is to act in accordance with the code of another, is to act in "bad faith". The notion of bad faith is thus generalized and indeed radically altered from its normal meaning of disloyalty or cheating towards some-one. Here it means disloyalty or cheating toward one's own person. In ordinary parlance, what matters is a person's own integrity. It is, of course, a fairly common experience for people to feel undermined if circumstances damage their integrity, and they sometimes go to great lengths of sacrifice to preserve their integrity. This has all been high-lighted by Sartre's notion of bad faith. Very possibly he has done no mean service in making this important feature of life much more a focus of deliberate intention than used to be the case.

Correlative with this is the notion of a project. If a householder calls in a plumber to mend a pipe, the plumber is engaging in a project not of his own making. A project that does not involve bad faith is one that stems from the being of a person himself. The illustration, of course, exaggerates the difference because a plumber has, in all likelihood, adopted the trade of plumbing, at least in part, because plumbing is a project that springs from him. Nonetheless, many such activities can become mainly, and on occasion completely, merely *roles*. Most plumbers probably like plumbing, most bus drivers probably like driving. No one example is certain to come off but one may hazard a try with that of a waiter. Assume, as Sartre seems to do, that a waiter often does not choose his job because this project stems from himself, but perhaps be-cause he can find nothing else that he can do. (The more sinister pos-sibility that he takes this up in order to serve or be servile will be discussed later.) Suppose this is a genuine example. Then the waiter, in waiting, enacts a role, and *as a waiter* he is no more than a role. Here the project is permeated entirely with bad faith. When one acts from bad faith, there is no difficulty about carrying out the action; the rules are given. All that has to be done is to follow them even though in a yes-man fashion. Being existential, on the other hand, is a refusal of acceptance merely for acceptance's sake, and only thus can one enter vitally into existence—hence the notion so widespread in the subject of being "thrown into the world". This may conjure up imagery of being thrown into the deep end with no rules to go on. All one can do is flounder, and we sink or we swim according to what comes from ourselves.

PHENOMENOLOGY

Although existentialism disavows the notion of an essence, it does have family affiliations with phenomenology, which in a certain sense deplores essences. The apparent paradox would seem to arise because essence in a rejected Platonic sense is a petrified aspect of existence and thus taken outside the experiencing of experience altogether. In phenomenology, however, essence in an accepted sense is located within experiencing and is its inner core. It is, so to speak, the purest distillate of experience itself and thus not outside experiencing but within it. Whether or not this is a valid notion, it is, I think, what is meant. And the message of phenomenology for existentialism would seem to be that by attending to the phenomenology of experience, that is to say, to the description with all its nuances, of an experience, one is in a better position to penetrate to the fulness of the experience or grasp what the experience is. For example, the waiter brings the potatoes and holds out the dish in front of one, and the diner helps himself. He replaces the serving spoon and the waiter takes away the dish. Phenomenologically, however, the diner either sees the waiter's face or he does not. If he does, he sees it simply as one face among many or he sees more than this. Perhaps he sees a flicker indicating servility, or a flicker indicating contempt for the diner's manners. Perhaps the diner senses in his own attitude a tinge of superiority of position, or perhaps a tinge of awe at an august waiter. Thus developed, the experiencing, or the experience, is not just a bad-faith situation of food presented, received, removed, but of a slave before a master, or a "slave" who is master of the "master". Such might be the essence and might be the reality of the experience of which the ordinary description would not be so much an abstraction as an opting out from the experience.

EXISTENTIALISM, FREEDOM, AND ANXIETY

The relation to Plato and to phenomenology is a convenience of exegesis only. The emphasis is an emphasis on existence as an experience, on what one achieves rather than has automatically. If one lives a life of bad faith, one does not exist unless one cares to call it a bare vegetable existence. To exist is to live, in the richness of the essence of experiencing phenomenologically. This is the basic notion; correlative with it is that of freedom, freedom of choice whether to decide or to act. If one acts from codes that come from outside, not freely adopted from within and thus acts in bad faith or with bad faith, then one does not exist and one does not act freely. Existentialism is essentially a philosophy of freedom. However, the originality of the claim lies not so much in the buttressing of freedom of the will as in an unusual or concomitant attachment to it or a natural consequence of it. Since a person acting freely ipso facto cannot be acting in accordance with a code from without, the question arises what is he acting in accordance with. There are two cases. The first is when there is no delay in decision or action. The answer is obvious, the decision is taken, the action is carried out. This is hardly free in the existentialist sense because the action is fully determined by the needs of the situation, the objective factors involved, and an unambiguous set of inner desires. Thus, a man will not take his neighbour's drink perhaps because of a code he has been taught, but if he has a drink of his own and he is thirsty, the situation confronting him provides him with the means of handling it and he drinks. The significant case arises, however, when there is some doubt, evoking deliberation, in fact a gap between the situation awaiting action to be taken and the taking of it. There can be a temptation to fill this gap in accordance with precepts obtainable from outside, but the freeman will not take this course. Rejecting such precepts, how does he reach a decision? So long as the gap exists, there is, by reason of that very fact, no sufficient reason for a decision or action. The chasm that yawns between his inaction and what is required to be done is what is known as das Nichts, le Néant, or the Nothing, which is a very positive chasm. The Nothing creates in the man a state of Anxst, angoise, or anxiety. Thus, freedom can exist only in a situation in which the Nothing is the dominant feature and which is experienced as anxiety. Existentialism is thus a philosophy of anxiety and moreover a philosophy that places a high valuation on anxiety.

How does a man meet this anxiety? He can do so in one of two ways. He can abolish it by giving up his freedom, filling up the Nothing, and deciding and acting in accordance with precepts which he finds to hand. Existential living is the way of the free man to experience the Nothing in the form of anxiety and live this. If he does not appeal to outside precept, there may come a time when he simply takes a decision. The decision is not caused, it issues out of the Nothing, though in a different form. The Nothing from which it issues is the Nothing in the man himself as contrasted with the Nothing constituting the gap he has to fill. He is said to take a leap, as he takes a leap in the dark or jumps in at the deep end, but he is taking an uncaused leap.

The conception of the *absurd* is one of the most striking, peripheral though it may be. What this refers to is the essential absurdity of the human predicament. The cynic might laugh at man for assuming the poise of being a little god, whose megalomania assures him about his place in the eternal order of the universe; but the existentialist notion of the absurd is a rather more tragic one. It concerns the tremendous self-importance of man, of doing his duty, or conforming with his tremendous and lofty ideas in a universe where these values have no objective validity at all. In short, "man doth take himself too seriously".

This emphasis on the absurd is a salutary reminder that man, after all, is no more than man.

That is the philosophy of existentialism. It has nothing to do with logic. It is a statement about experience, namely that to attain the full richness of experience it is necessary to relinquish all precepts belonging to another, to face the Nothing resulting from this which therefore cannot be filled by known procedures, to accept the freedom that results, accepting the anxiety induced by the Nothing and the freedom, and to overcome this only by a leap. It is clearly a normative philosophy in the sense of advocating an ideal. It states in effect what is the norm in the sense of what is the richest attainable experience.

THE RELATION OF EXISTENTIALISM TO EMPIRICISM AND PHILOSOPHICAL ANALYSIS

Although English and European philosophy is as divided as East from West, nonetheless, there are some strange identities to be found. For instance, the anti-essentialism characterizing existentialism is the keynote of the entire movement of philosophical analysis throughout the whole of the twentieth century. The reasons for this are different and the goals served are different but both are anti-essentialistic in the sense of being anti-metaphysical.

There is a further intriguing identity between existentialism and empiricism in that both are rooted in experience. Now, this may amount to very little because they understand experience so very differently. The British empiricist understands experience to be constructed out of sense-data, or perhaps some more sophisticated form of immediate experience. In any case, the sensory reality is a shell, with object-reality concealed as behind a blind. Experience for an existentialist is a lived experience, in which phenomenological form of immediate experience gives access to the reality within, not as something concealed but as something revealed through the phenomenological form of experience. These senses

of experience are so very different that it may seem illegitimate philosophically to mention them as if they have a common ingredient, but
there is in fact something in common. It is true that what is common in
a positive sense differs from one to the other, but they also have in
common what is excluded by their views of experience. For the British
empiricist, as for his forebears in the Middle Ages and beyond, "Nihil in
intellectu quod non prius in sensu". In other words, there is nothing
independent of the senses. For the existentialist, this is equally true and
like empiricism it excludes highly abstract scientific concepts from its
purview even though relatable indirectly to experience. For existentialism
would insist that such a highly abstract concept must be discernible
within experience itself. This deficiency incidentally constitutes a criticism of them both.

The two philosophies differ, oddly enough, in their position over one
interesting problem, mainly that of other minds. Empiricism quite
naturally founders on this difficulty. It has always done so and it still
does so. Berkeley obviated the problem by making an arbitrary postulate about having "notions" of persons. Hume ended up in sceptical
defeat. The latter-day empiricists have had the same fate. Russell
admitted that there was no way of defeating or arguing or disproving
solipsism. John Wisdom made the problem vanish but it was never quite
clear how the trick was done, and philosophers are not allowed con-
jurors' license. Ayer wrote a whole book trying to get around it, setting
his problem, interestingly enough in terms which admitted that the
sceptic must win (ending up by claiming that since the sceptic loaded the
dice unfairly, it was not a fair game, so the sceptic cheated and was
expelled). It is not clear to me from a rational point of view why philosophers for so many centuries have tried to get round this difficulty, seeing
that solipsism is an inevitable conclusion of one of the basic empiricist
premisses. The basic premiss is that what is given in experience is factual
observation and notably it is uninterpreted. To this we add the logical
point that facts cannot speak, or more academically phrased, from a
statement of fact no conclusion follows different from itself. From these
two the conclusion follows that from the data of experience it is impossible to infer the existence of other minds. Existentialism, on the other
hand, has no difficulty with this problem, because other minds are
revealed as manifest in certain experiences. Possibly the existentialist has
a formidable problem in explaining just what this relation consists of,
that is, just how a mind is revealed through experience, but he has
solved the problem in a general way even if he has substituted a new one.

If we consider the relation of existentialism to logical positivism, while
all the foregoing remarks about empiricism and philosophical analysis

do not have to be repeated, since logical positivism is but one phase of this movement, there is one point of identity to remark upon. Those who either liquidate what lies beyond their immediate experience or have difficulty in dealing with explanations in terms of it have both aimed at eliminating the world of the supersensible from intellectual moral influence.

EXISTENTIALISM AS A RATIONAL GOAL

Existentialism attempts to lay down an ideal of living, a universal norm, not turning away from this anxiety but taking a leap. This is the general framework, no matter what particular ingredients might be put into it. So far as I know, no proof whatever for this position has been offered, nor does it seem possible to seek a proof. This is no criticism, but it is salutary to bear it in mind.

EXISTENTIALISM AND RATIONALITY

The question of rationality arises because existentialism gives the impression of being highly subjective; that is to say, what it is a man's duty to do depends not on any objective norm but on what it seems to him he ought to do. The difference between this and a more orthodox view is not so great as might be imagined at first sight. For what it is in the ordinary way a man's duty to do is his interpretation of the norm, and this is not very different from an existentialist's outgoingness. However, the main point would seem to be that existentialism places a premium on *self*-responsibility and this is universalized. It seems to me to be just as universal as was, for example, Kant's categorical imperative. The particularization of both are open to individual construction and variation, but that does not make the general principle subjective. The question might be raised about whether this form of responsibility constitutes a theory of individual action in isolation from other human beings, for the emphasis certainly lies on being true to oneself. But then, being true to oneself for an existentialist is always in a context, not just of tables and chairs, but of other people, and existentialism might reasonably hold that responsibility towards other people has its roots in being true to oneself.

EXISTENTIALISM, PSYCHO-ANALYSIS, AND SOCIAL STRUCTURE

Existentialism makes a ploy of the particular fact that people's behaviour, even symbolic, can be explained fully in terms of consciousness, where this is understood in an existentialist or "intentionality" sense deriving from phenomenology, with the claim that there is no need to invoke the concept or theory of the unconscious. In fact, the theory of the unconscious would be precluded for exactly the same reason as high-level abstract scientific theories of any sort would be. The existentialist approach is that what is claimed by psycho-analysts to be unconscious must reveal itself in consciousness to be part of the existentialist phenomenological experience, and therefore is not properly speaking, in the fully technical psycho-analytic sense, unconscious. So far so good. This is the correct interpretation of the unconscious according to the existentialist premisses, but how the trick is turned is not made plain.

However, the main point to be made is one's reluctance to see a theory of a powerful type such as that of the unconscious, or some theory of dynamic social structure ruled out a priori by a philosophy. It might turn out that such theories are empirically unfruitful. If that should be so, then let us cease to struggle after them. But they should not be ruled out a priori, especially where no disproof is offered, only a quasi-self-evident philosophy, mainly a phenomenology.

If a critic should try to claim that the unconscious makes nonsense of the existentialist claim to freedom before the yawning Nothing, in that decision and action are certainly caused by unconscious factors, then let this be accepted. For it could be fitted into a wider existentialist type of framework: it is in no way incompatible with the *phenomenological* account offered by existentialism, which is an account of a purely conscious kind, a description of the Nothing, the freedom, and the anxiety, and the leap in the dark that constitute conscious experience, and this existentialism seems to characterize with amazing acuity. The incompatibility lies only between the unconscious explanation of these conscious phenomena, i.e. the contention that a phenomenological description proscribes a theoretical explanatory concept as not being immanent in experience. But this could be dropped; it is not necessary to existentialism as such.

EXISTENTIALISM AND THE TWENTIETH-CENTURY WELTANSCHAUUNG

It is no accident that existentialism arose when it did. It caught on after World War II. It is said to have been started by Kierkegaard in the last century, and other founding fathers have been located, such as Nietzsche, but these ancestors have been hunted down *post facto*. The movement was essentially a post-war phenomenon, so far as it caught on in intellectual society as a group. And here it clearly reflects the breakdown of social values after World War II. This breakdown has left man floundering, but has also thrown man back on himself, and indeed one can see modern man taking a kind of pride in throwing out all existing standards and becoming self-reliant, not necessarily effectively, but in a sense of deciding that there he stands. He can do none other but be responsible for his own decisions. It is as if mankind had said, however humble its members that for each of us "the buck stops here".

Existentialism is also obviously a cri de coeur to bolster up one's confidence in oneself, after man has felt let down by the decay of standard values and feels that he has no guiding prescriptions left to show the way.

Existentialism also faithfully reflects the wide experience of the chasm of the Nothing that yawns before man in the human predicament, and also the dawning recognition of the absurd in placing the huge emphasis on the person and willy-nilly upon interpersonal relations, which perhaps reaches its acme in Buber's I-Thou relationship. Existentialism is, perhaps, making a contribution to social theory by pointing out how much of a man consists of social roles (even though it makes the point in an idealistic way by claiming that the dignity of man lies in the ratio by which he exceeds those social roles).

It is, however, unfortunate that some of its exponents have linked existentialism with political activism, whereas of course no one has a duty to be a political activist on existentialist grounds unless he owes this to himself.

In short, existentialism would seem to have provided a new type of philosophy depicting very finely the phenomenological psychology of the problem of decision, freedom, anxiety, and the leap into the dark, the admission of bad faith, deterioration into social roles, the absurd in the human condition and the nature of human *self*-responsibility. It denies unnecessarily explanatory components by supplementary theses obtainable, for example, from psycho-analysis or from theories of social structure, but it faithfully reflects twentieth-century man in his disillusionment, despair, need for support, and possibility for self-reliance.

CHAPTER XXIX

The Rationale of Duty

WITH THE downfall of inherited Weltanschauungen, objective grounds for ethics, if not removed, are undermined. There is bound to be a widespread adoption, in practice, of a subjectivist approach to questions of obligation. With the advent of existentialism, there is bound to be an aura of "right you are if you think so", even if, as I would claim, existentialism does not really carry this repudiation of obligation. Enough doubt arises to make necessary an excursion into the, or one of the, fundamental problems of ethics: if there are no objective grounds for duty, what is its rationale—if any; or is there no place for the notion of duty at all?

In a broadcast a few years ago Bertrand Russell drew attention to a fundamental unresolved dilemma of ethics, which strangely is little discussed or even mentioned. It is constituted as follows: the arguments for subjectivism are unanswerable, but subjectivism is wholly incapable of serving as a basis for morals.

This puts the matter in a nutshell. In my view, one ought to retain a healthy acknowledgement of the force of this dilemma. One ought to be impressed by the cogency of the subjectivist arguments. One ought also to realize that objectivism is essential if moral judgements are to be true.

This is tantamount in my opinion to admitting the overwhelming force of the subjectivist position on the one hand and to admitting the overwhelming need for objective moral judgments on the other. These have always seemed to be completely incompatible. It is no use turning a blind eye to one of these two factors just because they are inconsistent, because we want to sweep the other under the carpet. We begin soberly, therefore, by realizing that we cannot accept one of these alternatives, however powerful an argument we find for it, unless we at the same time satisfy the force of the other alternative. I introduce below a new idea in an attempt to resolve this dilemma.

The inadequacy of certain contemporary approaches can be made to reveal something of what is required. On the one hand, "negative utilitarianism", while a great improvement on classical utilitarianism, in that it has considerable (if incomplete) and often accurate practical application, is obviously inadequate as a theory. In practice, when confronted with a situation in which every alternative is from an intuitive point of view "wrong", one may wisely try to inflict the least pain. But there are situations in which respect for a person requires the infliction of pain. (Of course, as with classical utilitarianism, the negative version can be saved by ad hoc widening of the concept of "pain".) The reason is simply that there are higher values, to do with persons, even than the non-infliction of pain.

This brings me to an approach through an impersonal value-theory that attempts to give "guide-lines" on "what one ought to do" : act against a value whenever this is for the sake of a greater value. Very good : this theory supersedes both utilitarianism in its traditional sense and the intuitionist ethics of prima facie obligation. (One wonders, however, how near it is to being a tautology.) The difficulty is that, unsupported by explicit scales of values, it can be used to justify anything, even for example, Nazism, and (if we do not wish to press this extreme case) there would be no difficulty whatever in using it to justify disregard for, and injustice to, persons; for, unless qualified, it implies that the end justifies the means, and obnoxious actions can be carried out under the banner of over-riding interests or even saintliness.

Qualified, however, by a suitable scale of values involving (not necessarily exclusively) persons, it might be made satisfactory.

But these theories, and most others with the great exception of Kant's, while they inevitably have some bearing on personhood, fail to give it the dominating position it obviously should have. In what follows an attempt is made to make personhood central.

Let us ask what are some of the elementary things involved in being a person. It means at least having desires and needs, or, to use a colourless short expression, having interests. I suggest that it also involves the *recognition* of interests in others. "Recognition" seems to me to be a good word for this. It means more than awareness. One hungry dog may be aware of another hungry dog's desire to gobble the only piece of food available. But "recognition" conveys something more than this : it conveys an *acceptance* or at least a *toleration* or at least the *possibility of toleration* of the other person's interests, which is commonly (and I think rightly) attributed to a capacity to put oneself in other people's shoes. It should be stressed that what is meant here is not merely the possibility of tolerating other men's interests and actions but also of recognising their feelings, that is, how their desires and needs feel to them. The importance of this is that con-

J

cern about the well-being of another person would be out of the question without recognition of his feelings. And indeed one could say the same about the sense of duty: it is hard to see how one could feel under a moral obligation to a person without having some recognition of his feelings. Thus concern for others and a sense of duty belong to a context of being a person who recognises desires, needs and feelings in others. I would even add that social living must always involve the mutual recognition of these things in others in some measure (however minimised it is or however qualified it must be in certain situations).

I have developed this point to do with recognition of persons because I wish now to discuss the ethics of obligation or moral imperatives, and in particular to ask what is the bearing on these of the psychological theory of the pleasure-principle when it involves recognition of persons.

The theme of obligation takes us to the Golden Rule, sometimes expressed as "Do as you would be done by". The most famous treatment of this by any ethical writer was, of course, that given by Kant, whose view may be put like this: "Do not carry out an action unless you would want all other men who are confronted with the possibility of acting in the same way to carry out that action also". Kant also enunciated his basic point in another way, which may be put thus: "Never treat other men or yourself as a means only". Closely connected though these two maxims are, they are not the same, for the first is concerned with a type of action, without *explicit* reference to whatever persons may be involved in the action, while the second supplies this deficiency. I would prefer here, however, to discuss not the Kantian principle but a form of it given by Leonard Nelson, which brings out in a direct way what seems to be the kernel of Kant's view. We may attempt to express Nelson's principle in the following way: (a) "In deciding between alternative actions, take into account the interests of others who are affected by your action *equally* with your own"; and (b) "Do not carry out an alternative you could not consent to if you had in mind not only your own interests but *equally* the interests of those others".

This principle has several advantages. It recognises the importance of not treating other men as a means only, without asserting that this should never be done. And it is a universal principle which permits of greater flexibility in practical application than Kant's. While it may not be able to stand up to all objections and may be in need of one sort of modification or another, it gives clear expression to a considerable part of the unvoiced moral outlook shared by many people and—the important point in the present context—expresses the deep relevance of recognition of the interests of other men to the idea of obligation. No doubt this is implied also in other forms of ethical theory, but it fails to come out clearly in them and indeed one can see it in them after one has discerned the point by some other means.

How much can we in fact get out of the principle? One result of the first part, if limited, is of some importance, namely what we might call a *hypothetical injunction* that, *if* you wish to be at all fully a person and treat others seriously as persons then the way to do this is to take serious account of their felt desires and needs; it tells us that *if* we subscribe to a certain goal then there is a definite way of attaining it.

What this part does not do is to offer us anything categorical: it does not tell us that we *ought* to do anything; in particular, it does not tell us that we *ought* to take into account the interests of others, when we adopt some course of action. But this is given by the second part of Nelson's principle, and it is this part that purports to offer us something categorical.

I wish now to discuss the position of each part of the principle. It is plain that the first part, to do with what I have called a hypothetical injunction, requires no special justification. Either psychological recognition of other persons exists or it does not; if it does, the hypothetical injunction at once comes into play. The second part is in a much more curious position; for if we consider the psychological facts it looks as though the categorical part has no possible application. What is involved in an attempt to use it? It would be relevant if a person is trying to avoid recognising the interests of another; for then one may say that he *ought* to do something in respect of that other; in other words obligation enters as a counter to an overexclusive self-concern. But it seems to me that the real problem at such a point is not an ethical one in the categorical sense but a psychological one of succeeding or failing to recognise a person. On the other hand the categorical part of the principle could also be relevant in a totally different way, namely if a person is trying to *avoid avoiding* the recognition of another's interests; for he may in this way give excessive weight to the interests of the other and be unable to do justice to his own interests. Here the problem would also not be fundamentally an ethical one but a psychological one of trying to over-compensate for a failure to recognise the interests of another person. Either way I would conclude that Ought implies Can't: obligation implies that one cannot do what one desires to do in the way of treating others as persons. Hence to the question: 'Is there a principle that will tell you whether to fall in with the interests of others or to disregard them?', it seems clear that the answer is: "No". The essence of all moral problems that give rise to the question of what *ought* to be done is conflict between one's own interests and the attempt to treat another as a person and thus recognise his interests.

Is the conclusion, then, that there is no rôle for the injunction "you ought ...." or "you ought not to ....", "I ought ...." or "I ought not to ...?" This would be in a certain way an overstatement. It would be generally held that it is more difficult to give due weight to the interests of others than to one's own; the rôle of ethical injunctions, like "you ought to ....", may simply be to remind a person of the interests of others that he is in danger of overlooking. We might complete the "you ought to ...." by "you ought to .... otherwise you will disregard the interests of another person". But this brings us back from the categorical to a hypothetical injunction. Thus an apparently categorical injunction would remind a person of the hypothetical, and to be reminded thus of the interests of others may be all that is ethically relevant. Action would then depend on whether the person did in fact wish to take full account of the interests of others.

It seems to me that a hypothetical injunction would suffice for dealing with actual situations and that a categorical ethical injunction would be no stronger. For, if a man could not be taught to recognise the interests of others, he could not be taught to use anything like the categorical imperative. And if he could be taught to recognise them fully, which implies that he will want to satisfy them in some degree, the hypothetical injunction will suffice and the categorical would add nothing. The practical case of course is almost always between the two : where there is recognition of the interests of others with only a partial wish to satisfy them. Here the categorical might have some effect. But I think it would be a veiled order with a suggestion of threat; and it would operate as a categorical injunction. In short, I wonder whether it might not be just as effective to inculcate the idea "think of what so and so wants" as the form of actions that ought always or ought never to be done. Once you have got people, when trying to assess what they ought to do, to look into the felt interests of others, you have gone a long way towards getting them to confront themselves with the really significant facts before coming to a moral decision.

Thus the ethical type of imperative would seem to divide into one part that goes no further than what is involved in the recognition of persons by persons and another part that has no significant rôle.

It is of interest to compare this position with the doctrine of "nature red in tooth and claw", in other words that "might is right". In a disintegrating society or in war, it may come to a case of "every man for himself". This seems to imply, not that there are two principles, one for anarchy, and one for a society in which there is recognition of persons, but a desperate attempt to cut oneself off from recognising the interests of others.

It may be of some interest to consider how the "naturalistic fallacy" fares within this framework.

The naturalistic fallacy, so named by Moore (1903) though first put forward by Hume (1738-40) and later by Kant, is that no statement about values can be deduced from statements of fact, that no statement about "ought" follows from statement about "is", that all accounts (or definitions) of such conceptions as obligation in naturalistic terms are invalid. For if a deduction is offered, the statement about value, or about "ought", could be denied without contradiction, while accepting the factual statements from which it was supposedly deduced. Or, of any suggested naturalistic equivalent of a value, we can question whether it has that value. Thus if the value, say the rightness of keeping a promise, is equated with a social attitude of approval for doing so, we can contest whether the attitude of approval is right—which shows that the rightness and the attitude of approval are not the same. Hare (1964) has given an admirably clear way of exposing the fallacy :

Let us suppose that someone claims that he can deduce a moral or other evaluative judgment from a set of purely factual or descriptive premises, relying on some definition to the effect that V (a value-word) means the same as C (a conjunction of descriptive predicates). . . . we have . . . to ask whether its advocate ever wishes to commend anything for being C. If he says that he does, we have only to point out to him that his definition makes this impossible, for the reasons given. And clearly he cannot say that he never wishes to commend anything for being C; for to commend things for being C is the whole object of his theory.

I assume that Hume, Kant, Moore, and Hare are correct in the contention—and proof—that statements of value cannot be deduced from statements of fact. It is of no little interest to find quite a movement of rebellion against this result. One recent concerted attack on it was made by three symposiasts forming a panel dealing with fact and value. All three took pot-shots at it in the hope of showing that the "naturalistic fallacy" is not a fallacy—even while *recognising* and even quoting (and understanding) the exposure of the fallacy. What is indicated by this restiveness? They want to preserve rational discussion of moral issues, to keep people remembered as persons, to have values accepted as *immanent* in society, to find a universal principle underlying the varieties of moral codes, and to allow in morals for culture evolution, but by no means to admit anarchy or free-for-all subjectivism. And somehow they chafe at the naturalistic fallacy which somehow, they think, is a barrier to these goals.

On my view, the "naturalistic fallacy" is definitely a fallacy, but not at all in my way : for it seems to me that the fallacy, quite validly exposed, is irrelevant to our great ethical problem. And this is because we can solve the problem by means of a *hypothetical injunction* without the need for categorical obligability. It boils down very simply to a choice : if you choose—and you may prefer to eradicate the tendency as much as you can—to be human, you are ipso facto committing yourself to considering the position of other persons from their point of view.

Thus existentialism does not carry with it a subjectivist ethic. For existentialism is not a theory of human action and responsibility constructed for a universe containing one and only one "person"[1]; on the contrary, it is concerned with a person "thrown" into a world of persons. And my argument above amounts simply to this : that if one takes the existentialist "decision" to be a person, this is ipso facto a "decision" to treat others as persons.

How does this treatment of the matter meet the difficulties of negative utilitarianism and of the impersonal graded-value theory scale of values?

The main defect of negative utilitarianism is that it may be necessary to inflict pain in order to take a person seriously as a person (even though this is rare in practice); and this is taken care of on the present account.

The impersonal graded-value theory can accommodate a great achievement, such as the building of the pyramids, above the lives of those building them. The defect of the theory is to permit of such a judgement which would either be excluded or else seriously questioned on the present view.

If the present view is an improvement over these, it still leaves us with grave moral problems. This is not necessarily a defect; it is only a defect if it accommodates wrong judgements. The kind of problem that remains is that of balancing an end involving persons against the means involving persons when there will be a sacrifice of persons whether we opt for the end or the means.

There can be no formula for solving such a problem.

It is, however, an advantage in a theory if it makes explicit one of the main moral problems confronting mankind, and if it places emphasis on the factors most in need of being considered. Concretely, when you have a great end in view, but it involves some hardship for persons who would have to be sacrificed for it, the present view, unlike negative utilitarianism and unlike the impersonal graded-value theory, tells you to consider their position most carefully.

To summarise :

I. Being a person means at least having desires and needs—say, having vital interests. Further it involves recognition of interests in others, where "recognition" conveys the possibility of toleration of another's interests. Thus you cannot be a person unless you recognize others as persons and tolerate their interests.

II. Consider Leonard Nelson's version of the categorical imperative : (a) "In deciding between alternative actions, take into account the interests of others who are affected by your action *equally* with your own", and (b) "Do not carry out an alternative you could not consent to if you had in mind not only your own interest but *equally* the interests of those others."

III. Corresponding to this, let us construct a *hypothetical injunction: if* you wish to be even in part a person, which involves treating others as persons, *then* you can do this only by taking account of their felt interests.

IV. This hypothetical injunction does not tell us we *ought* to recognize the interests of others—it does not include categorical obligation. It involves only a form of utility-appropriateness : recognizing the interests of others is what you should show *if* you wish to be a person—but if you do not wish to be a person, the hypothetical does not tell you you ought to.

V. The extent to which men take into account the felt interest of others is the extent to which they succeed in being persons.

VI. Thus the *categorical* imperative—apart from exhortation and the like—has no ethical role. Otherwise expressed, deontological concepts are otiose.

VII. But given the intention of being a person then certain rules become obligatory—thus explaining the appearance of absoluteness pertaining to ethics.

VIII. The hypothetical injunction is a compound of psychological fact about recognition and of philosophical theory about personhood. It would seem to provide a basis for the appearance of universality that characterizes moral imperatives, while at the same time allowing variation and change. For, the appearance of universality, or the sense of objectivity, would stem from a common conception of personhood, while variation (or cultural relativism) would reflect variation and development in the awareness of others.

IX. An extreme form of change occurs if a person decides to opt out of recognition of the interests of others; but if he opts out, he ceases to be a person.

FOOTNOTES

[1]On my view, of course, there could not exist one and only one person; for there exists a person only if there exist other persons mutually recognizing one another as persons.

REFERENCES

Hare, M. (1964).
Hume, David (1938–40), *A Treatise of Human Nature*.
Moore, G. E. (1903), *Principia Ethica*, Cambridge.

CHAPTER XXX

Quod Vitae Sectabor Iter?

THE TITLE of this chapter is taken from one of Descartes' dreams, in which he was much exercised by the question of what path he should pursue.

We could say there are three sorts of people: those who never ask "What path should I pursue?" because they know, at least intuitively; those who know what they want but do not know how to get it, which is a purely practical difficulty; and those who do not know where they are/ought to be going. An increasing number fall into this last category, and it is only with them that I am concerned here. It is one of the (two) questions, or an aspect of the main question, with which many approach philosophy. The basic question in the tyro's mind is "the Riddle of Existence", i.e. how did everything all come to be and what is it all for. If only one knew what it was all for, one would know one's place in it and what path one ought to pursue. It would seem that only the raw student and the philosopher (of a certain sort) are concerned with such questions.

After examining individual philosophers of various schools and also whole schools themselves, the outcome is that philosophers of multifarious positions have indeed been vitally involved—not always wittingly it is true—with just these issues. But, on studying philosophy, in most of our universities, the student quickly or slowly discovers that academic philosophy does not deal with such unsophisticated matters. Those who spot this quickly probably get out. The others soldier on believing it will come. The vast majority adjust gradually and imperceptibly by smothering their desire to penetrate the Riddle, and identify with their proximate peer-group, their teachers, who by a combination of silence about it and waving it aside, should it somehow intrude, inculcate that it is not the serious subject-matter of philosophy. Those who press the Riddle will not be accepted into the periphery of the establishment, i.e. appointed to the faculty, and thus there is a law of natural selection which perpetuates the establishment, in the sense of epiphilosophers: that is to say, those who deal with any philosophical question subject only to one proviso—that the questions are handled circumspectly so as never to touch the Riddle. And hence the history of philosophy is interpreted and taught in such a way that penultimate questions and even subsidiary questions constitute the core—volumes on Descartes' cogito, Berkeley's arguments against abstract general ideas, Hume's attack on causation, Kant's transcendent deduction, all of them important and essential to sort out but only in the setting of the philosopher's extra-philosophical goal or the Riddle—while the riddle is excluded from lectures and examination questions, and dismissed with the innuendo that it was an excrescence originating in the superstitions of the past which even the great philosophers succumbed to. My present concern is with such faculty as may not have wholly eradicated their interest in the Riddle, with those who have taken a quick sample of philosophy and decided it had nothing to offer of "relevance", and with those pillars from the history of philosophy who, faced with the Riddle, regarded philosophy as a Search.

How does the Riddle or the Search relate to the various forms of philosophy already described?

Mode (1), metascience, is taken to be a specific enquiry about science, on the road towards being a discipline on its own rather like logic. Mode (2), epistemology, is partly a more general form of Mode (1), and to this extent does not need to be considered further here; but it is also closely related to the Search insofar as it is an avenue to metaphysics. Mode (3), the ontology of science, is related closely to Mode (1), but it bears on the present topic sofar as it raises questions that are insoluble. Mode (4), on parascientific ontology, is an enquiry about the nature of things, which though it resembles Mode (3) is in this context more closely related to the ultimate enquiry into the nature of the universe, i.e. Mode (5), cosmological ontology. In short the more philosophical drive in these modes is cosmological, the nature of things. If you like, the aim of traditional epistemology and metaphysics is rerum cognoscere naturam (to put it somewhat more broadly than Epicurus who said it was to know the causes, rather than the nature, of things). Mode (6), which I have called meta-ontological negativism, is essentially an anti-philosophical philosophy—it asserts "the Riddle does not exist", a form of denial that rings hollow—which seems to rest upon a Search called off by the reassuring answer that there is nothing to look for. Mode (7), on the way to life, admits the Riddle and the Search.

These have been the modes of enquiry. I have urged that they conceal an attempt to provide a Weltanschauung. For the enquiry into cosmological philosophy is not just to satisfy curiosity about the nature of things as such but to find out what sort of place the universe is, what sort of setting the cosmos must have; and the enquiry into the way of life overtly presupposes or proposes a Weltanschauung.

Now the point of a Weltanschauung is that it enables us to know where we stand vis-à-vis the universe : whether we must take careful account of many immortal gods and obey them; whether they care nothing for us; so that our only concern is to eat, drink, and be merry, for tomorrow we die; whether the poor are poor by divine ordinance or because of their own laziness, so that it would be wrong to succour them; what sort of destiny man may have; and so on. Man's Search is the endeavour to find a Weltanschauung that shall be the answer to the Riddle of Existence.

The formulation in terms of the physical universe, namely, how does anything come to be at all and what is it all for, covers over the more pertinent question : unde quo veni? That is to say, why are *we* here and have *we* a function?

The question has both an individual and a social meaning. As Descartes asked it, it was an individual question—whether to live life, which following Ausonius he felt was an absurdity, or to pursue knowledge with the extraphilosophical goal of establishing communication with his fellows, in the face of the Riddle of Existence which inexplicably rendered this contact taboo. But obviously the question has often been general.

Whichever of the two we investigate, we work in a totally new framework of civilization as compared with all past ages. The question, though asked at times, was hardly pressing when the divine hierarchical social structure was secure : man was put into the world to carry out some mission. Now all forms of mission are imposed from without : that is to say, man interpreted his mission as willed by some divinities. So the effect of the twentieth-century Götterdämmerung is to bury all missions in this sense. Man is therefore lost because he has no mission. The obvious alternative solutions are either to find a new one or to live without one (a third possibility that is likely to escape attention). Thus (i) man has discarded the old mission. (ii) he cannot find a new one, for this is precluded by the downfall of all divinities which alone gave a mission its sense. And (iii) supposably to live without one is to feel one has reverted to animality and to feel empty and hopeless. It is true, a desperate attempt has been made to find new missions, allotted not by the immortal gods above but by the State below : the communist ideology erected the State into a divinity which gave life its meaning for its inhabitants; the Nazis substituted for the immortal gods not the State but the Aryan Race with similar objectives. These social structures, incidentally, share with traditional ones the feature of locating the goal in the far future.

But if man repudiates these attempts to put old wine in new bottles, and accepts being thrown back on himself, i.e. if he dares to entertain the third alternative (but cannot live without some substitute for a mission), he has to find some source of meaningfulness in himself. And this is what existentialism has sought to do. And it is what men of all sorts try to do as they fling themselves into a round of "absurd" activities.

Man's efforts swing between collecting new status symbols and miscellaneous distractions. Often these are connected: the distractions are selected so as to provide status. Status which was once either present automatically by reason of birth or unobtainable, is now obtainable. One used not to be able to join certain clubs unless one had the requisite status already (though joining might increase it); now one can join the jet-set by competitive examination, that is, if one can climb the business executive's ladder. There is no longer the awe shown by the village for the doctor, but there is the bank-balance of the prosperous manifested by expensive if tasteless acquisitions, especially when chosen for their social effect rather than personal enjoyment, i.e. when the social effect excludes personal enjoyment.[1] Men do the rounds of sports, hobbies, social activities, and, apparently increasingly, sex. This last is an interesting development in the new structure.

There have arisen unbelievable sexual freedoms, from widespread promiscuity to group-sex, the legalization of male homosexuality (here men have at last attained equality of rights with women), social sanction to mention orally or in print every aspect of sex in every kind of way (though severally these may have been paralleled at earlier times, collectively they have not). It used to be thought that this kind of freedom would be highly beneficial. It probably is mildly beneficial; but it is hardly likely to solve any deep-seated problems. The freedom to have extra-marital sex, while it has undoubtedly brought about a good deal of relish, has probably proved a disappointment to many. This is not to say they should give it up; what I mean is that many have sought something thinking it lay in sex, when in fact they were searching for something else, not knowing it was something else. Sex has, perhaps, turned out in large measure to be only one more of the benefits available in an affluent society.

'You never had it so good", though true, is ironically false. Luxury is necessary—but not sufficient. Luxury—and sex—are excellent as a top-dressing to an integrated personality with a meaningful life. They are no substitute if one or the other is wanting. Indeed the paradox of luxury and sex is that satiation by these means alone faces man with his own emptiness. When life was materially difficult, when you did not eat till you had hunted your dinner or did not drink till you had milked your goat, there was no time to feel lonely. But modern man has to fill copious leisure hours—sometimes by doing some more of his routine work. And modern woman can no longer use her ingenuity by preserving fruit in bottles, for she buys once a week at the supermarket, and is left with only two occupations, either how to remain attractive to her husband or how to find a new one. The welfare state, undoubtedly one of the greatest blessings and most humane measures ever introduced, exacts a terrible price in the human emptiness it makes men face. Since men will not give up the welfare state—even if this were feasible—they have to pay the price, or solve the problem of loneliness perhaps by a development of personality.

Man has abolished his divinities above and tried to fill the vacuum with status and goods. These, too, leave him empty. Homo Americanus in particular, but also in some measure his counterpart in Europe, begins by trying to make money in order to get somewhere, a specific position; this turns out to be a place that enables him to make more money, so as to go somewhere else; and so on. Many know that it leads only to the executive's ulcer or the coronary thrombosis grave. The epitaph: "Here lies the body of a man who attained status n, who realised that n is succeeded by $n + 1$, and who realised too late that n is empty".

The answer to this, which is to be found in Martin Buber, is not to go anywhere. Or rather, one may go somewhere provided going somewhere is not itself the main objective. For Buber has proclaimed that meaningfulness lies in the I-thou relationship.

And, even if this is too exacting for most, he has surely made a fundamental point.

It would be easy to be too much of a purist and require of us to spend every minute of our lives in I-thou relationships. But more reasonable would be to make such a relationship the dominant centre, and hook on to it all the other activities and goods that are relevant or desired. The weighting of these and the working out of the relationships between them needs much consideration. Here I will say only that the meaningful life involves the following:

I-thou relationship: to spouse (or another)
I-group relationship: to children/parents; and other peer-groups
Relationship between underlying sense of meaningfulness and day-today satisfactions.
Career/status

The main mistake that could be committed about the I-thou relationship would be to restrict significance to the I or to the thou or to the two in combination, if we allow that groups we belong to do not consist solely of thou's, for a group may have, say, a tradition, which is different both from individuals and also from a divinity.

With the loosening up of individual and social restrictions, I would expect the third revolution (the Copernican being the first, the Darwinian the second, and now the revolution of social structure) to involve fundamental developments in social theorizing and the relationship of man to society. There is at present no subject devoted to it, for the social science with the most general name is severely restricted in its concerns—sociology does not go beyond the questions of the origin, relationships, and functions of social institutions to study social dynamics. Meanwhile there is no objective to philosophizing about it.

We have seen that parascientific ontology was pursued in the absence of appropriate empirical science. Progress was scanty, perhaps absent. But questioning and discussion are not without value. The only caveat required is to remember—one of the few philosophical achievements however salutary—that no certainty can be attached to conclusions, indeed neither proof nor disproof. Given this outlook, I see no reason why, just as over the past 2000 years philosophers asked whether space was infinite or finite, they should not now ask questions about the basic structure of society.

I wish now to comment on a fundamental difficulty confronting contemporary man.

We have seen that his identifications have been undermined, so that he is not sure of himself in his groups or even in his family relationships. And this is a phenomenon resulting from the disintegration of the divine hierarchical social stratification. But we have also seen that it was a basic difficulty besetting some of the great philosophers of the past. Descartes had, it would seem, an unconscious personal problem over communication with his fellows, and this apparently stemmed from his being unable to identify with them. And this led to his being unsure of his place in the world. What the current situation of man and the unconscious difficulties of past philosophers add up to is that having an assured place in the world, knowing where one stands, finding life meaningful even without props, depend on fundamental identifications, and, correlatively, relationships to others as objects. It is not that a pathology has developed in man's identifications for the first time: I would suppose that the pathology was present all along; but that the social stratification mopped it up and prevented it from being pressing; and now this is no longer so.[2]

One could say that man is back at the problem, though now in a new, social, setting, of his being a subject confronting man as an object.

The problem can be investigated from either end, the subject-object relationship or the identification between subjects, and they are but different aspects of one problem; but I suspect that the identification problem is rather the more fundamental of the two, in that object-relationship presupposes basic identifications. A man who has firm identifications is not lonely when alone; a man who has not is lonely in the presence of others.

Looking back over the psychological difficulty common to the philosophers whose goals have been studied above, it seems to me that, considered both individually and as a group, the syndrome was a social product with a striking social Weltanschauung; they nearly all suffered from an unrecognized inability to communicate with their fellows, failed to identify normally with them, lacked the normal relationship to the opposite sex as objects, and lived in a purely male world, where men were not identified with but at most objects to beware of. Such a constellation goes below that of the Oedipus situation, and I am inclined to describe it as the Hippolytus complex. It may be recalled that the chaste Hippolytus rejected the incestuous advances of Phaedra, and was led, after a chain of consequences, to his death when a dog-seal or a white bull terrified his team of horses (Graves, 1959)[3]. Naming the constellation does not of course explain anything, but it may help to sharpen the syndrome.

We need a theory of identification-formation and of identification-dysfunction. I would suppose that identification is a result of adjusting to what is experienced as goodness and badness in oneself.

We need a method of handling dysfunction. I would suppose it to be a useful if painful exercise to concentrate on the evils that men do and that groups induce, and to dwell on these as if they somehow formed part of oneself.

If after all this time we are no wiser than Socrates, perhaps we may amplify the content of his maxim concerning self-knowledge: to know that neither he nor I nor any group is at all like the pure specimen we thought. So perhaps the path to pursue is a path without, towards an I-thou relationship, seen in terms of a path within, towards a knowledge of the evil that is sensed as residing there.

FOOTNOTES

[1]Social effect may be present *along with* personal enjoyment; indeed personal enjoyment that excludes the social effect amounts to eccentricity.

[2]This is exascerbated, as it were "mechanically", by increasing horizontal social mobility, particularly in America.

[3]I am indebted to Dr. Allan Cobb for suggesting this myth as being the closest to my requirements.

BIBLIOGRAPHY

Graves, Robert (1959), *The Greek Myths*, New York, §101 f.

CHAPTER XXXI

Philosophy and the Future Weltanschauung of Man and Society

WHAT IS the thesis of this book?

The discriminations into seven Modes of philosophizing is, I think, interesting in itself: to display the disparate subjects that found themselves bed-fellows, to show why philosophers of different Modes could not communicate with one another, and to show why philosophy is despised by some thinkers from other disciplines and regarded as providing salvation by others. But to raise the question of the relevance of philosophy to culture requires that we raise the question in terms of some Mode. The most "professional" Modes are (1) Metascience, (2) Epistemology, also to a small extent (5) Cosmological ontology, and (6) forms of meta-ontological negativism, though (7) way of life has now found a stable in some universities even if usually frowned upon. This book has required by contrast (3) the ontology of science, not officially on the books, though it would hardly arouse opposition. It functions here mainly as a jumping off ground enabling us to discriminate the vital (4) parascientific ontology and (5) cosmological ontology, which are the modes of philosophy that bear on culture; and (7) way of life is central.

Since there has been much self-questioning by philosophy—which must be credited to the meta-ontological negativists—about its methods, validity, limits, and so on, it is necessary to assess the weeding and pruning that has been done and to add to it, to know where we stand with philosophy as an instrument of human knowledge. By accepting that nothing philosophical can be proved or disproved, in particular by showing apparently that meta-ontological negativism can not provide disproof nor can synthetic a priori metaphysics provide proof—philosophy and its residual living problems, i.e. the interesting ontological issues, end up in limbo.

But many valuable functions remain even after it is seen, however sadly, that there is no future in the search for philosophical truth. It is good to raise questions, even if we cannot answer them, that are of moment to man; the question and the answers, whether accepted confidently or tentatively, throw light on man himself and on society. And this I have endeavoured to explore in the intellectual history brought out by the psychological and social sources of philosophy.

Thus the aims of the first three parts are: to solve a question about Modes of philosophy; to give a coup de grace to the age-old attempt, whether rational or rationalized, to discover or refute a philosophical claim; and to use the residue for exploring the nature of man and society. Yet these aims are, if partly ends in themselves, partly preliminary.

The chief value of philosophy for this book concerns the tentative use of ontological questions in the social field. We thus come to the final part. Philosophy, in the sense of cosmological philosophy, conveys a Weltanschauung. Although this has not been an explicit Mode of philosophy, I think it should be introduced as a Mode; for in a very real sense it is what most Modes are about, namely how we see the universe and how we stand in relation to it. Philosophy as a Weltanschauung is significant in several ways. The point is overt that it is neither provable or disprovable. A Weltanschauung governs our lives. It is usually scarcely recognized. It is usually hard to unearth. For those reasons it is all the more powerful whether for good or ill. It even governs the hard empirical core of science itself in certain ways. It determines our approach to society and its problems. It provides a new factor in rationality: the importance of questioning not merely what lies within a Weltanschauung but of questioning the Weltanschauung itself.

Thus the way is opened up to make a new approach to the study of society by investigating its Weltanschauung. In developing this, I have endeavoured to state the Weltanschauungen of post-Renaissance times, the period following World War I, and that following World War II (the first and second overlapped, then the second and third overlapped). These I called the Divine Hierarchial Social Structure, the Pragmatic Social Structure, and the Inter-Personal, Identificationless Social Structure. This last contains internal strains and is not free of the influence of its rival, the Pragmatic. Thus society still searches for a new Weltanschauung, a new Social Structure, a new set of values.

The effect upon philosophy has been to throw up two Modes—one, meta-ontological negativism in all its phases over seventy years, despairs with the downfall of the old Weltanschauung and its values which I have described as die Götterdämmerung, and plods on goalless and ritualised, reflecting the disillusionment of the age. The other, the way of life (existentialism) takes a new view of man, conveying a Weltanschauung of self-responsibility, without props before the unknown; it reflects the possibility of a great new social age dawning—though man has to be strong enough to face it, for though it takes great courage to die on behalf of one's ideals, it may take just as much courage, even if a different kind, to live the future.

Human beings are caught in a maelstrom because of there being no settled Weltanschauung. What does it mean any longer to do one's duty? I have tried to give a new answer to this in terms of the existentialist decision between opting to be a person or opting out (it is of course a matter of degree). And then comes the final question for man as a searcher: What path shall I pursue? The answer is in part existentialist, following Buber: the path lies in person-to-person relations. A slender answer if viewed without realising what it includes—and equally what it excludes. But existentialism omits the role of groups—paradoxically seems to forget society. We might perhaps combine these in the following:—

A PERSON-PERSON, PERSON-GROUP WELTANSCHAUUNG

That life is meaningful.

That man is no more than human—and no less.

To be a person is a supreme value.

Having a meaningful life.

Having a set of meaningful human relationships :
(i) spouse/other
(ii) children
(iii) parents

Friendship.

Amicable work relationships.

Sense of belonging to a work-group.

That Weltanschauungen are open to challenge.

That understanding alien Weltanschauungen fosters growth of the person.

Learning to live with one's ignorance.

Hobbies.

Sense of belonging to hobby-groups.

That society is unitary (without castes, ghettos, second class citizens).

That men are otherwise unequal.

Interest in community, national, world affairs.

Feeling part of the community, the nation, the world.

Replacement of a classical hard-core identity by a variable identity constituted by varying infusions of the above.

Goods.

Recognition that evil (i.e. hate, violence, sadism, autocratic power, subjugation, trouble-making, etc.) is shared by all groups and all individuals.

That the primary individual and group problem is to harness evil.

This Weltanschauung, or most of it, may be seen to be an amplification of the following principles :—

Man is a person in varying degrees; the most he can achieve is a high-degree of personhood.

Man is man in society.

Man achieves exalted ideals.

Man also contains evil inherently.

Acknowledgements

I wish to thank particularly Professor Ian Jarvie, Professor Joseph Agassi, and Dr. Jagdish Hattiangadi, who gave me helpful comments and criticisms, though it is not their responsibility if I have failed to meet them adequately. I am grateful to Mr. Russell McRae and Mr. Philip Antonacci for correcting the proofs and to Mr. Antonacci also for compiling the index.

Various chapters and portions of chapters, with minor alterations and some tailoring, were given in papers or talks in a variety of circumstances :—

Chapter 1 was first given as a talk to the Faculty Luncheon Club at the University of Southern California, 27 October 1965. Part I was given as campus talks at the State University College of New York at Fredonia, during 1967–8.

Chapter 3 utilizes parts of "Scientific Theory: Empirical Content, Embedded Ontology, and Weltanschauung", which appeared in *Philosophy and Phenomenological Research*, 1972, **33**, 62–77. I wish to thank the Editor for permission to reprint.

Chapter 10 "On the Refutability of Metaphysics" was given at the Pacific Division of the American Philosophical Association, San Francisco, 27–29 December 1965; and at the Boston Colloquium for the Philosophy of Science, 17 January 1966. It was published in *Boston Studies in the Philosophy of Science*, ed., Cohen & Wartofsky, Reidel, Dordrecht, 1969, Vol. 4, 523–37. I wish to thank the publisher for permission to reprint.

Chapters 11 and 12, "The Refutation of Logical Positivism" and "The Refutation of Semantic Ontology" were given to the London University Philosophy Faculty and appeared as a single paper in *Mind*, 1963, **72**, 335–47 under the title "Metamorphoses of the Verifiability Theory of Meaning." I wish to thank the publishers, Blackwell, Oxford, for permission to reprint.

Parts of Chapter 15, on the goal of Descartes and on the goal of Spinoza were given respectively at the Los Angeles City College, 9 December 1965, and at the State University of New York at Albany, 10 May 1968.

A brief passage in Chapter 16 is taken from "The Unconscious Origin of Schopenhauer's Philosophy", *Inter. J. Psycho-Analysis*, 1945, **26**, 44–52. I wish to thank the Editor for permission to reprint.

Chapter 17, "One Dogma of Apriorism and Empiricism", was given as "The Metaphysics of Empiricism" at the State University of New York at Stoney Brook, 19 February 1969.

Chapter 19, "Rationalist Tendencies in Twentieth-Century Thought and Chapter 20, "Anti-Rationalist Tendencies in Twentieth-Century Thought" were given together under a slightly different title to the Oswego Philosophical Club, 23 April 1968, and with a different slant at Glendon College, York University, Toronto, 13 October 1970 and at Carleton University, Ottawa, 16 October 1970.

Chapter 26, "Ultimate Social Values: Current Options", was given to a Social Science Division Seminar, York University, Toronto, 3 December 1971. One passage is moved to the last chapter of all.

Chapter 27, "Pragmatism and the American Mom", was given to the Toronto Imago Group, 16 January 1972.

A different version of Chapter 28 on Existentialism was given at Oxford many years ago.

Chapter 29, "The Rationale of Duty" contains bits from a paper, "Respect for Persons, the Pleasure-Principle, and Obligation", given at the International Congress of Philosophy, Venice 1958. This was published in *Proceedings of the XIIth International Congress of Philosophy*, Firenzi, 1961, **7**. I wish to thank Professor Felice Battaglie for permission to reprint. This chapter also contains a passage from "Why the Gap is Under Attack," Chairman's remarks at the Third Conference on Value Inquiry at the State University College of New York at Geneseo, 125–6, April 1969. It was published in *Human Values and Natural Science*, ed., Laszlo and Wilbur, Gordon and Breach, New York, 1970, 169–76. I wish to thank the publishers for permission to reprint.

Index